THE TROLLOPE CRITICS

Also by N. John Hall

THE NEW ZEALANDER (*editor*)
SALMAGUNDI: BYRON, ALLEGRA, AND THE TROLLOPE FAMILY
TROLLOPE AND HIS ILLUSTRATORS

THE TROLLOPE CRITICS

Edited by
N. John Hall

First published 1981 by
THE MACMILLAN PRESS LTD
London and Basingstoke
Companies and representatives
throughout the world

ISBN 0 333 26298 0

Typeset in 10/12pt Press Roman by
STYLESET LIMITED · *Salisbury · Wiltshire*
and printed in Hong Kong

Contents

Introduction

The criticism of Trollope's works brought together in this collection has been drawn from books and articles published since his death. Much of the material contemporary with Trollope is available in Donald Smalley's *Critical Heritage* (1969), and David Skilton in *Anthony Trollope and His Contemporaries* (1972) has provided judicious commentary on this criticism and greatly extended the bibliography of such reviews and articles. Studies of individual novels have not been included since it would have been impossible to make a representative selection for an author who produced forty-seven novels of surprisingly even quality. For the 'essential Trollope' was there at the very start, in *The Macdermots of Ballycloran*, published in 1847, as it was in the *The Landleaguers*, left unfinished at his death in 1882. Moreover, the never-ending practice of ranking the novels goes on with little consensus. Among the forty-seven titles are at least twenty first-rate novels and some half dozen — or is it a dozen? — masterworks of Victorian fiction, but one is hard put to find two Trollopians in agreement about which are which. However, the reader, with the help of the index, may easily find substantial discussions of particular novels, including those of the Barsetshire and Palliser series, as well as, for instance, *He Knew He Was Right, Ayala's Angel* and *Mr. Scarborough's Family*.

From a reading of the books and articles on Trollope published since his death there emerges the chief justification for concentrating on evaluations of his work as a whole: the unanswered question of exactly wherein Trollope's distinctive excellence lies. Each of these essays attempts to solve 'the Trollope problem', each tries 'to declare his quiddity'. In 1927 Michael Sadleir wrote: 'Trollope's quality remains intangible, baffles resolution. In theme familiar, in treatment undistinguished, his work is nevertheless potent in appeal, unrivalled in its power to hold the attention of readers of any kind and of any generation . . . it is almost irritating that books in themselves so lustily prosaic should be so hard of definition'.[1] More than fifty years later, the mystery of Trollope's appeal still eludes anything like complete explanation. But a prodigious amount of criticism has been produced, and the writers represented in this collection have, I believe, contributed much that is enlightening and provocative.

The twenty essays range from Henry James's appraisal, written in 1883 shortly after Trollope's death, to examples from the upsurge of critical work done within the past few years. Arranged in chronological order, these essays tell something, however indirectly, of Trollope's critical reputation. But the story of his reputation is a large subject in itself. The history of the 'Trollope revival' since the early 1920s is fairly clear, associated as it rightly is with Michael Sadleir's publications of that decade and the extensive reissues of some thirty Trollope titles by Oxford's World's Classics in the 1920s and 1930s. It is noteworthy, however, that when Sadleir's important *Trollope: A Commentary* was published in 1927, nearly two dozen Trollope titles were already in print. Trollope's great following among British readers during the Second World War is well known, and Elizabeth Bowen gave a convincing account of this wartime popularity in her radio play published as *Anthony Trollope: A New Judgement* (1946). In recent years the number of his readers has again increased, doubtless to some extent as a result of the popular television series 'The Pallisers'. Readers today on both sides of the Atlantic find many Trollope titles in print.

In academic circles, acceptance of Trollope has been decidedly slow. He has always been more of a favourite with 'ordinary readers' and fellow novelists than with academics and professional critics. Perhaps the most celebrated dismissal of Trollope came from F. R. Leavis, who spoke of Henry James and George Eliot as far above 'the ruck of Gaskells and Trollopes and Merediths' and quoted with approval an examination paper that called Trollope 'a lesser Thackeray', explaining in turn that even Thackeray has 'nothing to offer the reader whose demand goes beyond "creation of characters" and so on . . . for the reader it is merely a matter of going on and on; nothing has been done by the close to justify the space taken — except, of course, that time has been killed'.[2] Van Wyck Brooks's estimate is more qualified but nearly as dismissive: 'one has to be interested in England·to enjoy Trollope, but to enjoy Balzac, all one needs is to be interested in life'.[3] It is certainly a fact that Trollope has received less than his due in books surveying English literature or the novel, and still less recognition in university curricula and reading lists. But slowly, and after the at first relatively isolated labours of Professor Bradford Booth, who founded *The Trollopian* in 1945 (later renamed *Nineteenth-Century Fiction*), edited Trollope's *Letters* in 1951, and published widely on his chosen subject, academic eminence has at last come to Trollope. In 1977–8 alone, eight full-length studies of Trollope were published. The selected bibliography appended to this collection, large as it is, includes only part of the published work on Trollope and omits altogether the numerous Ph.D. dissertations concerning him.

More controversial, and requiring more consideration, is the story of Trollope's reputation from his death until the First World War. The received account, largely that given in 1927 by Michael Sadleir in his *Commentary*, was that after Trollope's heyday in the 1860s, his popularity with both readers and critics gradually declined, to the extent that upon his death he was decidely *démodé* and headed for oblivion. Then came Trollope's post-humous *Autobiography*, with its emphasis upon craftsmanship rather than inspiration and its tale of 'mechanical' work habits. This book, we are told, extinguished Trollope's reputation altogether with the new generation. Sadleir's reading of events has been challenged, most effectively and most recently by R. C. Terry in his book *Anthony Trollope: The Artist in Hiding*. Terry contends that the legend of Trollope's downfall and oblivion has been much exaggerated. Sadleir, says Terry, 'saw himself as a lonely pioneer for a writer with fairly dubious claims on posterity . . . he made more than he need have done of the alleged disappearance of the novelist'. In the first place, Trollope's following at his death was still immense, and practically all the obituary notices proclaimed his continued popularity. Even *The Times*' notice, by Mrs Humphry Ward, which Sadleir quoted to prove his point, was distinctly more positive than Sadleir thought. Terry examines the obituary notices and the criticism of the following years, including very favourable reviews of the supposedly death-dealing *Auto-biography*, and demonstrates satisfactorily that 'the period of neglect lasted at most some dozen years between the eighties and the turn of the century'. He assembles a list of critics from both America (where, if any-thing, the revival began still earlier) and England who supported or took notice of the renewed interest in Trollope. 'It is quite clear', concludes Terry, 'from reprints and articles that the early years of the century saw Trollope's reputation rising rapidly. On 9 September 1909, *The Times Literary Supplement* devoted its entire front page to the novelist. Trollope was back in vogue.'[4]

One aspect of Trollope's alleged disappearance that ought to receive more attention (although Terry says something on the subject and offers some evidence that Trollope 'remained a sound commercial investment for Mudie for at least seventy years'), is the republication of his books. The number of titles brought back into print in a given period is of course a more accurate barometer of an author's popularity than critical response during those years. In England, during the 1880s and 1890s, Ward, Lock's 'Select Library of Fiction' – taken over from Chapman & Hall – issued no fewer than thirty-two Trollope titles at two shillings (2s. 6d in cloth). The Select Library comprised some 500 works, undated but numbered, and it is worth noting that Trollope's were the first in the series, numbers 1–32:

Doctor Thorne	*Is He Popenjoy?*
The Macdermots of Ballycloran	*An Eye for an Eye*
Rachel Ray	*Cousin Henry*
The Kellys and the O'Kellys	*Dr. Wortle's School*
Tales of All Countries	*Harry Heathcote*
Castle Richmond	*Orley Farm*
The Bertrams	*Can you Forgive Her?*
Miss Mackenzie	*Phineas Finn*
The Belton Estate	*He Knew He Was Right*
Lotta Schmidt	*The Eustace Diamonds*
An Editor's Tales	*Phineas Redux*
Ralph the Heir	*The Prime Minister*
La Vendée	*The Duke's Children*
Lady Anna	*Ayala's Angel*
The Vicar of Bullhampton	*South and West Australia*
Sir Harry Hotspur	*New South Wales, Victoria, and Tasmania*

The omission of all the Barsetshire novels except *Doctor Thorne* was doubtless by arrangement with Chapman & Hall, who brought out the series in 1878, 1887 and 1891–3.

The following is an incomplete tally[5] of other London publishers' Trollope titles, issued during the period of neglect, or supposed neglect, 1885–1915:

Chatto & Windus:	*John Caldigate*, 1885, 1909
	Marion Fay, 1885, 1889, 1899
	The Landleaguers, 1885
	The American Senator, 1886
	Kept in the Dark, 1891
	Why Frau Frohmann Raised Her Prices, 1892
	The Way We Live Now, 1907
Smith, Elder:	*The Small House at Allington*, 1885, 1894, 1902, 1903
	Framley Parsonage, 1886, 1890, 1896
Longman:	*The Warden*, 1886
	Barchester Towers, 1886, 1891, 1900

Macmillan:	*Thackeray*, 1892, 1900, 1902, 1906, 1909, 1912
	The Three Clerks, 1900
Bentley:	*The Three Clerks*, 1900
John Lane, New	*Doctor Thorne*, 1901
Pocket Library:	*The Warden*, 1901 ˇ
	Barchester Towers, 1901
	Framley Parsonage, 1903
	The Bertrams, 1904
	The Three Clerks, 1904
	Castle Richmond, 1905
	The Macdermots of Ballycloran, 1905
	Orley Farm, 1906
	The Small House, 1906
	Rachel Ray, 1906
	The Kellys and the O'Kellys, 1906
	Can You Forgive Her?, 1908
Blackie:	*Barchester Towers*, 1903
	Framley Parsonage, 1904
Long:	*The Three Clerks*, 1903
Bell:	The six Barsetshire novels, 1906 (with frequent reprintings of individual titles e.g. *The Warden,* 1909, 1910, 1913)
	Phineas Finn, 1911
	Phineas Redux, 1911, 1913
Dent:	The six Barsetshire novels, 1906–9
	The Golden Lion of Granpère, 191–?
Oxford, World's	
Classics:	*The Three Clerks*, 1907
Cassell:	*Barchester Towers*, 1909
Collins:	*Barchester Towers*, 1909
	Framley Parsonage, 1909
	Orley Farm, 1910
	The Claverings, 1910
Routledge:	The six Barsetshire novels, 1909
Nelson:	Five of the six Barsetshire novels, 1913–15
Bohn's Popular	
Library:	The six Barsetshire novels, 1913

In America, Trollope's works were at least equally accessible. The thirty-two titles of Ward, Lock were distributed in New York, as were the thirteen John Lane titles (in some cases one year later) and those of Nelson. The six Dent titles were of course available from Dutton in New York. But the American house that did the most to keep Trollope before his readers was Dodd, Mead, with nineteen titles. Publishers with Trollope on their list during the thirty-year period include:

Munro, Seaside Library:	*The Warden*, 1885 *Harry Heathcote*, 1885 *The Prime Minister*, 1885 *Ralph the Heir*, 1886 *The Golden Lion*, 1886, 1896
Millar:	*An Old Man's Love*, 1885
Dodd, Mead:	The six Barsetshire novels, 1892 (with frequent reprintings of individual titles, e.g. *The Warden*, 1893, 1894, 1900, 1901, 1902, 1903, 1905, 1908, 1912, 1913) The six Parliamentary novels, 1892–3 (with frequent reprintings of individual titles, e.g. *Can You Forgive Her?*, 1893, 1897, 1900, 1902, 1903, 1904, 1906, 1908, 1911, 1912) *An Autobiography*, 1905, 1911 *Orley Farm*, 1905, 1906, 1911, 1913 *The Vicar of Bullhampton*, 1906, 1910, 1913 *Is He Popenjoy?*, 1907, 1913 *John Caldigate*, 1907, 1911, 1913 (these last four titles also issued together as 'The Manor House Novels') *The Belton Estate*, 1912
Knight (Boston):	*Christmas at Thompson Hall*, 1894
Lupton:	*The Macdermots of Ballycloran*, 1894?
Lovell, Corgell:	*The Prime Minister*, 1895?
Page (Boston):	*Christmas at Thompson Hall*, 1897
Harper:	*Thackeray*, 1899, 1902
Gebbie (Philadelphia):	The six Barsetshire novels, 1900. The six Palliser novels, 1900–2

Fowle: *Thackeray*, 189–?, 1905?
Century: *Barchester Towers*, 1902, 1903, 1904, 1906

It is clear that Trollope never suffered anything resembling total eclipse: evidently the commonplace about Trollope being much *read* has proved true during every decade since he first rose to great popularity in the 1860s. Trollope's novels continued to be commercially attractive to publishers, even, to some extent, during the years of his poorest showing, the 1890s; and during the first decade of the twentieth century there was a veritable flood of reprintings.

To this brief overview of the early years of Trollope's reputation I wish to add excerpts from writers who, although omitted from this collection because of limitations of space, produced criticism important either in its own right or as representative of a generation. The first such critic, George Saintsbury, can in fact represent two generations, so far apart were his pronouncements on Trollope. In 1895, his stance was doubtless typical of other members of the critical establishment:

> I admit that in the days of the 'Chronicles of Barset', Mr. Trollope gave me a very great deal of pleasure. . . .
>
> I do not know that I myself ever took Mr. Trollope for one of the immortals; but really between 1860 and 1870 it might have been excusable so to take him. . . . From almost the beginning until quite the end, Mr. Trollope . . . showed the faculty of constructing a thoroughly readable story. You might not be extraordinarily enamoured of it; you might not care to read it again; you could certainly feel no enthusiastic reverence for or gratitude to its author. But it was eminently satisfactory . . . .
>
> And yet even such work is doomed to pass—with everything that is of the day and the craftsman, not of eternity and art. . . . The fault of the Trollopian novel is in the quality of the Trollopian art. It is shrewd, competent, not insufficiently supported by observation, not deficient in more than respectable expressive power, careful, industrious, active enough. But it never has the last exalting touch of genius, it is everyday, commonplace, and even not infrequently vulgar. These are the three things that great art never is.[6]

'Comparative oblivion' is prophesied for Trollope. But a quarter of a century later Saintsbury forthrightly revised his estimate of 'this amazingly prolific, and at the same time singularly substantial, novelist'. The later novels, Saintsbury admits, are better than he had thought, though not coming up to the standard of those of the Barsetshire period. But *Barchester Towers* he calls 'one of the best of English novels short of the absolute "Firsts" '. Moreover, *The Small House at Allington* and *Can You Forgive Her?* fall very little short of *The Last Chronicle* and *Barchester Towers*. 'There are few *men* in fiction I *like* better, and should more like to have known, than Archdeacon Grantly.' Saintsbury sums up: 'I do not think that [Trollope] will, by the best judges, ever be thought worthy of the very highest place among novelists or among English novelists. He has something no doubt of the "*for* all time", but he is not exactly "*of* all time". Or, to put the calculus the other way, he is by no means only "*for* an age"; but he is to a certain lowering though not disqualifying degree "*of* an age".' This may seem grudging praise, but when it comes to naming names Saintsbury puts only Jane Austen, Scott, Dickens and Thackeray before Trollope among nineteenth-century English novelists.[7]

Herbert Paul, writing in 1897, was even more pessimistic about Trollope's hold on posterity than Saintsbury had been in 1895:

> Trollope was in his lifetime more popular than any of his contemporaries. Twenty years ago it would hardly have been an exaggeration to say that half the novels on the railway bookstalls were his. Now his books are never seen there, and seldom seen anywhere else. Why was he popular? Why has he ceased to be so? . . . It is to be feared that Trollope's books are dead. But it is a pity. . . . *Barchester Towers* is one of the most readable of books, and I do not envy the man who preserves his gravity over Bertie Stanhope or Mrs. Proudie. . . . His popularity was due partly to his cleverness, liveliness, and high spirits, but partly also to his never overtaxing the brains of his readers, if, indeed, he can be said to have taxed them at all. The change in the position of his books produced, and produced so rapidly, by the death of the author may, I think, be thus explained. He stimulated the taste for which he catered. He created the demand which he supplied.[8]

The early Saintsbury and Paul essays, with their somewhat wistful dismissal of Trollope, mark the low point in the novelist's reputation. Both critics slip into the practice of praising the readability of something they then proceed to belittle. It is an old and continuing habit of critics of Trollope's fiction. As early as 1863 an anonymous reviewer of *Rachel Ray* touched upon this phenomenon: 'It may seem rather hard that critics should read Mr. Trollope's novels and enjoy them, and then abuse them for being what they are.'[9] (Two years later, the young Henry James began

a review of *Miss Mackenzie*: 'We have long entertained for Mr. Trollope a
partiality of which we have yet been somewhat ashamed.')[10]

In 1901, Leslie Stephen, while not rating Trollope very high, foresaw
a modest revival. He told how he had at one time been a devoted reader of
the novels, but that on rereading one of his old favourites he found the
book 'as insipid as yesterday's newspaper':

> Of course I explained the phenomenon by my own improvement
> in good taste, and for a long time I held complacently that Trollope
> should be left to the vulgar herd. Lately I have begun to doubt this plaus-
> ible explanation. An excellent critic of Victorian novelists (Mr. Herbert
> Paul) told us, it is true, the other day that Trollope was not only dead,
> but dead beyond all hopes of resurrection. There are symptoms, how-
> ever, which may point rather to a case of suspended vitality. . . . No-
> body can claim for Trollope any of the first-rate qualities which strain
> the powers of subtle and philosophical criticism; but perhaps it would
> be well if readers would sometimes make a little effort to blunt their
> critical faculty. . . .
>
> We can see plainly enough what we must renounce in order to enjoy
> Trollope. We must cease to bother ourselves about art. We must not ask
> for exquisite polish of style. We must be content with good homespun
> phrases which give up all their meaning on the first reading. We must
> not desire brilliant epigrams suggesting familiarity with aesthetic doc-
> trines or theories of the universe. A brilliant modern novelist is not only
> clever, but writes for clever people. . . . Trollope writes like a thorough
> man of business or a lawyer stating a case. . . . To accept such writing in
> the corresponding spirit implies, no doubt, the confession that you are
> a bit of a Philistine, and can put up with the plainest of bread and
> butter, and dispense with all the finer literary essences. I think, however,
> that at times one's state is the more gracious for accepting the position.
> There is something so friendly and ample and shrewd about one's tem-
> porary guide that one is the better for taking a stroll with him and
> listening to gossiping family stories, even though they be rather rambling
> and never scandalous. . . .
>
> But taking Trollope to represent the point of view from which there
> is a certain truthfulness in the picture – and no novelist can really do
> more than give one set of impressions – posterity may after all consider
> his novels as a very instructive document. . . . The middle of the nine-
> teenth century – our descendants may possibly say – was really a time
> in which a great intellectual, political, and social revolution was begin-
> ning to make itself perceptible. . . . And yet in this ancient novelist we

see the society of the time, the squires and parsons and officials, and
the women whom they courted, entirely unconscious of any approaching
convulsions. . . . Then [our descendants] will look back to the early
days of Queen Victoria as a delightful time, when it was possible to
take things quietly, and a good, sound sensible optimism was the prevalent state of mind. How far the estimate would be true is another question; but Trollope, as representing such an epoch, will supply a soothing
if rather mild stimulant for the imagination, and it will be admitted that
if he was not among the highest intellects of his benighted time, he was
as sturdy, wholesome, and kindly a human being as could be desired.[11]

Stephen clearly was not among those who like art that conceals art. It is
one of the curious twists of literary history, that in Stephen's case one can,
through the comments of his own daughter, see the difference a generation
makes. Virginia Woolf had high, if qualified, praise for Trollope. For her
he represented an earlier tradition brought to perfection. In 1928 she applauded Meredith for his innovations because 'it is a possible contention
that after those two perfect novels, *Pride and Prejudice* and *The Small
House at Allington*, English fiction had to escape from the dominion of
that perfection'.[12] In an essay written the following year, she placed
Trollope among the 'Truth-tellers' (with Defoe, Swift, Borrow, W. E. Norris
and Maupassant): 'We get from their novels the same sort of refreshment
and delight that we get from seeing something actually happen in the
street below.' And again, 'We believe in Barchester as we do in the reality
of our own weekly bills. Nor, indeed, do we wish to escape from the consequences of our belief, for the truth of the Slopes and the Proudies, the
truth of the evening party where Mrs. Proudie has her dress torn off her
back under the light of eleven gas jets, is entirely acceptable. At the top
of his bent Trollope is a big, if not first-rate novelist.'[13]

By 1906, Lewis Melville, although apparently unaware of the recent
republication of many Trollope titles, discussed the novelist in an essay
that can be taken as representative of the gradually progressing critical
acceptance that accompanied the first Trollope revival:

Every writer has his ups and downs in the estimation of the generations immediately succeeding his own; but of all the mighty none have
fallen so low as Anthony Trollope. His has been the worst fate that can
befall a writer: he has not been abused: he has been ignored; and he is
not disappearing: he has disappeared. . . .

Perhaps the temporary eclipse of Trollope is due largely to his

Autobiography.... The public naturally has not gone below the surface; and it has accepted Trollope's statements without reservation.

Melville then lists his favourite Trollope titles: the six Barsetshire novels, as well as *The Three Clerks, Orley Farm, Can You Forgive Her?*, the two Phineas books, *The Prime Minister* and 'perhaps' *The Eustace Diamonds*. Upon this 'very sound basis' Trollope's fame depends. Melville continues: 'Trollope did not take for his province the matters of life and death. He was pre-eminently a chronicler of small-beer, and at his best when dealing with such trifles as the appointment to a deanery or a wardenship, and the subsequent intrigues.' Of the passage where Mr Crawley, his pride conquered, thanks Lucy Robarts for her services to his stricken family, Melville says 'There is nothing finer in Trollope, and perhaps nothing better in English fiction.' The essay concludes:

Trollope's best books are veritable human documents, and his scenes are as true to life as are his characters. . . . Within his limits he did excellent work; and the fact that he was for many years prior to his death the most popular of English writers of fiction is a tribute alike to his powers and to the public which had the discernment to recognise them. He must for ever rank high among the exponents of English country life in mid-Victorian times; and the day cannot be far distant when he will take his place, not perhaps with the greatest English novelists, but certainly not far below them.[14]

One can be reasonably certain that Sadleir's version of the 'disappearance' and the critical disparagement of Trollope was based largely on Paul and Melville.[15] At any rate he did not base it upon William Dean Howells. For during the very years of severest critical neglect, the prominent American novelist and man of letters was giving an altogether different reading. Were it not that Howells's references to Trollope are scattered and brief (except for some essays on heroines in which Howells is not at his best), he would certainly be included in the collection proper. Howells, who knew Trollope but disliked him strongly, came late to an appreciation of his novels. But by 1889 he was saying:

The art of fiction, as Jane Austen knew it, declined from her. . . . The only observer of English middle-class life since Jane Austen worthy to be named with her was not George Eliot. . . . It was Anthony Trollope who was most like her in simple honesty and instinctive truth, as unphilosophized as the light of common day; but he was so warped

from a wholesome ideal as to wish at times to be like the caricaturist
Thackeray, and to stand about in his scene, talking it over with his
hands in his pockets, interrupting the action, and spoiling the illusion
in which alone the truth of art resides. Mainly, his instinct was too
much for his ideal, and with a low view of life in its civic relations and a
thoroughly *bourgeois* soul, he yet produced works whose beauty is surpassed only by the effect of a more poetic writer in the novels of
Thomas Hardy.[16]

Six years later he was setting a still higher value on that 'simple honesty
and instinctive truth':

> You cannot be at perfect ease with a friend who does not joke, and I
> suppose this is what deprived me of a final satisfaction in the company
> of Anthony Trollope, who jokes heavily or not at all, and whom I
> should otherwise make bold to declare the greatest of English novelists;
> as it is, I must put before him Jane Austen, whose books, late in life,
> have been a youthful rapture with me. Even without much humor
> Trollope's books have been a vast pleasure to me through their simple
> truthfulness. Perhaps if they were more humorous they would not be so
> true to the British life and character present in them in the whole
> length and breadth of its expansive commonplaceness. It is their
> serious fidelity which gives them a value unique in literature, and which
> if it were carefully analyzed would afford a principle of the same quality
> in an author who was undoubtedly one of the finest of artists as well as
> the most Philistine of men.[17]

In 1899 Howells wrote in an essay that was unpublished during his lifetime:

> In all that time [the nineteenth century] the most artistic, that is to say
> the most truthful English novelist was Anthony Trollope, and he was
> so unconscious of his excellence, that at times he strove hard for the
> most inartistic, the most untruthful attitudes of Thackeray.[18]

And finally, in 1901, Howells began a discussion of Trollopian heroines
by lamenting that the Victorian period should be represented by Dickens
and Thackeray rather than by the 'far greater artists' George Eliot and
Trollope. In his view Trollope's 'immense acquaintance with society in all
its ranks and orders has taken the mind of his critics from his profound
and even subtle proficiency in the region of motive'. Of Lily Dale's career

in *The Small House at Allington*, Howells says, 'It is a great story, whose absolute fidelity to manners, and whose reliance on the essential strength of motive must exalt it in the esteem of those accustomed to think of what they read.' He begins his discussion of Mrs Proudie by asserting that Trollope is 'the most English of the English novelists'. And in this essay, revising his earlier judgement, he now finds Trollope a 'true humorist' as well as a 'profound moralist':

> He surpassed the only contemporaries worthy to be named with him in very essential things as far as he surpassed those two great women [Jane Austen and George Eliot] in keeping absolutely the level of the English nature. He was a greater painter of manners than Thackeray because he was neither a sentimentalist nor a caricaturist; and he was of a more convincing imagination than Dickens because he knew and employed the probable facts in the case and kept himself free of all fantastic contrivances.

And in regard to his specific subject, heroines, Howells concludes:

> Upon the whole I should be inclined to place Trollope among the very first of those supreme novelists to whom the ever-womanly has revealed itself. . . it is not the very soul of the sex that shows itself in [his portraits] but it is the mind, the heart, the conscience, the manner; and this for one painter is enough. . . . Trollope has shown them as we mostly see them when we meet them in society and as we know them at home; and if it were any longer his to choose, he might well rest content with his work. For my part I wish I might send my readers to the long line of his wise, just, sane novels, which I have been visiting anew for the purposes of these papers, and finding as delightful as ever, and, thanks to extraordinary gifts for forgetting, almost as fresh as ever.[19]

The first essay in this collection is that by Henry James, published in July 1883 after Trollope's death in December 1882. It is a fitting beginning because, aside from James's pre-eminence as novelist, critic and theoretician of the novel, this piece has become for many the cornerstone of Trollopian criticism. For James himself, it was something of an *amende honorable* for the scathing remarks he had made in reviewing Trollope in the mid-1860s. Of *Can You Forgive Her?* he had said, 'Of course we can, and forget her, too, for that matter.' He had called *The Belton Estate* 'a *stupid* book. . . . It is essentially, organically, consistently stupid. . . . It is without a single

idea.'[20] Twenty years later, as an established novelist, he made large
though circumscribed claims for Trollope, in the process putting the questions that have dominated Trollope criticism ever since, set down in the
phrases that have been ringing in the ears of Trollope's critics for nearly
a hundred years: Trollope's 'great, his inestimable merit was a complete
appreciation of the usual'; he 'takes the good-natured, temperate conciliatory view' of all human complexities; he 'represents in an eminent degree
[the] natural decorum of the English spirit'; he was 'a man of genius'
in virtue of his 'happy instinctive perception of human varieties.... He
had no airs of being able to tell you *why* people in a given situation
would conduct themselves in a particular way; it was enough for him that
he felt their feelings and struck the right note, because he had, as it were,
a good ear. If he was a knowing psychologist, he was so by grace.' James
stresses the social and moral interest of Trollope's stories. He says Trollope
should be judged 'in the lump'. Of Trollope's presentation of the English
girl, James writes, 'he took possession of her, and turned her inside out';
he 'plant[s] her so well on her feet.... She is always definite and natural.'
In a most notable commendation – coming from Henry James – he
declares that Trollope's American portraits 'hit it off more happily than
the attempt to depict American character from the European point of
view is accustomed to do' and that with regard to the American girl,
'Trollope's treatment of this complicated being is full of good humour
and of that fatherly indulgence, that almost motherly sympathy, which
characterizes his attitude, throughout toward the youthful feminine.'
Trollope, says James, often 'achieved a conspicuous intensity of the
tragical'; he points out Trollope's extraordinary facility in using letters
as an 'unfailing resource' in his fiction. Will Trollope endure? 'Trollope
did not write for posterity ... but these are just the writers whom posterity is apt to put in its pocket.... Trollope will remain one of the
most trustworthy, though not one of the most eloquent, of the writers
who have helped the heart of man to know itself.' On the other hand,
James's reservations are almost as pointed as his praise: Trollope's 'fertility
was gross, importunate.... He abused his gift, overworked it, rode his
horse too hard. As an artist he never took himself seriously.'

     The political novels James finds 'distinctly dull'; indeed he confesses
that he has 'not been able to read them.' Trollope 'had no "views" whatever on the subject of novel-writing'. As for style, 'he is seated on the back
of a heavy-footed prose'. He 'had as little as possible of the quality of
irony'. And, most damagingly, Trollope 'took suicidal satisfaction in reminding the reader that the story he was telling was only, after all, make
believe.... These little slaps at credulity... are very discouraging.' James's

pronouncements, those of censure as well as those of approbation, are returned to again and again by the critics included in this volume.

Frederic Harrison is the other representative of Trollope's century to be included in this collection, and his essay, written in 1895, may be somewhat more apologetic than he himself would have preferred had the critical climate been different. 'In view of the enormous popularity he once enjoyed', writes Harrison, 'I cannot altogether omit him from these studies.' Harrison was one of the first to defend Trollope's style, calling his 'command over plain English almost perfect for his limited purpose'. Harrison applauds Trollope for never sinking to affectation or extravagance, for his unity of texture and harmony of tone, his lack of discordant notes, 'a mastery which conceals itself'. In producing conversation Trollope has 'hardly any equal' in 'absolute realism of spoken words'. Harrison claims for Trollope something more than 'photographic accuracy' in depicting English society, namely 'very subtle insight and delicate intuition' in portraying character.

W. P. Ker, whose University College lecture, although not published until 1955, was probably written about 1912,[21] attacks the thesis that, because Trollope's works were written with mechanical regularity they were hackwork. Realism such as Trollope's is 'inventive and imaginative'. Ker takes up a classic example of Trollope's intrusive narrator: when the author comes forward early on in *Barchester Towers* and announces that the widow Bold will marry neither of her unsatisfactory wooers, 'this confidence does not mean that the spectator knows all the story beforehand. It means that what is going on is comedy; that. . . there is no great stress or strain.' For Ker, Trollope's ability to keep up a created world through sequels is unequalled by any English author; Ker admires not only the Barsetshire but also the political or Palliser series; moreover, he likes the *politics* therein. (He also likes the ubiquitous foxhunting scenes.) He is not afraid of the comparison with Balzac.

Had Ker's lecture been printed earlier it might have served later Trollopians well, perhaps even Michael Sadleir himself, whose extensive and crucial work on Trollope is marred by nagging elements of apology. However, the excerpt reprinted here from *Trollope: A Commentary* (1927) is not only free from apology but noteworthy for its statement, quoted above, of the Trollope dilemma, and its attempts to solve that dilemma, to get at Trollope's peculiar excellence. In doing so Sadleir added to the list of phrases well-known in Trollope criticism. He begins where Trollope would have wanted him to, namely with 'power of characterization',[22] but, of course, one asks more than that as an explanation for Trollope's 'strange potency'. For Sadleir the answer lies in Trollope's 'acceptance and his profound understanding of ordinary daily life', something close to James's 'complete appreciation of the usual'. But Sadleir refines the concept: Trollope is 'never a writer in revolt', his 'extreme acquiescence' is such that 'he is not even a critical despot over the society of his imagination'. Towards his characters he is 'at once genially disposed but fundamentally detached'. It is 'this almost pugnacious acceptance of reality that distinguishes him from all other novelists of standing'. Prominent in Trollope's work Sadleir finds the 'power of dramatization of the undramatic'; at the same time he draws attention to Julian Hawthorne's observation that Trollope unobtrusively inserted considerable violence and sensation in his fiction, but in such a manner as not to 'alarm' the reader.

In an appendix to his *Commentary* Sadleir printed a classification of Trollope's fiction into ten categories and gave asterisks — one to three — 'Baedeker fashion', to recommended works. Ranking Trollope's works has always been a source of disagreement (and fun), for every critic must, however indirectly, pick and choose among the forty-seven novels.[23] Sadleir did so in the most forthright and elaborate fashion, and I have reprinted his much-disputed ratings.

Paul Elmer More's essay, 'My Debt to Trollope', was in part occasioned by the publication of Sadleir's *Commentary*, More objecting to its 'recurrent note of apology'. When told, for example, that Trollope could not do what Balzac, and Dostoevsky, and Turgenev and Manzoni did, More asks whether they could have written the chronicles of Barsetshire. He believes Sadleir's 'conciliatory' approach compels him to present Trollope as 'intellectually without ideas and imaginatively without wings', something one could do only if he identifies thought with 'fussy activity of mind' and subscribes, however unconsciously, to what More calls 'the current theory of the dehumanization of art'. At any rate, More's complaint — and, as we have seen, it is an old one in Trollope criticism — leads him to attempt to explain 'why a reader so acute otherwise belittles critically what instinctively he admires'. More also places special emphasis upon Trollope's ethical concern, a subject frequently returned to by later critics.

Lord David Cecil's discussion of Trollope begins by asserting that in 1934 Trollope was 'the only Victorian novelist whom our sensitive intelligentsia appear to be able to read without experiencing an intolerable sense of jar'. He explains this by claiming a kind of negative superiority in Trollope, who avoided the mistakes of his contemporaries, namely sentimentality, melodrama, inconsistency of characterisation, and absolute goodness or evil in characters. But Trollope's imagination is weak; he falls short of his great contemporaries 'as an artist'. Of style, in the sense of a marked style, 'Trollope has none at all'. His dialogue, however, is 'the most realistic ... of any English novelist's', although, if true to life, 'it is also sometimes as dull as life'.

For Chauncey Brewster Tinker, whose essay first appeared in 1947, Trollope's fecundity is an important and decided strength. Tinker stresses evenness of quality: 'Trollope has no *juvenilia*'. Trollope's style does not 'date'; perhaps his 'perfect clarity and unpretentiousness may ... prove to be a saving grace, in that his very lack of manner keeps him from becoming antiquated'. The special quality that makes the novels so warm and readable is our 'association with the author himself, a man wordly-wise, yet kindly and, above all, fairminded. . . . Not even Henry Fielding associates with his readers on more agreeable terms.'

A. O. J. Cockshut's *Anthony Trollope* (1955) was the first full-length critical study of the novelist except for Hugh Walpole's disappointing volume for the English Men of Letters series in 1928. Cockshut, who takes Trollope's importance for granted, believes that he 'is a gloomier, more introspective, more satirical, and more profound writer than he is usually credited with being; and further, the Barsetshire series, fine as it is, is not fully characteristic of his genius'. Cockshut develops this theory in the latter half of his work, the section called 'Progress to Pessimism'. His book remains controversial, but there can be no doubting its importance, and the emphasis on works other than the early ones has proved groundbreaking. Because the progress to pessimism thesis is tied to chapters on individual novels, I have instead reprinted the discussion of Trollope's insights into human nature, with its helpful observations about the absence of children in Trollope's fiction, about self-deception, endurance and obsession, and about outcasts.

Frank O'Connor, in *The Mirror in the Roadway* (1956), despite an initial misplaced emphasis upon the importance of the *Autobiography* in downgrading Trollope's reputation, has engaging and important things to say about Trollope. His discussion, to some extent, addresses itself to Cecil's. O'Connor says that Trollope's 'favorite device is to lead his reader very gently up the garden path of his own conventions and prejudices and then to point out that the reader is wrong'. Again, and just as provocatively, O'Connor sees Trollope's special essence not in realism, in loyalty to facts, but in 'a certain attitude to the facts, to a humility and passivity in the face of life'. He claims that 'Trollope is whatever the opposite of a moralist may be' — an idea that stated baldly sounds off the mark; refined, it can probably be made to support Ruth apRoberts's thesis that Trollope advocated something akin to situation ethics.

Bradford Booth, for so many years Trollope's academic champion, is represented by the final chapter of his book, *Anthony Trollope: Aspects of His Life and Art* (1958). Entitled 'The Chaos of Criticism', it states succinctly and with telling examples the extraordinarily divergent opinions held on individual Trollope novels. As for an explanation of this lack of agreement among critics, Booth suggests that the source of Trollope's power is the 'keeness of his sensibility and the warmth of his sympathy' and that these qualities are perhaps just the kind that, in a particular novel, one reader and not another is likely to sense. This is well enough. On the other hand, the final paragraph of this last chapter epitomises the entire book in its spelling out of Trollope's supposed shortcomings. As late as 1958, Trollope was underrated, even, apparently, by his leading academic advocate.

Novelists, as I have said, have been much less circumspect in their approval of Trollope than have academic critics. Gerald Warner Brace, writing in 1961, said unabashedly that Trollope is the kind of writer who doesn't need critical endorsement: 'his hold over the future is as sure as Chaucer's'. For Brace, Trollope's fertility of invention, that productivity that James found 'almost indecent' is a 'miraculous gift'. His true peers are Dumas and Balzac. Especially noteworthy is Trollope's manipulation of material in such fashion as to keep forty or fifty characters, as in *The Last Chronicle*, in a state of 'living suspension', giving them a vitality and relevance that makes the reader believe in and follow these characters 'from moment to moment'. As for Trollope's often disparaged style, Brace finds it 'molded and shaped into an instrument of his honesty, and . . . in its own way, it may be said to have the strengh of ten'.

For readers who eschew chronological order, Gordon Ray's discussion of 'Trollope at Full Length', published in 1968, might be the place to begin. His presentation contains an enormous amount of information, bibliographical and critical, marshalled with conciseness and ease. It is a remarkable overview of Trollope's accomplishment and one which, unlike that of so many critics, is not based on a partial reading of the novels. The section reprinted here ends with the words that closed down for good the apologetic note in academic criticism: 'Trollope was a great, truthful, varied artist, who wrote better than he or his contemporaries realized, and who left behind him more novels of lasting value than any other writer in English.'

Those who think Trollope's novels are little more than simple stories of young romantic love that end happily in marriage are urged to ponder J. Hillis Miller's 'Self and Community' from his *Form of Victorian Fiction* (1968). Miller examines Trollope's treatment of self-fulfilment through love in its relation to society, together with such varied but pertinent considerations as the stubbornness of Trollope's heroines, the use of paralleling subplots, the function of the narrator, resolution through assimilation of the protagonists into the community, and, finally, 'open-ended-ness'. His analysis includes a distinctly structuralist, extended analogy between language and interpersonal relations in fiction.

From Ruth apRoberts's book, *Trollope: Artist and Moralist* (1971), I reprint her celebrated if sometimes controversial discussion called 'The Shaping Principle'. Trollope's constant ethical concern, she says, is rooted in a consideration of particular circumstances, a stance that today is called situation ethics: 'It is Trollope's art to be advocate for each one of his characters; he makes the best case possible for one, and then juxtaposes this with the demands of the other, defended with a similar passionate sympathy. . . . His great achievement, often just called being "good at characterization," may be really that he communicates his characters' sense of self.' Hers is a bold and striking attempt to circumscribe and define the 'Trollope mystery'. (The words about making the best possible case for each of his characters bring to mind Max Beerbohm's *mot*, 'Trollope isn't always turning out his characters' pockets to see what he can find against them.')[24]

James Gindin, in *Harvest of a Quiet Eye: The Novel of Compassion* (1971), sees Trollope's novels, especially the later ones, as ethically descriptive rather than prescriptive. Trollope, Gindin writes, 'maintains a sense of compassion towards most human creatures', a compassion that dominates the novels 'in direct proportion to the recognition that a meaningful code of virtue cannot be followed and applied in the unjust world'. For Trollope, despite his apparent piety, 'does not establish a world that operates on any principle beyond itself, does not develop a Christian universe'. And hence, 'compassion becomes an attitude in the fictional world that is unsystematized and unregulated, becomes a substitute for the metaphysical assurance man seeks without finding'.

David Skilton, in the concluding chapter to *Anthony Trollope and His Contemporaries* (1972), takes up Trollope's 'realism'. Skilton's distinctions and insights help clear the air on a subject that has been the source of much misguided discussion since the days of the first reviews of the novels. He notes, for example, that the belief that the nearly perfect illusion of reality in Trollope's fictional world is somehow particularly close to 'objective reality' need not mean that his fictional world is not an 'artistic construct'. Nor should it direct our attention away from 'one of the most important features of Trollopian realism – its independence'. All the 'rules' of the fictional world are built into the books, and, as it is the narrator who teaches us how to interpret what is happening, the 'narrative presence of Trollope's persona in the novels is essential to their illusion, and not damaging to it'.

C. P. Snow, whose own career as novelist and civil servant has similarities to Trollope's, is an enthusiastic and sensitive reader of Trollope. Reprinted here from *Trollope: His Life and Art* (1975) is his considered opinion: Trollope is the 'finest natural psychologist of all nineteenth-century novelists'.[25] Specifically, Lord Snow posits 'percipience' as Trollope's greatest gift: 'he could see a person as others saw him; he could also see him as he saw himself. He had both insight and empathy, working together in exceptional harmony. Further . . . he could not only see a person in the here-and-now . . . but also in the past and in the future'. (Snow remarks that readers without at least some shred of Trollopian percipience themselves cannot see anything in Trollope.) Snow's analysis, which is a development of James's, concludes that Trollope, by telling 'so much of the truth about his great characters', achieved 'one of the peaks of realistic novel writing'.

John Halperin's essay, an abridgement of the introductory chapter of *Trollope and Politics: A Study of the Pallisers and Others* (1977) shows Trollope's political novels, very much to the fore today, to be firmly rooted in a keen and informed knowledge of politics. These books are not, as Leopold Amery claimed, political novels with 'the politics left out'. Rather, insists Halperin, 'it is hard to see how novels about Victorian politics and politicians could tell us more about these subjects'. Halperin's discussion is important, for it indicates how subtly Trollope founded his fiction upon the real world, at the same time blending life and art so skilfully that some readers believe his work mere 'social photography', while others aver it to be essentially, predominantly, imaginative.

James Kincaid's provocative and decidedly modern discussion of Trollope's narrator, taken from his book *The Novels of Anthony Trollope* (1977) brings us full circle to James. But if James found it 'suicidal' for Trollope's narrator to remind the reader that the story he was telling was only 'make believe', for Kincaid 'Trollope's most serious and pressing claim to be recognized as a major artist rests principally with his subtle and organic use of the dramatized narrator'. For James, the only analogy appropriate here is between novelist and historian, and no more should Trollope remind us that we are reading something made-up than Macaulay should intimate that William of Orange was a myth. For Trollope, the analogy is between novelist and shoemaker. Trollope's comparison is partly humorous self-depreciation, but, Kincaid maintains, 'the assumption that art is not something observed but something made is a serious one'. Trollope continually tells us that the novel we are reading is 'art, not life, and that art, unlike life, is an affair of convention, tradition, pure artifice'.

Juliet McMaster's essay, a slightly abridged version of the concluding chapter of *Trollope's Palliser Novels: Theme and Pattern* (1978) also postulates authorial presence as crucial to Trollope's artistic success. Her discussion is less theoretical, more descriptive, than Kincaid's, although the two are in fact complementary. McMaster examines the narrator's tone; she observes, for example, that 'Trollope reminds one often of an accommodating lecturer, a personal presence responding to the needs of a present audience, humorous often, and patient, and engagingly concerned with his students' full understanding of the subject in hand.' Trollope's tone makes us sympathetic and interested readers; he has 'endowed us with his own sense of his characters' life'.

Trollope criticism, then, although it has not altogether solved the 'Trollope problem', has arrived at full maturity. In effect it has caught up with the ordinary reader (not to mention many fellow-novelists) in admiration for and loyalty to Trollope.

The essays are reprinted with minimal alteration. All ellipses are indicated by spaced stops. The original spelling and punctuation have been retained, though single quotation marks have been used throughout and a few misspelled proper names have been silently corrected. References in the text to Trollope's novels have been standardised to chapter (and volume, where necessary) of the first edition. (There exists a 'chaos of texts' in Trollope because there is no standard or even collected edition.) The notes are printed in their original form, except that some renumbering has been necessary; moreover, shortened second citations that appear in an excerpt for the first time are expanded to accord with the actual first citation. I wish to thank Miss Nina Burgis for her helpful advice and for assistance in proofreading.

New York, 1979   *N.J.H.*

NOTES

1. *Trollope: A Commentary*, 3rd edn (London: Oxford University Press, 1961), pp. 366–7.
2. *The Great Tradition* (London: Chatto & Windus, 1948), pp. 15, 21.
3. *The Opinions of Oliver Allston* (New York: Dutton, 1941), p. 295.
4. R. C. Terry, *Anthony Trollope: The Artist in Hiding* (London: Macmillan, 1977), pp. 49–54.

5. This list and that of the American publishers draw upon the recently published vol. 602 of *The National Union Catalog: Pre-1956 Imprints* (New York: Mansell, 1978) and upon Albert H. Gordon, 'Anthony Trollope: The Fall and Rise of His Popularity', *Gazette of the Grolier Club*, n.s. 24–5 (June–Dec. 1976 [1978]), 60–73. Gordon gives prominence to the John Lane series and discusses the introductions that Algar Thorold supplied for these editions.

6. *Corrected Impressions: Essays on Victorian Writers* (London: Heinemann, 1895), pp. 173, 175–7.

7. 'Trollope Revisited', *Essays and Studies by Members of the English Association* (Oxford: Clarendon Press, 1920), VI, 41, 55, 64–6.

8. 'The Apotheosis of the Novel under Queen Victoria', *Nineteenth Century*, 41 (May 1897), 783–4.

9. *Saturday Review*, 16 (24 Oct. 1963), 554–5; reprinted in *Anthony Trollope: The Critical Heritage*, ed. Donald Smalley (London: Routledge & Kegan Paul, 1969), p. 187.

10. *Nation* (New York), 1 (13 July 1865), 51–2; reprinted in Smalley, p. 233.

11. 'Anthony Trollope', *The National Review*, 38 (Sep. 1901), 68–9, 78–9, 84.

12. 'The Novels of George Meredith', *Collected Essays* (New York: Harcourt, Brace & World, 1967), I, 230–1; written in 1928; originally published in *The Common Reader: Second Series* (1932).

13. 'Phases of Fiction', *Collected Essays*, II, 57, 62; originally published in *The Bookman* (April, May and June, 1929) and reprinted in *Granite and Rainbow* (1958).

14. *Victorian Novelists* (London: Constable, 1906), pp. 168–9, 171, 174–5, 182, 184, 186–7. George Gissing, a few years earlier, wrote that Trollope 'at his best . . . is an admirable writer of the pedestrian school, and this disappearance of his name does not mean final oblivion'. On the question of whether the *Autobiography* damaged Trollope's reputation, Gissing added his own twist, saying that he hoped it were true, namely that 'the great big stupid public' was 'really, somewhere in its secret economy, offended by that revelation of mechanical methods' (*The Private Papers of Henry Ryecroft* [London: Constable, 1903] p. 213).

15. R. C. Terry (pp. 52–3) makes this connection; he also points out that Sadleir quoted Melville's phrase 'a chronicler of small-beer' while ascribing it to Richard Garnett.

16. 'Effectism', from 'The Editor's Study', *Harper's Monthly* (Nov. 1889) and reprinted in *W. D. Howells as Critic*, ed. Edwin H. Cady (London: Routledge & Kegan Paul, 1973), pp. 169–70.

17. *My Literary Passions* (New York: Harper, 1895), p. 247.

18. 'Novel-Writing and Novel-Reading: an Impersonal Explanation', ed. William M. Gibson, *Bulletin of the New York Public Library*, 62 (Jan. 1958), 21.

19. *Heroines of Fiction* (New York and London: Harper, 1901), II, 94, 96–7, 122–3, 137; originally published in *Harper's Bazar* in April and June, 1901. Another American, A. Edward Newton, in an important

early essay, cites Howells's assertion that Trollope was 'the greatest of the Victorians', and then venture his own judgment that 'Dickens and Thackeray aside, Trollope will outlive all the other novelists of his time' ('A Great Victorian', in *The Amenities of Book-Collecting* [1920; Boston: Little, Brown, 1929], pp. 251, 252–3; an earlier version of the essay was privately printed as *Trollopeana* in 1911).

20. *Nation* (New York), 1 (28 Sept. 1865), 409–10; and 2 (4 Jan. 1866), 21–2; reprinted in Smalley, pp. 249–53 and 254–8.

21. Donald Smalley (*Victorian Fiction: A Guide to Research*, ed. Lionel Stevenson [Cambridge, Mass.: Harvard University Press, 1964], p. 198) believed the essay was probably written 'not long after 1906, doubtless because of reference to the "recent" preface by Frederic Harrison to a new edition of the Barsetshire novels published that year, but another reference, that to Émile Faguet's *Rousseau contre Molière*, 1912, suggests later composition'.

22. Trollope wrote: 'I do not think it probable that my name will remain among those who in the next century will be known as the writers of English prose fiction—but if it does, that permanence of success will probably rest on the characters of Plantagenet Palliser, Lady Glencora, and the Rev. Mr. Crawley' (*An Autobiography*, ed. Frederick Page [London: Oxford University Press, 1950], p. 361).

23. A recent example is found in the introductory chapter of P.D.Edwards's book, *Anthony Trollope: His Art and Scope* (University of Queensland Press, 1977), p.7:

> My own grading . . . is limited to singling out what seem to me the very best and the very worst of the novels. In respect of the much larger number in between, I generally indicate those which I see as falling little short of Trollope's best novels, *The Warden, Phineas Finn, The Vicar of Bullhampton, Ralph the Heir, Lady Anna, Is He Popenjoy?, John Caldigate,* and *Cousin Henry* are works that I place in this category. Above them . . . I place *Barchester Towers, Doctor Thorne, The Claverings, He Knew He Was Right, The Eustace Diamonds, The Way We Live Now,* and *Mr. Scarborough's Family,* all of which seem to me among the major Victorian novels. At the opposite end, I regard as Trollope's distinct failures the following: *The Kellys and the O'Kellys, La Vendée, Castle Richmond, The Struggles of Brown, Jones and Robinson, The Golden Lion of Granpère, Harry Heathcote of Gangoil, The Prime Minister, Kept in the Dark, Marion Fay, The Fixed Period,* and *The Landleaguers.*

24. Quoted in David Cecil, *Max: A Biography* (Boston: Houghton Mifflin, 1965), p. 365.

25. These words are quoted, not from the section reprinted here, but from the opening paragraph of the book (p. 9).

HENRY JAMES
Anthony Trollope*

When, a few months ago, Anthony Trollope laid down his pen for the last time, it was a sign of the complete extinction of that group of admirable writers who, in England, during the preceding half century, had done so much to elevate the art of the novelist. The author of *The Warden*, of *Barchester Towers*, of *Framley Parsonage*, does not, to our mind, stand on the very same level as Dickens, Thackeray and George Eliot; for his talent was of a quality less fine than theirs. But he belonged to the same family — he had as much to tell us about English life; he was strong, genial and abundant. He published too much; the writing of novels had ended by becoming, with him, a perceptibly mechanical process. Dickens was prolific, Thackeray produced with a freedom for which we are constantly grateful; but we feel that these writers had their periods of gestation. They took more time to look at their subject; relatively (for to-day there is not much leisure, at best, for those who undertake to entertain a hungry public), they were able to wait for inspiration. Trollope's fecundity was prodigious; there was no limit to the work he was ready to do. It is not unjust to say that he sacrificed quality to quantity. Abundance, certainly, is in itself a great merit; almost all the greatest writers have been abundant. But Trollope's fertility was gross, importunate; he himself contended, we believe, that he had given to the world a greater number of printed pages of fiction than any of his literary contemporaries. Not only did his novels follow each other without visible intermission, overlapping and treading on each other's heels, but most of these works are of extraordinary length. *Orley Farm, Can You Forgive Her?, He Knew He Was Right*, are exceedingly voluminous tales. *The Way We Live Now* is one of the longest of modern novels. Trollope produced, moreover, in the intervals of larger labour a great number of short stories, many of them charming, as well as various

* From *Partial Portraits* (London: Macmillan, 1888), pp. 97–133. First published in slightly different form in the New York *Century Magazine*, n.s. 4 (July 1883), 385–95.

books of travel, and two or three biographies. He was the great *impro-visatore* of these latter years. Two distinguished story-tellers of the other sex — one in France and one in England — have shown an extraordinary facility of composition; but Trollope's pace was brisker even than that of the wonderful Madame Sand and the delightful Mrs. Oliphant. He had taught himself to keep this pace, and had reduced his admirable faculty to a system. Every day of his life he wrote a certain number of pages of his current tale, a number sacramental and invariable, independent of mood and place. It was once the fortune of the author of these lines to cross the Atlantic in his company, and he has never forgotten the magnificent example of plain persistence that it was in the power of the eminent novelist to give on that occasion. The season was unpropitious, the vessel overcrowded, the voyage detestable; but Trollope shut himself up in his cabin every morning for a purpose which, on the part of a distinguished writer who was also an invulnerable sailor, could only be communion with the muse. He drove his pen as steadily on the tumbling ocean as in Montague Square; and as his voyages were many, it was his practice before sailing to come down to the ship and confer with the carpenter, who was instructed to rig up a rough writing-table in his small sea-chamber. Trollope has been accused of being deficient in imagination, but in the face of such a fact as that the charge will scarcely seem just. The power to shut one's eyes, one's ears (to say nothing of another sense), upon the scenery of a pitching Cunarder and open them upon the loves and sorrows of Lily Dale or the conjugal embarrassments of Lady Glencora Palliser, is certainly a faculty which could take to itself wings. The imagination that Trollope possessed he had at least thoroughly at his command. I speak of all this in order to explain (in part) why it was that, with his extraordinary gift, there was always in him a certain infusion of the common. He abused his gift, overworked it, rode his horse too hard. As an artist he never took himself seriously; many people will say this was why he was so delightful. The people who take themselves seriously are prigs and bores; and Trollope, with his perpetual 'story', which was the only thing he cared about, his strong good sense, hearty good nature, generous appreciation of life in all its varieties, responds in perfection to a certain English ideal. According to that ideal it is rather dangerous to be explicitly or consciously an artist — to have a system, a doctrine, a form. Trollope, from the first, went in, as they say, for having as little form as possible; it is probably safe to affirm that he had no 'views' whatever on the subject of novel-writing. His whole manner is that of a man who regards the practice as one of the more delicate industries, but has never troubled his head nor clogged his pen with theories about the nature of his business. Fortunately he was not obliged to do so, for he had an easy road to success; and his honest, familiar, deliberate way of treating his readers as if he were one of them, and shared their indifference to a general view, their limitations of knowledge, their love of a comfortable ending, endeared him to many persons in England and America. It is in the name of some chosen form that, of late years, things have been made most disagreeable for the novel-reader, who has been treated by several votaries of the new experiments in fiction to unwonted and bewildering sensations. With Trollope we were always safe; there were sure to be no new experiments.

His great, his inestimable merit was a complete appreciation of the usual. This gift is not rare in the annals of English fiction; it would naturally be found in a walk of literature in which the feminine mind has laboured so fruitfully. Women are delicate and patient observers; they hold their noses close, as it were, to the texture of life. They feel and perceive the real with a kind of personal tact, and their observations are recorded in a thousand delightful volumes. Trollope, therefore, with his eyes comfortably fixed on the familiar, the actual, was far from having invented a new category; his great distinction is that in resting there his vision took in so much of the field. And then he *felt* all daily and immediate things as well as saw them; felt them in a simple, direct, salubrious way, with their sadness, their gladness, their charm, their comicality, all their obvious and measurable meanings. He never wearied of the pre-established round of English customs — never needed a respite or a change — was content to go on indefinitely watching the life that surrounded him, and holding up his mirror to it. Into this mirror the public, at first especially, grew very fond of looking — for it saw itself reflected in all the most credible and supposable ways, with that curiosity that people feel to know how they look when they are represented, 'just as they are', by a painter who does not desire to put them into an attitude, to drape them for an effect, to arrange his light and his accessories. This exact and on the whole becoming image, projected upon a surface without a strong intrinsic tone, constitutes mainly the entertainment that Trollope offered his readers. The striking thing to the critic was that his robust and patient mind had no particular bias, his imagination no light of its own. He saw things neither pictorially and grotesquely like Dickens; nor with that combined disposition to satire and to literary form which gives such 'body', as they say of wine, to the manner of Thackeray; nor with anything of the philosophic, the transcendental cast — the desire to follow them to their remote relations — which we associate with the name of George Eliot. Trollope had his elements of fancy, of satire, of irony; but these qualities were not very highly developed, and he walked mainly by the light of his good sense, his clear, direct vision

of the things that lay nearest, and his great natural kindness. There is
something remarkably tender and friendly in his feeling about all human
perplexities; he takes the good-natured, temperate conciliatory view – the
humorous view, perhaps, for the most part, yet without a touch of pessimistic prejudice. As he grew older, and had sometimes to go farther afield
for his subjects, he acquired a savour of bitterness and reconciled himself
sturdily to treating of the disagreeable. A more copious record of disagreeable matters could scarcely be imagined, for instance, than *The Way We
Live Now*. But, in general, he has a wholesome mistrust of morbid analysis,
an aversion to inflicting pain. He has an infinite love of detail, but his
details are, for the most part, the innumerable items of the expected.
When the French are disposed to pay a compliment to the English mind
they are so good as to say that there is in it something remarkably *honnête*.
If I might borrow this epithet without seeming to be patronizing, I should
apply it to the genius of Anthony Trollope. He represents in an eminent
degree this natural decorum of the English spirit, and represents it all the
better that there is not in him a grain of the mawkish or the prudish. He
writes, he feels, he judges like a man, talking plainly and frankly about
many things, and is by no means destitute of a certain saving grace of
coarseness. But he has kept the purity of his imagination and held fast to
old-fashioned reverences and preferences. He thinks it a sufficient objection
to several topics to say simply that they are unclean. There was nothing in
his theory of the story-teller's art that tended to convert the reader's or
the writer's mind into a vessel for polluting things. He recognised the right
of the vessel to protest, and would have regarded such a protest as conclusive. With a considerable turn for satire, though this perhaps is more
evident in his early novels than in his later ones, he had as little as possible
of the quality of irony. He never played with a subject, never juggled with
the sympathies or the credulity of his reader, was never in the least paradoxical or mystifying. He sat down to his theme in a serious, business-like
way, with his elbows on the table and his eye occasionally wandering to
the clock.

To touch successively upon these points is to attempt a portrait, which
I shall perhaps not altogether have failed to produce. The source of his
success in describing the life that lay nearest to him, and describing it ivy
without any of those artistic perversions that come, as we have said, from
a powerful imagination, from a cynical humour or from a desire to look, as
George Eliot expresses it, for the suppressed transitions that unite all
contrasts, the essence of this love of reality was his extreme interest in
character. This is the fine and admirable quality in Trollope, this is what
will preserve his best works in spite of those flatnesses which keep him

from standing on quite the same level as the masters. Indeed this quality is so much one of the finest (to my mind at least), that it makes me wonder the more that the writer who had it so abundantly and so naturally should not have just that distinction which Trollope lacks, and which we find in his three brilliant contemporaries. If he was in any degree a man of genius (and I hold that he was), it was in virtue of this happy, instinctive perception of human varieties. His knowledge of the stuff we are made of, his observation of the common behaviour of men and women, was not reasoned nor acquired, not even particularly studied. All human doings deeply interested him, human life, to his mind, was a perpetual story; but he never attempted to take the so-called scientific view, the view which has lately found ingenious advocates among the countrymen and successors of Balzac. He had no airs of being able to tell you *why* people in a given situation would conduct themselves in a particular way; it was enough for him that he felt their feelings and struck the right note, because he had, as it were, a good ear. If he was a knowing psychologist he was so by grace; he was just and true without apparatus and without effort. He must have had a great taste for the moral question; he evidently believed that this is the basis of the interest of fiction. We must be careful, of course, in attributing convictions and opinions to Trollope, who, as I have said, had as little as possible of the pedantry of his art, and whose occasional chance utterances in regard to the object of the novelist and his means of achieving it are of an almost startling simplicity. But we certainly do not go too far in saying that he gave his practical testimony in favour of the idea that the interest of a work of fiction is great in proportion as the people stand on their feet. His great effort was evidently to make them stand so; if he achieved this result with as little as possible of a flourish of the hand it was nevertheless the measure of his success. If he had taken sides on the droll, bemuddled opposition between novels of character and novels of plot, I can imagine him to have said (except that he never expressed himself in epigrams), that he preferred the former class, inasmuch as character in itself is plot, while plot is by no means character. It is more safe indeed to believe that his great good sense would have prevented him from taking an idle controversy seriously. Character, in any sense in which we can get at it, is action, and action is plot, and any plot which hangs together, even if it pretend to interest us only in the fashion of a Chinese puzzle, plays upon our emotion, our suspense, by means of personal references. We care what happens to people only in proportion as we know what people are. Trollope's great apprehension of the real, which was what made him so interesting, came to him through his desire to satisfy us on this point — to tell us what certain people were and what they did in consequence of being so. That is the purpose of each of his tales; and if these things produce an illusion it comes from the gradual abundance of his testimony as to the temper, the tone, the passions, the habits, the moral nature, of a certain number of contemporary Britons.

His stories, in spite of their great length, deal very little in the surprising, the exceptional, the complicated; as a general thing he has no great story to tell. The thing is not so much a story as a picture; if we hesitate to call it a picture it is because the idea of composition is not the controlling one and we feel that the author would regard the artistic, in general, as a kind of affectation. There is not even much description, in the sense which the present votaries of realism in France attach to that word. The painter lays his scene in a few deliberate, not especially pictorial strokes, and never dreams of finishing the piece for the sake of enabling the reader to hang it up. The finish, such as it is, comes later, from the slow and somewhat clumsy accumulation of small illustrations. These illustrations are sometimes of the commonest; Trollope turns them out inexhaustibly, repeats them freely, unfolds them without haste and without rest. But they are all of the most obvious sort, and they are none the worse for that. The point to be made is that they have no great spectacular interest (we beg pardon of the innumerable love-affairs that Trollope has described) like many of the incidents, say, of Walter Scott and of Alexandre Dumas: if we care to know about them (as repetitions of a usual case), it is because the writer has managed, in his candid, literal, somewhat lumbering way, to tell us that about the men and women concerned which has already excited on their behalf the impression of life. It is a marvel by what homely arts, by what imperturbable button-holing persistence, he contrives to excite this impression. Take, for example, such a work as *The Vicar of Bullhampton*. It would be difficult to state the idea of this slow but excellent story, which is a capital example of interest produced by the quietest conceivable means. The principal persons in it are a lively, jovial, high-tempered country clergyman, a young woman who is in love with her cousin, and a small, rather dull squire who is in love with the young woman. There is no connection between the affairs of the clergyman and those of the two other persons, save that these two are the Vicar's friends. The Vicar gives countenance, for Christian charity's sake, to a young countryman who is suspected (falsely, as it appears), of murder, and also to the lad's sister, who is more than suspected of leading an immoral life. Various people are shocked at his indiscretion, but in the end he is shown to have been no worse a clergyman because he is a good fellow. A cantankerous nobleman, who has a spite against him, causes a Methodist conventicle to be erected at the gates of the vicarage; but afterward, finding that he has no title to the land used for this obnoxious purpose, causes the conventicle to be pulled down, and is reconciled with the parson, who accepts an invitation to stay at the castle. Mary Lowther, the heroine of *The Vicar of Bullhampton*, is sought in marriage by Mr. Harry Gilmore, to whose passion she is unable to respond; she accepts him, however, making him understand that she does not love him, and that her affections are fixed upon her kinsman, Captain Marrable, whom she would marry (and who would marry her), if he were not too poor to support a wife. If Mr. Gilmore will take her on these terms she will become his spouse; but she gives him all sorts of warnings. They are not superfluous; for, as Captain Marrable presently inherits a fortune, she throws over Mr. Gilmore, who retires to foreign lands, heart-broken, inconsolable. This is the substance of *The Vicar of Bullhampton*; the reader will see that it is not a very tangled skein. But if the interest is gradual it is extreme and constant, and it comes altogether from excellent portraiture. It is essentially a moral, a social interest. There is something masterly in the large-fisted grip with which, in work of this kind, Trollope handles his brush. The Vicar's nature is thoroughly analysed and rendered, and his monotonous friend the Squire, a man with limitations, but possessed and consumed by a genuine passion, is equally near the truth.

Trollope has described again and again the ravages of love, and it is wonderful to see how well, in these delicate matters, his plain good sense and good taste serve him. His story is always primarily a love-story, and a love-story constructed on an inveterate system. There is a young lady who has two lovers, or a young man who has two sweethearts; we are treated to the innumerable forms in which this predicament may present itself and the consequences, sometimes pathetic, sometimes grotesque, which spring from such false situations. Trollope is not what is called a colourist; still less is he a poet: he is seated on the back of heavy-footed prose. But his account of those sentiments which the poets are supposed to have made their own is apt to be as touching as demonstrations more lyrical. There is something wonderfully vivid in the state of mind of the unfortunate Harry Gilmore, of whom I have just spoken; and his history, which has no more pretensions to style than if it were cut out of yesterday's newspaper, lodges itself in the imagination in all sorts of classic company. He is not handsome, nor clever, nor rich, nor romantic, nor distinguished in any way; he is simply rather a dense, narrow-minded, stiff, obstinate, common-place, conscientious modern Englishman, exceedingly in love and, from his own point of view, exceedingly ill-used. He is interesting because he suffers and because we are curious to see the form that suffering will take in that particular nature. Our good fortune, with Trollope, is that the person put

before us will have, in spite of opportunities not to have it, a certain
particular nature. The author has cared enough about the character of such
a person to find out exactly what it is. Another particular nature in *The
Vicar of Bullhampton* is the surly, sturdy, sceptical old farmer Jacob
Brattle, who doesn't want to be patronised by the parson, and in his
dumb, dusky, half-brutal, half-spiritual melancholy, surrounded by domestic
troubles, financial embarrassments and a puzzling world, declines altogether
to be won over to clerical optimism. Such a figure as Jacob Brattle, purely
episodical though it be, is an excellent English portrait. As thoroughly
English, and the most striking thing in the book, is the combination, in the
nature of Frank Fenwick — the delightful Vicar — of the patronizing,
conventional, clerical element with all sorts of manliness and spontaneity;
the union, or to a certain extent the contradiction, of official and personal
geniality. Trollope touches these points in a way that shows that he knows
his man. Delicacy is not his great sign, but when it is necessary he can be as
delicate as any one else.

I alighted, just now, at a venture, upon the history of Frank Fenwick; it
is far from being a conspicuous work in the immense list of Trollope's
novels. But to choose an example one must choose arbitrarily, for examples
of almost anything that one may wish to say are numerous to embarrassment. In speaking of a writer who produced so much and produced always
in the same way, there is perhaps a certain unfairness in choosing at all. As
no work has higher pretensions than any other, there may be a certain
unkindness in holding an individual production up to the light. 'Judge me
in the lump,' we can imagine the author saying; 'I have only undertaken to
entertain the British public. I don't pretend that each of my novels is an
organic whole.' Trollope had no time to give his tales a classic roundness;
yet there is (in spite of an extraordinary defect), something of that quality
in the thing that first revealed him. *The Warden* was published in 1855. It
made a great impression; and when, in 1857, *Barchester Towers* followed
it, every one saw that English literature had a novelist the more. These
were not the works of a young man, for Anthony Trollope had been born
in 1815. It is remarkable to reflect, by the way, that his prodigious fecundity (he had published before *The Warden* three or four novels which
attracted little attention), was enclosed between his fortieth and his sixty-
seventh years. Trollope had lived long enough in the world to learn a good
deal about it; and his maturity of feeling and evidently large knowledge of
English life were for much in the effect produced by the two clerical tales.
It was easy to see that he would take up room. What he had picked up, to
begin with, was a comprehensive, various impression of the clergy of the
Church of England and the manners and feelings that prevail in cathedral

towns. This, for a while, was his speciality, and, as always happens in such cases, the public was disposed to prescribe to him that path. He knew about bishops, archdeacons, prebendaries, precentors, and about their wives and daughters; he knew what these dignitaries say to each other when they are collected together, aloof from secular ears. He even knew what sort of talk goes on between a bishop and a bishop's lady when the august couple are enshrouded in the privacy of the episcopal bedroom. This knowledge, somehow, was rare and precious. No one, as yet, had been bold enough to snatch the illuminating torch from the very summit of the altar. Trollope enlarged his field very speedily – there is, as I remember that work, as little as possible of the ecclesiastical in the tale of *The Three Clerks*, which came after *Barchester Towers*. But he always retained traces of his early divination of the clergy; he introduced them frequently, and he always did them easily and well. There is no ecclesiastical figure, however, so good as the first – no creation of this sort so happy as the admirable Mr. Harding. *The Warden* is a delightful tale, and a signal instance of Trollope's habit of offering us the spectacle of a character. A motive more delicate, more slender, as well as more charming, could scarcely be conceived. It is simply the history of an old man's conscience.

The good and gentle Mr. Harding, precentor of Barchester Cathedral, also holds the post of warden of Hiram's Hospital, an ancient charity where twelve old paupers are maintained in comfort. The office is in the gift of the bishop, and its emoluments are as handsome as the duties of the place are small. Mr. Harding has for years drawn his salary in quiet gratitude; but his moral repose is broken by hearing it at last begun to be said that the wardenship is a sinecure, that the salary is a scandal, and that a large part, at least, of his easy income ought to go to the pensioners of the hospital. He is sadly troubled and perplexed, and when the great London newspapers take up the affair he is overwhelmed with confusion and shame. He thinks the newspapers are right – he perceives that the warden is an overpaid and rather a useless functionary. The only thing he can do is to resign the place. He has no means of his own – he is only a quiet, modest, innocent old man, with a taste, a passion, for old church-music and the violoncello. But he determines to resign, and he does resign in spite of the sharp opposition of his friends. He does what he thinks right, and goes to live in lodgings over a shop in the Barchester High Street. That is all the story, and it has exceeding beauty. The question of Mr. Harding's resignation becomes a drama, and we anxiously wait for the catastrophe. Trollope never did anything happier than the picture of this sweet and serious little old gentleman, who on most of the occasions of life has shown a lamblike softness and compliance, but in this particular matter

opposes a silent, impenetrable obstinacy to the arguments of the friends
who insist on his keeping his sinecure — fixing his mild, detached gaze on
the distance, and making imaginary passes with his fiddle-bow while they
demonstrate his pusillanimity. The subject of *The Warden*, exactly viewed,
is the opposition of the two natures of Archdeacon Grantly and Mr.
Harding, and there is nothing finer in all Trollope than the vividness with
which this opposition is presented. The archdeacon is as happy a portrait
as the precentor — an image of the full-fed, worldly churchman, taking his
stand squarely upon his rich temporalities, and regarding the church
frankly as a fat social pasturage. It required the greatest tact and temperance to make the picture of Archdeacon Grantly stop just where it does.
The type, impartially considered, is detestable, but the individual may be
full of amenity. Trollope allows his archdeacon all the virtues he was likely
to possess, but he makes his spiritual grossness wonderfully natural. No
charge of exaggeration is possible, for we are made to feel that he is
conscientious as well as arrogant, and expansive as well as hard. He is one
of those figures that spring into being all at once, solidifying in the author's
grasp. These two capital portraits are what we carry away from *The Warden*,
which some persons profess to regard as our writer's masterpiece. We
remember, while it was still something of a novelty, to have heard a judicious
critic say that it had much of the charm of *The Vicar of Wakefield*.
Anthony Trollope would not have accepted the compliment, and would
not have wished this little tale to pass before several of its successors. He
would have said, very justly, that it gives too small a measure of his knowledge of life. It has, however, a certain classic roundness, though, as we
said a moment since, there is a blemish on its fair face. The chapter on
Dr. Pessimist Anticant and Mr. Sentiment would be a mistake almost
inconceivable if Trollope had not in other places taken pains to show us
that for certain forms of satire (the more violent, doubtless), he had
absolutely no gift. Dr. Anticant is a parody of Carlyle, and Mr. Sentiment
is an exposure of Dickens: and both these little *jeux d'esprit* are as infelici-
tous as they are misplaced. It was no less luckless an inspiration to convert
Archdeacon Grantly's three sons, denominated respectively Charles James,
Henry and Samuel, into little effigies of three distinguished English bishops
of that period, whose well-known peculiarities are reproduced in the
description of these unnatural urchins. The whole passage, as we meet it, is
a sudden disillusionment; we are transported from the mellow atmosphere
of an assimilated Barchester to the air of ponderous allegory.
　　I may take occasion to remark here upon a very curious fact — the fact
that there are certain precautions in the way of producing that illusion
dear to the intending novelist which Trollope not only habitually scorned

to take, but really, as we may say, asking pardon for the heat of the thing, delighted wantonly to violate. He took a suicidal satisfaction in reminding the reader that the story he was telling was only, after all, a make-believe. He habitually referred to the work in hand (in the course of that work) as a novel, and to himself as a novelist, and was fond of letting the reader know that this novelist could direct the course of events according to his pleasure. Already, in *Barchester Towers*, he falls into this pernicious trick. In describing the wooing of Eleanor Bold by Mr. Arabin he has occasion to say that the lady might have acted in a much more direct and natural way than the way he attributes to her. But if she had, he adds, 'where would have been my novel?' The last chapter of the same story begins with the remark, 'The end of a novel, like the end of a children's dinner party, must be made up of sweetmeats and sugar-plums.' These little slaps at credulity (we might give many more specimens) are very discouraging, but they are even more inexplicable; for they are deliberately inartistic, even judged from the point of view of that rather vague consideration of form which is the only canon we have a right to impose upon Trollope. It is impossible to imagine what a novelist takes himself to be unless he regard himself as an historian and his narrative as a history. It is only as an historian that he has the smallest *locus standi*. As a narrator of fictitious events he is nowhere; to insert into his attempt a back-bone of logic, he must relate events that are assumed to be real. This assumption permeates, animates all the work of the most solid story-tellers; we need only mention (to select a single instance), the magnificent historical tone of Balzac, who would as soon have thought of admitting to the reader that he was deceiving him, as Garrick or John Kemble would have thought of pulling off his disguise in front of the foot-lights. Therefore, when Trollope suddenly winks at us and reminds us that he is telling us an arbitrary thing, we are startled and shocked in quite the same way as if Macaulay or Motley were to drop the historic mask and intimate that William of Orange was a myth or the Duke of Alva an invention.

It is a part of this same ambiguity of mind as to what constitutes evidence that Trollope should sometimes endow his people with such fantastic names. Dr. Pessimist Anticant and Mr. Sentiment make, as we have seen, an awkward appearance in a modern novel; and Mr. Neversay Die, Mr. Stickatit, Mr. Rerechild and Mr. Fillgrave (the two last the family physicians), are scarcely more felicitous. It would be better to go back to Bunyan at once. There is a person mentioned in *The Warden* under the name of Mr. Quiverful — a poor clergyman, with a dozen children, who holds the living of Puddingdale. This name is a humorous allusion to his overflowing nursery, and it matters little so long as he is not brought to the front. But in *Barchester Towers*, which carries on the history of Hiram's Hospital, Mr. Quiverful becomes, as a candidate for Mr. Harding's vacant place, an important element, and the reader is made proportionately unhappy by the primitive character of this satiric note. A Mr. Quiverful with fourteen children (which is the number attained in *Barchester Towers*) is too difficult to believe in. We can believe in the name and we can believe in the children; but we cannot manage the combination. It is probably not unfair to say that if Trollope derived half his inspiration from life, he derived the other half from Thackeray; his earlier novels, in especial, suggest an honourable emulation of the author of *The Newcomes*. Thackeray's names were perfect; they always had a meaning and (except in his absolutely jocose productions, where they were still admirable) we can imagine, even when they are most figurative, that they should have been borne by real people. But in this, as in other respects, Trollope's hand was heavier than his master's; though when he is content not to be too comical his appellations are sometimes fortunate enough. Mrs. Proudie is excellent, for Mrs. Proudie, and even the Duke of Omnium and Gatherum Castle rather minister to illusion than destroy it. Indeed, the names of houses and places, throughout Trollope, are full of colour.

I would speak in some detail of *Barchesters Towers* if this did not seem to commit me to the prodigious task of appreciating each of Trollope's works in succession. Such an attempt as that is so far from being possible that I must frankly confess to not having read everything that proceeded from his pen. There came a moment in his vigorous career (it was even a good many years ago) when I renounced the effort to 'keep up' with him. It ceased to seem obligatory to have read his last story; it ceased soon to be very possible to know which was his last. Before that, I had been punctual, devoted; and the memories of the earlier period are delightful. It reached, if I remember correctly, to about the publication of *He Knew He Was Right*; after which, to my recollection (oddly enough, too, for that novel was good enough to encourage a continuance of past favours, as the shopkeepers say), the picture becomes dim and blurred. The author of *Orley Farm* and *The Small House at Allington* ceased to produce individual works; his activity became a huge 'serial'. Here and there, in the vast fluidity, an organic particle detached itself. *The Last Chronicle of Barset*, for instance, is one of his most powerful things; it contains the sequel of the terrible history of Mr. Crawley, the starving curate — an episode full of that literally truthful pathos of which Trollope was so often a master, and which occasionally raised him quite to the level of his two immediate predecessors in the vivid treatment of English life — great artists whose pathetic effects were sometimes too visibly prepared. For the most part, however, he should be judged by the productions of the first half of his career; later the strong wine was rather too copiously watered. His practice, his acquired facility, were such that his hand went of itself, as it were, and the thing looked superficially like a fresh inspiration. But it was not fresh, it was rather stale; and though there was no appearance of effort, there was a fatal dryness of texture. It was too little of a new story and too much of an old one. Some of these ultimate compositions – *Phineas Redux* (*Phineas Finn* is much better), *The Prime Minister, John Caldigate, The American Senator, The Duke's Children* – betray the dull, impersonal rumble of the mill-wheel. What stands Trollope always in good stead (in addition to the ripe habit of writing), is his various knowledge of the English world – to say nothing of his occasionally laying under contribution the American. His American portraits, by the way (they are several in number), are always friendly; they hit it off more happily than the attempt to depict American character from the European point of view is accustomed to do: though, indeed, as we ourselves have not yet learned to represent our types very finely – are not apparently even very sure what our types are – it is perhaps not to be wondered at that transatlantic talent should miss the mark. The weakness of transatlantic talent in this particular is apt to be want of knowledge; but Trollope's knowledge has all the air of being excellent, though not intimate. Had he indeed striven to learn the way to the American heart? No less than twice, and possibly even oftener, has he rewarded the merit of a scion of the British aristocracy with the hand of an American girl. The American girl was destined sooner or later to make her entrance into British fiction, and Trollope's treatment of this complicated being is full of good humour and of that fatherly indulgence, that almost motherly sympathy, which characterizes his attitude, throughout toward the youthful feminine. He has not mastered all the springs of her delicate organism nor sounded all the mysteries of her conversation. Indeed, as regards these latter phenomena, he has observed a few of which he has been the sole observer. 'I got to be thinking if any one of them should ask me to marry him,' words attributed to Miss Boncassen, in *The Duke's Children*, have much more the note of English American than of American English. But, on the whole, in these matters Trollope does very well. His fund of acquaintance with his own country – and indeed with the world at large – was apparently inexhaustible, and it gives his novels a spacious, geographical quality which we should not know where to look for elsewhere in the same degree, and which is the sign of an extraordinary difference between such an horizon as his and the limited world-outlook, as the Germans would say, of the brilliant writers who practise the art of realistic fiction on the other side of the Channel. Trollope was familiar with all sorts and conditions of men, with the business of life, with affairs, with the great world of sport, with every component part of the ancient fabric of English society. He had travelled more than once all over the globe, and for him, therefore, the background of the human drama was a very extensive scene. He had none of the pedantry of the cosmopolite; he remained a sturdy and sensible middle-class Englishman. But his work is full of implied reference to the whole arena of modern vagrancy. He was for many years concerned in the mangement of the Post-Office; and we can imagine no experience more fitted to impress a man with the diversity of human relations. It is possibly from this source that he derived his fondness for transcribing the letters of his love-lorn maidens and other embarrassed persons. No contemporary story-teller deals so much in letters; the modern English epistle (very happily imitated, for the most part), is his unfailing resource.

There is perhaps little reason in it, but I find myself comparing this tone of allusion to many lands and many things, and whatever it brings us of easier respiration, with that narrow vision of humanity which accompanies the strenuous, serious work lately offered us in such abundance by the votaries of art for art who sit so long at their desks in Parisian *quatrièmes*. The contrast is complete, and it would be interesting, had we space to do so here, to see how far it goes. On one side a wide, good-humoured, superficial glance at a good many things; on the other a gimlet-like consideration of a few. Trollope's plan, as well as Zola's, was to describe the life that lay near him; but the two writers differ immensely as to what constitutes life and what constitutes nearness. For Trollope the emotions of a nursery-governess in Australia would take precedence of the adventures of a depraved *femme du monde* in Paris or London. They both undertake to do the same thing – to depict French and English manners; but the English writer (with his unsurpassed industry) is so occasional, so accidental, so full of the echoes of voices that are not the voice of the muse. Gustave Flaubert, Emile Zola, Alphonse Daudet, on the other hand, are nothing if not concentrated and sedentary. Trollope's realism is as instinctive, as inveterate as theirs; but nothing could mark more the difference between the French and English mind than the difference in the application, on one side and the other, of this system. We say system, though on Trollope's part it is none. He has no visible, certainly no explicit care for the literary part of the business; he writes easily, comfortably, and profusely, but his style has nothing in common either with the minute stippling of Daudet or the studied rhythms of Flaubert. He accepted all the common restrictions, and found that even within the barriers there was plenty of material. He attaches a preface to one of his novels – *The Vicar of Bullhampton*, before mentioned – for the express purpose of explaining why he has introduced a young woman who may, in truth, as he says, be called a 'castaway'; and in relation to this episode he remarks that it is the object of the novelist's art to entertain the young people of both sexes. Writers of the French school would, of course, protest indignantly against such a formula as this, which is the only one of the kind that I remember to have encountered in Trollope's pages. It is meagre, assuredly; but Trollope's practice was really much larger than so poor a theory. And indeed any theory was good which enabled him to produce the works which he put forth between 1856 and 1869, or later. In spite of his want of doctrinal richness I think he tells us, on the whole, more about life than the 'naturalists' in our sister republic. I say this with a full consciousness of the opportunities an artist loses in leaving so many corners unvisited, so many topics untouched, simply because I think his perception of character was naturally more just and liberal than that of the naturalists. This has been from the beginning the good fortune of our English providers of fiction, as compared with the French. They are inferior in audacity, in neatness, in acuteness, in intellectual vivacity, in the arrangement of material, in the art of characterizing visible things. But they have been more at home in the moral world; as people say to-day they know their way about the conscience. This is the value of much of the work done by the feminine wing of the school – work which presents itself to French taste as deplorably thin and insipid. Much of it is exquisitely human, and that after all is a merit. As regards Trollope, one may perhaps characterize him best, in opposition to what I have ventured to call the sedentary school, by saying that he was a novelist who hunted the fox. Hunting was for years his most valued recreation, and I remember that when I made in his company the voyage of which I have spoken, he had timed his return from the Antipodes exactly so as to be able to avail himself of the first day on which it should be possible to ride to hounds. He 'worked' the hunting-field largely; it constantly reappears in his novels; it was excellent material.

But it would be hard to say (within the circle in which he revolved) what material he neglected. I have allowed myself to be detained so long by general considerations that I have almost forfeited the opportunity to give examples. I have spoken of *The Warden* not only because it made his reputation, but because, taken in conjunction with *Barchester Towers*, it is thought by many people to be his highest flight. *Barchester Towers* is admirable; it has an almost Thackerayan richness. Archdeacon Grantly grows more and more into life, and Mr. Harding is as charming as ever. Mrs. Proudie is ushered into a world in which she was to make so great an impression. Mrs. Proudie has become classical; of all Trollope's characters she is the most often referred to. She is exceedingly true; but I do not think she is quite so good as her fame, and as several figures from the same hand that have not won so much honour. She is rather too violent, too vixenish, too sour. The truly awful female bully – the completely fatal episcopal spouse – would have, I think, a more insidious form, a greater amount of superficial padding. The Stanhope family, in *Barchester Towers*, are a real *trouvaille*, and the idea of transporting the Signora Vesey-Neroni into a cathedral-town was an inspiration. There could not be a better example of Trollope's manner of attaching himself to character than the whole picture of Bertie Stanhope. Bertie is a delightful creation; and the scene in which, at the party given by Mrs. Proudie, he puts this majestic woman to rout is one of the most amusing in all the chronicles of Barset. It is perhaps permitted to wish, by the way, that this triumph had been effected by means intellectual rather than physical; though, indeed, if Bertie had not despoiled her of her drapery we should have lost the lady's admirable 'Unhand it, sir!' Mr. Arabin is charming, and the hen-pecked bishop has painful truth; but Mr. Slope, I think, is a little too arrant a scamp. He is rather too much the old game; he goes too coarsely to work, and his clamminess and cant are somewhat overdone. He is an interesting illustration, however, of the author's dislike (at that period at least) of the bareness of evangelical piety. In one respect *Barchester Towers* is (to the best of our recollection) unique, being the only one of Trollope's novels in which the interest does not centre more or less upon a simple maiden in her flower. The novel offers us nothing in the way of a girl; though we know that this attractive object was to lose nothing by waiting. Eleanor Bold is a charming and natural person, but Eleanor Bold is not in her flower. After this, however, Trollope settled down steadily to the English girl; he took possession of her, and turned her inside out. He never made her a subject of heartless satire, as cynical fabulists of other lands have been known to make the shining daughters of those climes; he bestowed upon her the most serious, the most patient, the most tender, the most copious consideration. He is evidently always more or less in love with her, and it is a wonder how under these circumstances he should make her so objective, plant her so well on her feet. But, as I have said, if he was a lover, he was a paternal lover; as competent as a father who has had fifty daughters. He has presented the British maiden under innumerable names, in every station and in every emergency in life, and with every combination of moral and physical qualities. She is always definite and natural. She plays her part most properly. She has always health in her cheek and gratitude in her eye. She has not a touch of the morbid, and is delightfully tender,

modest and fresh. Trollope's heroines have a strong family likeness, but it
is a wonder how finely he discriminates between them. One feels, as one
reads him, like a man with 'sets' of female cousins. Such a person is inclined
at first to lump each group together; but presently he finds that even in
the groups there are subtle differences. Trollope's girls, for that matter,
would make delightful cousins. He has scarcely drawn, that we can remember, a disagreeable damsel. Lady Alexandrina de Courcy is disagreeable,
and so is Amelia Roper, and so are various provincial (and indeed metro-
politan) spinsters, who set their caps at young clergymen and government
clerks. Griselda Grantly was a stick; and considering that she was intended
to be attractive, Alice Vavasor does not commend herself particularly to
our affections. But the young women I have mentioned had ceased to
belong to the blooming season; they had entered the bristling, or else the
limp, period. Not that Trollope's more mature spinsters invariably fall into
these extremes. Miss Thorne of Ullathorne, Miss Dunstable, Miss Mackenzie,
Rachel Ray (if she may be called mature), Miss Baker and Miss Todd, in
The Bertrams, Lady Julia Guest, who comforts poor John Eames: these
and many other amiable figures rise up to contradict the idea. A gentleman
who had sojourned in many lands was once asked by a lady (neither of
these persons was English), in what country he had found the women most
to his taste. 'Well, in England,' he replied. 'In England?' the lady repeated.
'Oh yes,' said her interlocutor; 'they are so affectionate!' The remark was
fatuous, but it has the merit of describing Trollope's heroines. They are so
affectionate. Mary Thorne, Lucy Robarts, Adela Gauntlet, Lily Dale, Nora
Rowley, Grace Crawley, have a kind of clinging tenderness, a passive
sweetness, which is quite in the old English tradition. Trollope's genius is
not the genius of Shakespeare, but his heroines have something of the
fragrance of Imogen and Desdemona. There are two little stories to which,
I believe, his name has never been affixed, but which he is known to have
written, that contain an extraordinarily touching representation of the
passion of love in its most sensitive form. In *Linda Tressel* and *Nina Balatka*
the vehicle is plodding prose, but the effect is none the less poignant. And
in regard to this I may say that in a hundred places in Trollope the extremity
of pathos is reached by the homeliest means. He often achieved a conspicuous intensity of the tragical. The long, slow process of the conjugal wreck
of Louis Trevelyan and his wife (in *He Knew He Was Right*), with that
rather lumbering movement which is often characteristic of Trollope,
arrives at last at an impressive completenesss of misery. It is the history of
an accidental rupture between two stiff-necked and ungracious people —
'the little rift within the lute' — which widens at last into a gulf of anguish.
Touch is added to touch, one small, stupid, fatal aggravation to another;

and as we gaze into the widening breach we wonder at the vulgar materials of which tragedy sometimes composes itself. I have always remembered the chapter called 'Casalunga', toward the close of *He Knew He Was Right*, as a powerful picture of the insanity of stiff-neckedness. Louis Trevelyan, separated from his wife, alone, haggard, suspicious, unshaven, undressed, living in a desolate villa on a hill-top near Siena and returning doggedly to his fancied wrong, which he has nursed until it becomes an hallucination, is a picture worthy of Balzac. Here and in several other places Trollope has dared to be thoroughly logical; he has not sacrificed to conventional optimism; he has not been afraid of a misery which should be too much like life. He has had the same courage in the history of the wretched Mr. Crawley and in that of the much-to-be-pitied Lady Mason. In this latter episode he found an admirable subject. A quiet, charming, tender-souled English gentlewoman who (as I remember the story of *Orley Farm*) forges a codicil to a will in order to benefit her son, a young prig who doesn't appreciate immoral heroism, and who is suspected, accused, tried, and saved from conviction only by some turn of fortune that I forget; who is further-more an object of high-bred, respectful, old-fashioned gallantry on the part of a neighbouring baronet, so that she sees herself dishonoured in his eyes as well as condemned in those of her boy: such a personage and such a situation would be sure to yield, under Trollope's handling, the last drop of their reality.

There are many more things to say about him than I am able to add to these very general observations, the limit of which I have already passed. It would be natural, for instance, for a critic who affirms that his principal merit is the portrayal of individual character, to enumerate several of the figures that he has produced. I have not done this, and I must ask the reader who is not acquainted with Trollope to take my assertion on trust; the reader who knows him will easily make a list for himself. No account of him is complete in which allusion is not made to his practice of carrying certain actors from one story to another — a practice which he may be said to have inherited from Thackeray, as Thackeray may be said to have borrowed it from Balzac. It is a great mistake, however, to speak of it as an artifice which would not naturally occur to a writer proposing to himself to make a general portrait of a society. He has to construct that society, and it adds to the illusion in any given case that certain other cases corres-pond with it. Trollope constructed a great many things — a clergy, an aristocracy, a middle-class, an administrative class, a little replica of the political world. His political novels are distinctly dull, and I confess I have not been able to read them. He evidently took a good deal of pains with his aristocracy; it makes its first appearance, if I remember right, in *Doctor Thorne*, in the person of the Lady Arabella de Courcy. It is difficult for us in America to measure the success of that picture, which is probably, however, not absolutely to the life. There is in *Doctor Thorne* and some other works a certain crudity of reference to distinctions of rank — as if people's consciousness of this matter were, on either side, rather inflated. It suggests a general state of tension. It is true that, if Trollope's consciousness had been more flaccid he would perhaps not have given us Lady Lufton and Lady Glencora Palliser. Both of these noble persons are as living as possible, though I see Lady Lufton, with her terror of Lucy Robarts, the best. There is a touch of poetry in the figure of Lady Glencora, but I think there is a weak spot in her history. The actual woman would have made a fool of herself to the end with Burgo Fitzgerald; she would not have discovered the merits of Plantagenet Palliser — or if she had, she would not have cared about them. It is an illustration of the business-like way in which Trollope laid out his work that he always provided a sort of underplot to alternate with his main story — a strain of narrative of which the scene is usually laid in a humbler walk of life. It is to his underplot that he generally relegates his vulgar people, his disagreeable young women; and I have often admired the perseverance with which he recounts these less edifying items. Now and then, it may be said, as in *Ralph the Heir*, the story appears to be all underplot and all vulgar people. These, however, are details. As I have already intimated, it is difficult to specify in Trollope's work, on account of the immense quantity of it; and there is sadness in the thought that this enormous mass does not present itself in a very portable form to posterity.

Trollope did not write for posterity; he wrote for the day, the moment; but these are just the writers whom posterity is apt to put into its pocket. So much of the life of his time is reflected in his novels that we must believe a part of the record will be saved; and the best parts of them are so sound and true and genial, that readers with an eye to that sort of entertainment will always be sure, in a certain proportion, to turn to them. Trollope will remain one of the most trustworthy, though not one of the most eloquent, of the writers who have helped the heart of man to know itself. The heart of man does not always desire this knowledge; it prefers sometimes to look at history in another way — to look at the manifestations without troubling about the motives. There are two kinds of taste in the appreciation of imaginative literature: the taste for emotions of surprise and the taste for emotions of recognition. It is the latter that Trollope gratifies, and he gratifies it the more that the medium of his own mind, through which we see what he shows us, gives a confident direction to our sympathy. His natural rightness and purity are so real that the good things he projects must be real. A race is fortunate when it has a good deal of the sort of imagination — of imaginative feeling — that had fallen to the share of Anthony Trollope; and in this possession our English race is not poor.

FREDERIC HARRISON
Anthony Trollope*

Some of our younger friends who read the name which heads this essay
may incline to think that it ought to be very short indeed, nay, be limited
to a single remark; and, like the famous chapter on the snakes in Iceland, it
should simply run — that Anthony Trollope has no place at all in Victorian
literature. We did not think so in England in the fifties, the sixties, and
the seventies, in the heyday of Victorian romance; and I do not think we
ought to pass that judgment now in this last quinquennium of our century.
I shall have to put our friend Anthony in a very moderate and prosaic
rank; I shall not conceal my sense of his modest claims and conspicuous
faults, of his prolixity, his limited sphere, his commonplace. But in view of
the enormous popularity he once enjoyed, of the space he filled for a
whole generation, I cannot altogether omit him from these studies of the
Victorian writers. . . .

Trollope's sixty works no doubt exceed the product of any Englishman
of our age; but they fall short of the product of Dumas, George Sand, and
Scribe. And, though but a small part of the sixty works can be called good,
the inferior work is not discreditable: it is free from affectation, extravagance, nastiness, or balderdash. It never sinks into such tawdry stuff as
Bulwer, Disraeli, and even Dickens, could indite in their worst moods.
Trollope is never bombastic, or sensational, or prurient, or grotesque. Even
at his worst, he writes pure, bright, graceful English; he tells us about
wholesome men and women in a manly tone, and if he becomes dull, he
is neither ridiculous nor odious. He is very often dull: or rather utterly
commonplace. It is the fashion with the present generation to assert that
he is never anything but commonplace; but this is the judgment of a
perverted taste. His besetting danger is certainly the commonplace. It is
true that he is almost never dramatic, or powerful, or original. His plots are

* From *Studies in Early Victorian Literature* (London: Edward Arnold,
1895), abridged from pp. 183—95. First published in somewhat different
form in *Forum*, 19 (May 1895), 324—37.

of obvious and simple construction; his characters are neither new, nor subtle, nor powerful; and his field is strictly limited to special aspects of the higher English society in town and country. But in his very best work, he has risen above commonplace and has painted certain types of English men and women with much grace and consummate truth.

One of Trollope's strong points and one source of his popularity was a command over plain English almost perfect for his own limited purpose. It is limpid, flexible, and melodious. It never rises into eloquence, poetry, or power; but it is always easy, clear, simple, and vigorous. Trollope was not capable of the sustained mastery over style that we find in *Esmond*, nor had he the wit, passion, and pathos at Thackeray's command. But of all contemporaries he comes nearest to Thackeray in easy conversations and in quiet narration of incidents and motives. Sometimes, but very rarely, Trollope is vulgar, – for good old Anthony had a coarse vein: it was in the family: – but as a rule his language is conspicuous for its ease, simplicity, and unity of tone. This was one good result of his enormous rapidity of execution. His books read from cover to cover, as if they were spoken in one sitting by an *improvisatore* in one and the same mood, who never hesitated an instant for a word, and who never failed to seize the word he wanted. This ease and mastery over speech was the fruit of prodigious practice and industry both in office work and in literary work. It is a mastery which conceals itself, and appears to the reader the easiest thing in the world. How few out of many millions have studied that subtle mechanism of ear and thought which created the melodious ripple of these fluent and pellucid words.

His work has one special quality that has not been sufficiently noticed. It has the most wonderful unity of texture and a perfect harmony of tone. From the first line to the last, there is never a sentence or a passage which strikes a discordant note; we are never worried by a spasmodic phrase, nor bored by fine writing that fails to 'come off'. Nor is there ever a paragraph which we need to read over again, or a phrase that looks obscure, artificial, or enigmatic. This can hardly be said of any other novelist of this century, except of Jane Austen, for even Thackeray himself is now and then artificial in *Esmond*, and the vulgarity of *Yellowplush* at last becomes fatiguing. Now Trollope reproduced for us that simplicity, unity, and ease of Jane Austen, whose facile grace flows on like the sprightly talk of a charming woman, mistress of herself and sure of her hearers. This uniform ease, of course, goes with the absence of all the greatest qualities of style; absence of any passion, poetry, mystery, or subtlety. He never rises, it is true, to the level of the great masters of language. But, for the ordinary incidents of life amongst well-bred and well-to-do men and women of the world, the form of Trollope's tales is almost as well adapted as the form of Jane Austen.

In absolute realism of spoken words Trollope has hardly any equal. His characters utter quite literally the same words, and no more, that such persons utter in actual life. The characters, it is true, are the average men and women we meet in the educated world, and the situations, motives, and feelings described are seldom above or below the ordinary incidents of modern life. But within this very limited range of incident, and for this very common average of person and character, the conversations are photographic or stenographic reproductions of actual speech. His letters, especially his young ladies' letters, are singularly real, life-like, and characteristic. We have long got rid of the artificial eloquence and the studied witticisms of the older school. Richardson, Fielding, Goldsmith, and Scott put into the mouths of their heroes and heroines elaborate speeches, poetry, eloquence, and epigrams which are no more like real speech than the allocutions of kings and queens in Shakespeare are like natural talk. That has long been discarded. Jane Austen and Thackeray make their men and women discourse as men and women do. But perhaps with Thackeray, the talk is too racy, too brilliant, too rich with wit, humour, and character, to be quite literally truthful. Now, Trollope, taking a far lower and simpler line, makes his characters talk with literal truth to nature. . . .

We may at once confess to his faults and limitations. They are plain enough, constant, and quite incapable of defence. Out of his sixty works, I should be sorry to pick more than ten as being worth a second reading, or twenty which are worth a first reading. Nor amongst the good books could I count any of the last ten years. The range of characters is limited to the clergy and professional men of a cathedral city, to the county families and the respectabilities of a quiet village, to the life of clubs, public offices, and Parliament in London, and to the ways of 'society' as it existed in England in the third quarter of the present century. The plots are neither new nor ingenious; the incidents are rarely more than commonplace; the characters are seldom very powerful, or original, or complex. There are very few 'psychologic problems', very few dramatic situations, very few revelations of a new world and unfamiliar natures. There are some natural scenes in Ireland; now and then a cook-maid, a farmer, a labourer, or a clerk, come on the stage and play their short parts with faultless demeanour. But otherwise, the entire company appear in the frock-coats and crinolines of the period, and every scene is played in silk hats, bonnets, and regulation evening toilette.

But within this limited range of life, this uniformity of 'genteel comedy', Trollope has not seldom given us pieces of inimitable truthfulness and curious delicacy of observation. The dignitaries of the cathedral close, the sporting squires, the county magnates, the country doctors, and the rectory home, are drawn with a precision, a refinement, an absolute fidelity that only Jane Austen could compass. There is no caricature, no burlesque, nothing improbable or over-wrought. The bishop, the dean, the warden, the curate, the apothecary, the duke, the master of fox-hounds, the bishop's wife, the archdeacon's lady, the vicar's daughter, the governess, the undergraduate, – all are perfectly true to nature. So, too, are the men in the clubs in London, the chiefs, subordinates, and clerks in the public offices, the ministers and members of Parliament, the leaders, and rank and file of London 'society'. They never utter a sentence which is not exactly what such men and women do utter; they do and they think nothing but what such men and women think and do in real life. Their habits, conversation, dress, and interests are photographically accurate, to the point of illusion. It is not high art – but it is art. The field is a narrow one; the actors are ordinary. But the skill, grace, and humour with which the scenes are caught, and the absolute illusion of truthfulness, redeem it from the commonplace.

The stage of Trollope's drama is not a wide one, but it is far wider than that of Jane Austen. His plots and incidents are sufficiently trite and ordinary, but they are dramatic and original, if contrasted with those of *Emma* or *Mansfield Park*. No one will compare little Jane's delicate palfrey with Anthony's big-boned hunter; nor would any one commit the bad taste of treating these quadrupeds as if they were entered for a race; but a narrow stage and familiar incidents are not necessarily fatal to true art. If Trollope had done nothing more than paint ordinary English society with photographic accuracy of detail, it would not be a great performance. But he has done more than this. In the Barsetshire series, at any rate, he has risen to a point of drawing characters with a very subtle insight and delicate intuition. The warden, the bishop, Mrs. Proudie, Dr. Thorne, Mary Thorne, Lily Dale, Lady Arabella, and, above all, Mr. Crawley, are characters definitely conceived, profoundly mastered, and truly portrayed. Trollope evidently judged Crawley to be his greatest creation, and the *Last Chronicle of Barset* to be his principal achievement. In this he was doubtless right. There are real characters also in the two *Phineas Finn* tales. Chiltern, Finn, Glencora Palliser, Laura Kennedy, and Marie Goesler, are subtly conceived and truly worked out. This is enough to make a decent reputation, however flat be the interminable pot-boilers that precede and follow them.

The list of Trollope's real successes is not very long. The six tales of the Barsetshire cycle, *The Warden, Barchester Towers, Doctor Thorne, Framley Parsonage, The Small House at Allington, The Last Chronicle of Barset*, are unquestionably his main achievements; and of these either *Doctor Thorne* or *The Last Chronicle* is the best. The Crawley story is undoubtedly the finest thing Trollope ever did; but for myself, I enjoy the unity, completeness, and masterly scheme of *Doctor Thorne*, and I like Mary Thorne better than any of Trollope's women. If, to the six Barset tales, we add *Orley Farm, The Claverings*, the two *Phineas Finns*, and the *Eustace Diamonds*, we shall include, perhaps, more than posterity will ever trouble itself about, and almost exactly one-fifth of the novels he left behind. The ten or twelve of Trollope's best will continue to be read, and will, in a future generation, no doubt, regain not a little of their early vogue. This will be due, in part, to their own inherent merit as graceful, truthful, subtle observation of contemporary types, clothed in a style of transparent ease. Partly, it will be due to this: that these tales will reproduce for the future certain phases of life in the nineteenth century in England with minute fidelity and the most literal realism. . . .

W. P. KER
Anthony Trollope*

Anthony Trollope usually wrote for three hours in the morning early, and timed himself to write 250 words every quarter of an hour.[1] He also wrote in railway trains. These historical facts are fairly well known, and in consequence the imaginative work of Trollope is lightly valued and often neglected. It is taken as mechanical hackwork; what was so easily and regularly turned out is supposed to be of corresponding small value. Obviously there is a *petitio principii* here; it is assumed that the value varies inversely as the velocity. Further, Trollope never took to himself any great credit as a literary man; he does not seem to have thought much of literary fame; he was not ambitious, he was not jealous; he did not want to differ from the kindly race of men who played whist in clubs between five and seven in the afternoon. His own opinion about himself and his writings is worth some consideration from those who are curious about the lives and methods of artists. The books themselves are worth reading, whatever the author may have thought about them; I have a long acquaintance with many of them, and undiminished readiness for more, and I am still left wondering at the modesty of Anthony Trollope and his apparently low estimate of his own achievements in fiction. He had much to be proud of and good excuses for boasting, if his temper had led him that way. But in truth he was too proud and secure to boast; his even, balanced soul knew what it required from the world and what it was prepared to give, and so his business was carried on without any overdraft at the bankers.

It is always interesting to find out what artists think about their work, and Trollope has told a good deal about his aims and processes; much more than the common facts about his rate of words to the minute. He

*From *On Modern Literature: Lectures and Addresses by W. P. Ker*, eds Terence Spencer and James Sutherland (Oxford: Clarendon Press, 1955), abridged from pp. 136–46. Originally presented as a lecture at University College, London, probably about 1912. Reprinted by permission of Oxford University Press.

wrote a book on Thackeray for the 'English Men of Letters' series in 1879, and there he explains very clearly a far from easy standard of imaginative work. Fluency in writing is all very well. Trollope has so much of that talent by nature that he undervalues it. But he is not misled by his own fortunate, ready-running style to think that everything will do which comes on the spur of the moment, or that the pen may be trusted to write by itself. 'Whether I guide the pen or the pen me' is a problem that occurs at times to all of us. Dr. Johnson's advice to poets to sit down doggedly (which is the same as that given to Mr. Crawley in *The Last Chronicle of Barset* – 'it's dogged as does it', chap. lxi)[2] – this advice, to poets or prosers, is really confidence in the magic of the pen, which is not to be despised. The way to write is to write. But the magic of the pen will not do everything, not even for geniuses like Scott and Thackeray. They may think of glorious things as they write, but they must have done some thinking before they sit down; and Trollope is uncompromising, remarkably austere, in his rule for novelists. The loose construction of *Vanity Fair* and *Pendennis* he will not pass without censure; he distinguishes *Barry Lyndon* and *Henry Esmond* as showing more intellectual care than the rest, and *Henry Esmond* as the one book in which there is 'no touch of idleness'. Whether Trollope was right or wrong about Thackeray is not my concern; I wish to note what the ready writer of a thousand words an hour thought necessary before the hour began.

When we were young we used to be told, in our house at home, that 'elbow-grease' was the one essential necessary to getting a tough piece of work well done. If a mahogany table was to be made to shine, it was elbow-grease that the operation needed. Fore-thought is the elbow-grease which a novelist, – or poet, or dramatist, – requires. It is not only his plot that has to be turned and re-turned in his mind, not his plot chiefly, but he has to make himself sure of his situations, of his characters, of his effects, so that when the time comes for hitting the nail he may know where to hit it on the head, – so that he may himself understand the passion, the calmness, the virtues, the vices, the rewards and punishments which he means to explain to others, – so that his proportions shall be correct, and he be saved from the absurdity of devoting two-thirds of his book to the beginning, or two-thirds to the completion of his task. It is from want of this special labour, more frequently than from intellectual deficiency, that the tellers of stories fail so often to hit their nails on the head. To think of a story is much harder work than to write it. The author can sit down with the pen in his hand for a given time, and produce a certain number of words.

That is comparatively easy, and if he have a conscience in regard to his task, work will be done regularly. But to think it over as you lie in bed, or walk about, or sit cosily over your fire, to turn it all in your thoughts, and make the things fit, − that requires elbow-grease of the mind.[3]

In Trollope's strict requirement of preliminary hard work from the novelist there is evidently nothing pedantic or hypocritical; it is his rule and theory for himself in his own practice; he is neither conceited nor ashamed of it; to him it is the merest common sense. We know that his rule was not acknowledged by Scott or Thackeray. . . . . But what is here to the point is that Trollope, who has told us of his easy writing, tells us also of premeditation and careful planning; so that if any of his stories seem to be loose, rambling, ill constructed, we may be sure that the author has fallen short of his ideal method. A critic who has recently done good service in writing a preface to a new edition of *The Barsetshire Novels*[4] makes a contrast between Trollope and Flaubert, speaking as though Trollope had no literary principle or aim. Trollope on Thackeray has escaped his notice. Trollope did not trust to mere luck, and he thought not so poorly of his own writings as he sometimes in his *Autobiography* may appear to have done. If Trollope was not a great artist, he knew what the art of fiction demanded. I do not think that he failed, and I hope to give reasons for this opinion.

But first I should like to notice some other opinions of Trollope on the subject. One of them is specially interesting, because the subject of it − realism in fiction − has been discussed and debated so extensively and comprehensively by such eminent persons that it will probably figure in future histories of literature in the same way as the Dramatic Unities in former ages. I quote again from Trollope on Thackeray. I am strongly inclined to quote the whole chapter on 'Thackeray's style and manner of work', so full of plain good sense is it, resembling Aristotle in his literary judgements and discriminations. This is what Trollope says about Realism:

A novel in style should be easy, lucid, and of course grammatical. The same may be said of any book; but that which is intended to recreate should be easily understood, − for which purpose lucid narration is an essential. In matter it should be moral and amusing. In manner it may be realistic, or sublime, or ludicrous; − or it may be all these if the author can combine them. As to Thackeray's performance in style and matter I will say something further on. His manner was mainly realistic, and I will therefore speak first of that mode of expression which was peculiarly his own.
Realism in style has not all the ease which seems to belong to it.

It is the object of the author who affects it so to communicate with his reader that all his words shall seem to be natural to the occasion. We do not think the language of Dogberry natural, when he tells neighbour Seacole that 'to write and read comes by nature'. That is ludicrous. Nor is the language of Hamlet natural when he shows to his mother the portrait of his father;

> See what a grace was seated on this brow;
> Hyperion's curls; the front of Jove himself;
> An eye like Mars, to threaten and command.

That is sublime. Constance is natural when she turns away from the Cardinal, declaring that

> He talks to me that never had a son.

In one respect both the sublime and ludicrous are easier than the realistic. They are not required to be true. A man with an imagination and culture may feign either of them without knowing the ways of men. To be realistic you must know accurately that which you describe. How often do we find in novels that the author makes an attempt at realism and falls into a bathos of absurdity, because he cannot use appropriate language? 'No human being ever spoke like that,' we say to ourselves, — while we should not question the naturalness of the production, either in the grand or the ridiculous.

And yet in very truth the realistic must not be true, — but just so far removed from truth as to suit the erroneous idea of truth which the reader may be supposed to entertain.[5]

Is not the whole essence of the thing in that? Does it not explode the stupid realists? Realism is not mechanical imitation; it is inventive and imaginative; in fact, it is idealism. Trollope was clear in his own mind as to the scope and range, the limitations and the exigencies of the art of fiction. He knew that its business was an allusion to real life in which realities were not to be treated with superstitious respect. He knew also that the novel must itself be alive. And the result was, though now it is neglected, that Trollope's best novels compete with Jane Austen's in giving a sense of the movement of life, keeping the right relations and proportions between different characters and their surroundings, through changes of time, so that the reader finds himself moving along with a number of people who are all changing in different ways as their several lives are determined on the scene of the world.

Trollope reckoned himself a moralist, and he had no scruple in repeating the old commonplace about mingling amusement with instruction. He does not pretend to be indifferent about good and evil, nor yet to have any peculiar standard of conduct; ordinary sane common sense is good enough for him. But his moral judgements are not those of ordinary common sense, nor of the moral philosopher. He is more discriminating than the jury of common sense and less abstract than the philosopher, and so, for all his common sense there may be something paradoxical in his morality. There generally is, in comedy, and comedy is what the great novelists are mostly engaged in. . . .

In *Barchester Towers* Trollope makes another note about his theory of novel writing. The chief thread of the story is the life of Eleanor Bold (daughter of Mr. Harding, the Warden) between her widowhood and her marriage with Dr. Arabin, the new Dean of Barchester. This is all part of the ecclesiastical history. The Bishop and Mrs. Proudie, Archdeacon Grantly and his wife (Mrs. Bold's elder sister), the remarkable family of Dr. Stanhope, Mr. Slope the Bishop's chaplain – these are the other chief personages. Mrs. Bold is courted by Bertie Stanhope and by Mr. Slope, who are both in different ways absurd; and it looks as if the story were going to inflict some anxiety on the reader. Is Mrs. Bold to be given to either of these unsatisfactory wooers? But no! the author comes forward to explain that she is not, and that he has no wish to harrow our feelings in that way. His heroine is too good for either of them, and he does not intend us ever to think otherwise. Then he explains his general opinion about his work, viz. that the reader, the spectator, should be in the confidence of the author; the people on his stage have to play out their comedy of errors, but the audience must not be confused or in doubt which Antipholus or Dromio is which. Of course, this confidence does not mean that the spectator knows all the story beforehand. It means that what is going on is comedy; that the mistakes and misjudgements on the stage are understood as such, and interesting and amusing as such to the lookers-on. Hence it follows that, as in comedy, so in the novels of Anthony Trollope, there is no great stress or strain. Life and the conduct which is three parts of life, or possibly more, must not be taken too seriously.

This does not mean that the novelist or the comic poet does his work without any use of what are commonly reckoned tragic motives. It is certainly not true of Trollope, any more than of Miss Austen, what is sometimes said in depreciation of them – that all their matter is insipid, ordinary, conventional life, at best the small interests and humours of unheroic people. (Trollope does not seem to have cared for Jane Austen; he calls her conventional. It is a pity, but it can't be helped.) Trollope's stories of ordinary life are not wanting in the sensational elements; some

of them are 'full of novelty and crime'. Phineas Finn has to stand his trial
for the murder of Mr. Bonteen in the Curzon Street passage, which was
really the work of Mr. Emilius, Lady Eustace's eloquent Asiatic second
husband. Do not those names imply enough detective business? There is
much more than detective business, of course, in *The Eustace Diamonds*
and in *Phineas Redux*; but to say that Trollope is wanting in incident is a
proposition which can be plainly refuted without any cavilling as to what
is meant by incident. But cavilling (if that be the proper word) is unavoid-
able if one is not only to silence but to convert the objector. Surely at
this time of day one may be allowed to reckon as 'incident' in a story
whatever comes to affect the minds and lives of the personages. Is it
incident when Johnny Eames saves Lord de Guest from the bull or knocks
Mr. Adolphus Crosbie into Smith's bookstall at Paddington Station? (*The
Small House at Allington*, I, xxi, and II, iv). Most certainly and agreeably.
It is also incident when Crosbie's first letters to Lily Dale are delivered at
the small house at Allington, and equally when the letters cease, and much
more when Lily Dale's letter comes to Crosbie at Courcy Castle just after
he has engaged himself to Lady Alexandrina. 'He would have given all that
he had in the world three times told, if he could have blotted out that visit
to Courcy Castle from the past facts of his existence' (I, xxiv). Trollope's
work is comedy, the comic epic in prose. He is a prose author, not a poet.
Yet he is not to be reckoned among the prose authors who are that and
nothing else. He was a lover of poetry (as a reading man he threw Dr.
Johnson out of the window once,[6] in disgust at his treatment of 'Lycidas'),
and though his business was prose one can see that he kept away from the
tragic heights through a right understanding of his limitations and his
proper scope, not through any want of sense or sensibility. He tells,
in a plain easy-going way, of many things that might be matter for tragedy — adversities, sorrows, trials. Is he superficial? Certainly he is, with
regard to such passionate things as are represented in *Wuthering Heights* or
The Ordeal of Richard Feverel or *The Woodlanders*. But he always lets you
know that the tragic motives are at work when to ignore them would
falsify his record. The charges brought against Scott by Carlyle may be
brought against Trollope — with equal justice.

The best of Trollope's novels, it is pretty generally agreed, is *The Last
Chronicle of Barset*. In this there is more than usual of a continuous anxiety
throughout. It begins with the accusation of theft against the Reverend
Josiah Crawley, perpetual curate of Hogglestock. He had cashed a cheque
for £20 which did not belong to him, and for his possession of which he
could not account; and it is only at the end of the book that the matter is
happily cleared up. The reader is not allowed to have any doubts as to

Mr. Crawley's innocence, but he has to follow the stages of the long ordeal. It is the most serious thing Trollope wrote, and there are two heroic characters in it, Mr. Crawley and his wife, not to speak of Grace Crawley his daughter. His wife is of the finer temper and better judgement; Mr. Crawley full of pride, selfwill, bitterness, contempt, and anger, unmistakably true and courageous — all that was wanted for a tragic figure, if the author had been so inclined. The author's intention is different: he is a prose author and not a tragic poet; the pain of Mr. Crawley is left to be understood by the reader just as he chooses to take it; it is not brought to bear upon the reader's mind with the concentration of tragedy. The story is not simply Mr. Crawley Agonistes; it has a broad field and many other interests. Among these there is one which shows how well Trollope knew his own powers. *The Last Chronicle of Barset* tells the end of the story of the Warden. Old Mr. Harding has to suffer some cruelty, not comparable to the distress of Mr. Crawley, but still bad enough for an old weak man. Trollope has no particular delight in misery, but he understands what it means, and he also understands the limits of the novel (which is comedy) in dealing with miserable things. The story of Mr. Harding (in *The Warden* and *The Last Chronicle*) is a beautiful thing in itself if you follow it apart from the other stories; and, if there were any need to cavil about incident, one might maintain that this, too, is an adventurous story.

Trollope in his remarks on *Henry Esmond* is unexpectedly classical and exacting;[7] he is unjust, it may be, to *Vanity Fair* and *Pendennis*, and to Thackeray's conception of the unities of story-telling. His own books are most of them rather complicated. Many of them show great skill in managing a number of different interests and plots, and keeping them all together. Some of them are failures in this respect. There is a comic underplot in *Can you Forgive Her?* which might be taken out with no trouble and great advantage. It looks like the old style of farce; and Trollope in his *Autobiography* says that he worked it in from an early experiment of his in drama.[8] It is seldom, however, that there is so little meaning in Trollope's secondary characters or their stories. No English novelist has done anything to equal his Chronicles of Barset, and what may be called the later political series with all its branches, in keeping up through thousands of pages the image of a coherent world to which we return again and again — the world of Barchester, Bishop, Dean, Archdeacon, prebendaries, parsons, curates, of the county of Barset to which Freeman gave his approval on historical and philological grounds,[9] the Duke of Omnium and Plantagenet Palliser. the Greshams, Thornes, De Courcys, and then the London, and that extraordinary comic version of politics in which hardly any political motive is recognized except the glory and profit of being in and the discomfort of being out — more truly comic and more coherent even than the politics of *Coningsby* or *Sybil*. Nothing in Trollope except the fox-hunting scenes is better written than the politics of *Phineas Redux*: the disestablishment of the Church proposed by the leader of the Conservative party, the perplexity of the Liberals and particularly the speech of Mr. Daubeny the Conservative Prime Minister after his defeat in the House of Commons [I, xxxix]. As an author of political comedy Trollope had two advantages over Disraeli. He was disinterested and kept his politics purely superficial and imaginary; that is one thing. In the second place he had Disraeli himself to draw from and has caught exactly, as far as it suited his purpose, the attitude and gesture of that hero confronting his great antagonist in the House.

Thinking of Barsetshire, I do not forget Mrs. Oliphant[10] and Carlingford, and I am not competent to choose between Salem Chapel and Barchester Cathedral. But Trollope's scene is immensely larger. It is like Balzac's in extent; but I will not attempt a comparison, except in one respect. Wherever else Trollope may fall short — in dialogue, that is, in pure and proper comedy, he can do what the great Frenchman refuses. He makes people talk like life. He is a dramatist, and Balzac is not.

NOTES

1. *An Autobiography*, chap. xv (ed. F. Page, 'The Oxford Trollope', Oxford University Press [1950], pp. 271–2).
2. 'Somebody talked of happy moments for composition; and how a man can write at one time, and not at another — "Nay, (said Dr Johnson) a man may write at any time, if he will set himself *doggedly* to it." ' Boswell, *The Journal of a Tour to the Hebrides*, 16 August 1773 (Boswell's *Life*, &c., ed. Birkbeck Hill, rev. Powell, v. 40).
3. *Thackeray* ('English Men of Letters' series), pp. 122–3, 124.
4. *The Barsetshire Novels*, ed. F. Harrison, 8 vols (1906) &c.
5. *Thackeray*, pp. 184–5.
6. *An Autobiography*, chap. iii ('The Oxford Trollope', p. 53).
7. *Vanity Fair, Pendennis*, and *The Newcomes* 'are comparatively idle books. His only work, as far as I can judge them, in which there is no touch of idleness, is *Esmond*. . . . All his full-fledged novels, except *Esmond*, contain rather strings of incidents and memoirs of individuals, than a completed story. But *Esmond* is a whole from beginning to end, with its tale well told, its purpose developed, its moral brought home, — and its nail hit well on the head and driven in' (*Thackeray*, pp. 123–4).
8. Chap. x ('The Oxford Trollope', p. 180).
9. E. A. Freeman, 'Anthony Trollope' in *Macmillan's Magazine*, xlvii (1883), p. 239.
10. Author of nearly one hundred novels, including several with the general title, *Chronicles of Carlingford*.

MICHAEL SADLEIR
The Books*

I

The initial obstacle to a sober-minded definition of Trollope's novels is that they provide a sensual rather than an intellectual experience. A smell, a pain or a sound is not more difficult to describe than the effect — at once soothing and exciting — produced on the reader's mind by the leisurely, nonchalant commentaries on English social life which carry his name on their title-pages.

The phenomenon is partly explicable by the fact that a Trollope novel is of the very essence of fiction. At its best it represents a distillation of that element in story-telling on which all other elements depend, without which no blend — however skilful — of fact, incident, idea and description can be recognised for fiction at all — the element of characterisation.

There are novels more spiritual than his, more heroic and more beautiful; but there are none more faultless in this most delicate of all novel-writing problems. 'Trollope' one critic has declared 'is more than the painter or the sculptor of his people; he is the biographer of them all.' That is high praise, but it is praise deserved.

Power of characterisation, then, is the superlative quality of Trollope as a novelist. And as revealed by him, it is not a power of observation nor of imagination; not a power of knowledge nor of intuition; but a compound of all four, with a something added of the author's personality, giving to the whole a peculiar but elusive flavour.

For even granted characterisation, Trollope's quality remains intangible, baffles resolution. In theme familiar, in treatment undistinguished, his work is nevertheless potent in appeal, unrivalled in its power to hold the

*From *Trollope: A Commentary*, 3rd ed. (originally published 1927; 3rd edn 1945; [rpt. London: Oxford University Press, 1961]), pp. 366–76; excerpts from Appendix II, C, 'Classification of Trollope's Fiction', pp. 416–21. Reprinted by permission of Constable & Co. and of Mr Richard Sadler.

attention of readers of any kind and of any generation. And its elusiveness is the more extreme for being unexpected. It seems hardly fitting that a being, who in himself was so definite and so solid, who – like a solitary tower upon a hill – was visible for miles around in the wide landscape of Victorian England, should as a literary phenomenon be so difficult to seize and to describe; it is almost irritating that books in themselves so lustily prosaic should be so hard of definition.

There are, of course, certain qualities that Trollope as a novelist emphatically does not possess. He is no great philanthropist like Dickens; he has not Thackeray's pointed brilliance nor George Eliot's grave enthusiasm; he does not, like Meredith, paint a familiar scene in colours so vivid as to be of themselves a challenge; he has not the passionate sense of Nature's oneness with humanity that lights the sunset over Egdon Heath. Even in comparison with Jane Austen – the writer nearest to him as a novelist of manners – his curiosity seems suave rather than searching, his observation to have more of scope than of discrimination.

But not by elimination only can the quality of Trollope be appraised. He may be neither teacher nor word-painter, neither pantheist nor social reformer, but he is definitely something. What is he? Wherein lies that strange potency, which renders work so featureless, so sober and so undemonstrative an entertainment than which few are more enthralling?

It lies surely in his acceptance and his profound understanding of ordinary daily life. In the tale of English literature he is – to put the matter in a phrase – the supreme novelist of acquiescence.

I know there are artists [says a modern writer] whose work bears witness to a complete acquiescence in the world and in life as it is. But in the most clumsy and bungled work (if it has been born of the desire for beauty) we should doubtless find, could we but pierce through the dead husk of it to the hidden conception, that divine homesickness, that longing for an Eden from which each one of us is exiled.[1]

Trollope is the great exception that proves the rule herein laid down. He seeks for no doorway of escape. He is content with life, engrossed in it, never weary of its kaleidoscope of good and evil, of tears and laughter. Not only does he agree to the terms proposed by life, but he glories in them. And yet his work is born of a desire for beauty. He finds all of romance and courage and achievement within the unpretentious limits of the social existence of his day. He believes in individual capacity for perfection, but in terms of things as they are; his ideal of beauty and of proportion, whether in character or in happening, lies in the suave adjustment of personality to circumstance.

Trollope, then, is never a writer of revolt. But so complete is his acquiescence that he is not even a critical despot over the society of his imagination. Like a man in a crowded street who views his fellow-men, he is at once genially disposed but fundamentally detached. Also, to the point inevitable in detachment, he is cynical. He is without superiority; without presumption of omniscience. He has his own idea of what is right; but if the crowd of passers-by have a different idea and act accordingly, their ultimate salvation is no concern of his.

It is this almost pugnacious acceptance of reality that distinguishes him from all other novelists of standing. It lies at the root of his difference from Jane Austen, from Sir Walter Scott, from Dickens, from Thackeray and from George Eliot. It explains why his social pictures differ in basic impulse from theirs. And they do differ, even from such as belong in theme and treatment to an identical school of novels of manners. *Middlemarch*, for example – which is the most Trollopian of all George Eliot's novels[2] – is never wholly free of the intellectual superiority of its author towards the non-intellectual middle class. As Oliver Elton wisely says: 'George Eliot is apt to be hard on the upper bourgeois, and Trollope's light, unassuming way is really sounder than hers.'[3] As for Thackeray and Jane Austen, behind the whimsical elegance of the former, behind the latter's shy sense of the absurdity of other people, lies a conviction – unexpressed but unmistakable – that the satirist at least knows what is what. Thackeray when he tears at snobbery, Jane Austen when she laughingly lays bare the follies of the female heart, are passing judgment, basing a criticism on a code of manners of which they, at least, claim to possess the secret.

But Trollope arrogates to himself no general right of judgment, no knowledge of the true paths of virtue or of social decency more profound than that possessed by any of his characters. Punishment for wrong-doing he frequently inflicts; but it is punishment by one citizen of a fellow-citizen who has transgressed the civic code. For he himself, as has been said, is one of the throng of his imaginary persons. With the amusement of a casual acquaintance he can observe their little ambitions, disappointments, self-delusions. But if they are free to live their lives, so is he also. He will fall in love with his heroines as readily as he will take a hand in the discomfiture of villainy. Snobbery, infidelity, dishonesty are as displeasing to him in his fictional as in his real life; but in the former, no less than in the latter, he is pugnacious rather than censorious, touched in his sense of citizenship rather than in his moral consciousness. 'Such things are', he seems to say; adding, more tritely still, 'It takes all sorts to make a world.' But at certain crises he is roused. 'This sort of thing won't do,' he declares. 'We must put a stop to it.' With the result that Crosbie gets a thrashing at Paddington; that Lord Brotherton is knocked into the fireplace of his hotel sitting-room by an angry Dean; that Mountjoy Scarborough lies senseless on the flag-stones by the Junior United Service Club.

A curious, though not perhaps unnatural, result of Trollope's extreme acquiescence has been to set his work athwart the pattern of modern literary criticism. The long series of his books — so drab yet so mysteriously alive, so obvious yet so impossible of imitation — evade every criterion of what has become an academic judgment. They will stand no school-tests save those of the school of real life. They cannot but violate the modish canons of good fiction, as continually and as shamelessly as does life itself. Like life, they are diffuse, often tedious, seldom arrestingly unusual. Their monotony is the monotony of ordinary existence, which, although while actually passing it provides one small sensation after another, emerges in retrospect as a dull sequence of familiar things.

For in this queer sense of the absorbing interest of normal occupations lies the true realism of Trollope. He can reproduce the fascination of the successive happenings of the daily round, in the absence of which the human spirit would perish or go mad. Existence is made up of an infinite number of tiny fragments of excitement, interest and provocation, which carry men on from day to day, ever expectant, ever occupied. It is the second part of Trollope's claim to be a novelist that, by building up from just such multifarious trivialities the big absorptions which are his books, he gives the illusion that is of all illusions the most difficult to create — the illusion of ordinary life.

II

The art of Trollope, therefore, has two predominant qualities: power of characterisation and power of dramatisation of the undramatic. Within the limits of these rare capacities he designed and peopled a second England, virtually a replica of the London and counties of his day. But although in his imaginary England life seems (as indeed it is) utterly, almost exaspera-tingly, a series of unsensational sensations, a slow progression of meals and small ambitions, of love-making and disappointments, of sport and business, it would be an error to regard the Trollopian world as — other than superficially — without violent happenings. Accompanying a rather offensive 'Spy' cartoon of Trollope published in *Vanity Fair* in April 1873 was a still more offensive paragraph of critical text. 'Mr. Trollope has had by far the greatest success in writing books with the ordinary young lady always in mind – books sufficiently faithful to the external aspects of English life to interest those who see nothing but its external aspects, sufficiently removed from all the depths of humanity to conciliate all respected parents.' The implication of these words – that Trollope for profit's sake was a writer of goody-goody unreality – is grotesque. Julian Hawthorne in the article already quoted was much nearer the mark when he wrote: –

There may be, perhaps, as many murders, forgeries, foundlings, abductions, and missing wills, in Trolope's novels as in any others; but they are not told about in a manner to alarm us; we accept them philosophically; there are paragraphs in our morning paper that excite us more. And yet they are narrated with art, and with dramatic effect. They are interesting, but not uncourteously – not exasperatingly – so; and the strangest part of it is that the introduction and intermediate passages are no less interesting, under Trollope's treatment, than are the murders and forgeries.

And to murders and forgeries may be added – if one is agog for crime – adulteries and bigamies. It is one aspect of his amazing truth to life that he could contrive at the same time to be a novelist for the *jeune fille* and a most knowledgeable realist. For, his books are lifelike in this also – that though compounded both of innocent and guilty, the guilt (as in life) is shrouded from the innocent, so that only such as know the signs of it may realise its presence or its nature.

This fact indicates those two of his personal qualities which most influence his handling of an imaginary social scene – his worldly proficiency and his good manners. There is nothing that he does not know; there is very little that, in his quiet skilful diction, he is not prepared to say. Socially speaking he is the wisest of English novelists; but because a large part of social wisdom is restraint, alike of gesture and of word, his books are restrained – not in incident or necessarily in emotion – but in expression. He writes adult books for adult people. But because he writes in terms of polite society, because he is in the truest sense a 'man of the world', he is too civilised and too experienced to forget the social decencies for the sake of the social sins.

And not only had he a well-bred man's distaste for ugly realism; he was himself more interested in the deceptive calm of society's surface than in details of the hidden whirlpools beneath. The incident of Madame Max Goesler and the old Duke of Omnium in *Phineas Finn* provides a case in point. The inclination of the great nobleman to make the pretty widow his mistress is treated adequately but briefly; all of the author's skill in dramatic dialogue goes to the fashioning of the subsequent scene between Madame Goesler and Lady Glencora Palliser, in which the latter (representing the *convenances*) appeals to the former (as likely to represent irregularity) to forgo a personal triumph for the sake of social decency. Always, as here, the clash between conventional poise and secret catastrophe, the delicate adjustment of repute and disrepute which kept the life of upper-class England outwardly serene for all its inward hazard, appealed to Trollope's sophisticated and rather cynical mind.

For in all things he was sophisticated and in social things more than a little cynical. Carlyle compared his work to alum, and the fancy is a shrewd one. Contrast his books with those of the sensation-writers of his day or with those of novelists from a later generation who have been praised for their courageous realism. Trollope in geniality, in satire or in bitterness is calm; but to the others, in one way or another, existence is perpetually and disproportionately exciting. Wilkie Collins and Miss Braddon; Zola, Hardy and George Moore – all of these have beside Trollope a certain callowness. One or two of them may excel him in other, perhaps higher qualities; but none can rival his controlled indifference in the face of life. The sensationalists are thrilled by their own catalogues of crime; the reforming realist shudders to read his own exposures of cruelty and bestiality; the child of nature makes discoveries as to the shifts and sorrows of humanity that have been made in every generation for centuries; the amorist regards his love successes as of a piquancy unrivalled. But Trollope is beyond such elementary stimulus. To him everything is material for observation, nothing for declamation or for vanity. He approves virtue and deprecates vice, but he refuses to become excited either over ugliness or beauty. Like a connoisseur of wine he sips at this vintage and at that, selects to his taste and lays a cellar down. We, who inherit it, have but to drink at will, and in the novels that he left behind to savour the essence of life as once it was, as it still is, as in all likelihood it will remain.

III

Indeed, general observations apart, a reading of Trollope is worth a volume of critical analysis. But there is interest in a consideration of the evolution of his talent and of his changing tendencies as fiction-writer, while to a wholesale recommendation of the novels should be added some degree of special definition.

A schedule of the various categories into which the stories fall is given below. Some such classification is necessary in an age of scanty leisure and with work of such intimidating bulk. But toward actual comment on each

single novel no attempt can be made. Such book-by-book examination
would result only in repetitions, and it has seemed more practical to call
attention mainly to the less familiar tales, and to those more famous ones
which have a direct bearing on their author's literary development.

Trollope's work is of unusually constant quality, and at frequent intervals during his writing life he would revert to earlier loves and to earlier
models. Nevertheless, during his long and crowded career of authorship,
not only did he come to gradual technical mastery, but also his work
underwent a definite transformation in kind. There came a moment at
which – perhaps in unconscious obedience to the new tendency in fiction –
he sought to abandon pure narrative, to leave behind the type of novel
in which many characterisations are blended to produce a complex but
evolving tale, and to experiment in psychological analysis of one character
reacting to a single set of circumstances. There came another moment when,
stirred to indignant protest by what he deemed the vulgar degeneration of
his beloved England, he wrote one of the most savage satires in social
fiction and became, instead of an amused and tolerant observer, an en-
venomed castigator of the age.

That the early Irish novels and the historical romance *La Vendée*
were the unskilful fumblings of a writer who had not found himself, has
already been shown; and in a survey of his work those books can be ignored.
The Trollope of posterity appeared in 1855, when *The Warden* first gave
sign of a new and individual talent. One may salute *The Warden* and respect
it for the sake of the admirable books it heralded; but one may not deny
that this inaugural fiction, with its exaggerated sentiment and its clumsy
caricature, is very elementary Trollope. The two years that followed its
completion were years of vital education – how vital the author's next
novel was to prove. *Barchester Towers* shows a wonderful advance, alike in
literary technique and in forcible use of selected material *solely in the
interests of the novel's plot*. There is virtually no beating of the propa-
gandist air in *Barchester Towers*; hardly an incident or a character but
goes to strengthen the book's legitimate fictional aim – the portrayal of
society in a southern cathedral city.[4] '*Barchester Towers*' says Oliver Elton
'is crowded and rich and harsh'.[5] The epithets are happy, and may be applied
not only to this book, but to most of Trollope's successful work. He was
a generous writer. He loved to populate his novels thickly, and felt the
more at home the more his characters jostled one another in his mind.
Also, beneath the suavity, was always harshness – not the harshness of
cruelty, but the asperity of a man who was impatient of false sentiment,
on the rock of whose aggressive commonsense the waves of flummery beat
in vain.

But in the excellence of *Barchester Towers* was an element of fluke. That Trollope himself was not aware of the book's real quality was shown by its immediate successor. *The Three Clerks*, whatever its value as a document in autobiography, is a bad novel. Beside *Barchester Towers* it is shrill and facetious; its background is a mere 'painting in' and not a fertile soil from which spring character and happening. Indeed it is a novel born some fifteen years too late, and was, no doubt, written with a mistaken idea of emulating the picaresque novel of incident which bloomed and faded in the 'forties. Formless and flaccid for all its sprightliness, *The Three Clerks* is not redeemed even by the character of Undy Scott, who introduces what was to become a Trollopian speciality — the gentleman who is also a cad. Perhaps the book's female characters betray most completely its essential feebleness. The young women are pretty dolls in simpering bourgeois homes, or lovely daughters of the people, exposed to sordid sights and much temptation but with a virtue repellently impregnable. The freshness and frankness that distinguish the true Trollope girl are lacking even from Katie Woodward, for whom (and perhaps this is the reason of her unreality) Trollope himself cherished a romantic memory.

Undoubtedly *The Three Clerks* was derivative — in ultimate resort from Dickens, nearer at hand from such a Dickens imitator as Frank Smedley; and to the fact of its derivativeness may be attributed its popularity among contemporary intellectuals. Neither Thackeray nor the Brownings could have felt for such genuine Trollopianism as (for example) *The Belton Estate* the enthusiasm they had for a book written to a more familiar recipe. Thackeray was himself a novelist of the 'forties, and knew where he was in a novel written to the specification of his own period; the Brownings, out of touch with changing England and perforce judging their own country by its appearances in such fiction as came their way, accepted *The Three Clerks* for a continuing reality, whereas in fact it was a picture — and an inexpert picture — of a vanished age.

Trollope himself, although he clung — and for very obvious reasons — to his affection for this book of reminiscence, must during 1857 have had a vision of his real writer's destiny. How otherwise may be explained the sensational perfection of *Doctor Thorne*, one of the five (in a technical sense) faultless books he was to write? In nearly every novel — even in novels so outstanding as *The Small House at Allington*, *The Last Chronicle of Barset*, the two chronicles of Phineas Finn, *He Knew He Was Right*, *The Eustace Diamonds*, *The Vicar of Bullhampton*, *The Way We Live Now* and *Mr. Scarborough's Family* — it is impossible not to deplore a sub-plot or an exaggeration, a longwindedness or a more than normally aggressive repetition. But in five books — *Doctor Thorne, The Belton Estate, The*

Claverings, Sir Harry Hotspur of Humblethwaite and *Dr. Wortle's School* — though there may be an extreme of tranquillity there is not a loose end, not a patch of drowsiness, not a moment of false proportion.

Classification of Trollope's Fiction[6]

[Books recommended are marked with an asterisk — several Baedeker fashion, with a double asterisk, a very few (in restrained imitation of the A.A.) with a triple asterisk.]

I. THE CHRONICLES OF BARSETSHIRE

The Warden (1855).
*Barchester Towers (1857).
***Doctor Thorne (1858).
*Framley Parsonage (1861).
*The Small House at Allington (1864).
**The Last Chronicle of Barset (1867).

II. THE POLITICAL NOVELS

Can You Forgive Her? (1864).
**Phineas Finn: The Irish Member (1869).
**The Eustace Diamonds (1873).
**Phineas Redux (1874).
*The Prime Minister (1876).
*The Duke's Children (1880).

III. NOVELS OF MANNERS, CONVENTION AND SOCIAL DILEMMA

The Three Clerks (1858).
*Orley Farm (1862).
***The Belton Estate (1866).
***The Claverings (1867).
**The Vicar of Bullhampton (1870).
*Ralph the Heir (1871).
**Sir Harry Hotspur of Humblethwaite (1871).
Lady Anna (1874).

The American Senator (1877).
**Is He Popenjoy?* (1878).
Ayala's Angel (1881).
Marion Fay (1882).

IV. SOCIAL SATIRES

The Bertrams (1859).
*Rachel Ray (1863).
Miss Mackenzie (1865).
The Stuggles of Brown, Jones and Robinson (1870).
***The Way We Live Now (1875).
**Mr. Scarborough's Family (1883).

V. IRISH NOVELS

*The Macdermots of Ballycloran (1847).
The Kellys and the O'Kellys (1848).
Castle Richmond (1860).
The Landleaguers (1883).

VI. AUSTRALIAN NOVELS

Harry Heathcote of Gangoil (1874).
*John Caldigate (1879).

These two novels were, of course, the outcome of the author's visit to his son in Australia. The earlier shorter tale is a mere ranch episode — dramatic, vividly told and with good local colour, but frankly the 'Christmas Number' story that it set out to be. *John Caldigate* is more important. It is the only one of Trollope's books in which *for the purpose of his plot* he uses his knowledge and experience of the Post Office (the salvation of Caldigate from his enemies is achieved by an ingenuity not unworthy of the modern detective story), and the comments on the Civil Service contrast interestingly with those implicit in *The Three Clerks*, written twenty years earlier.

VII. HISTORICAL AND ROMANTIC NOVELS

> *La Vendée* (1850).
> **Nina Balatka* (1867).
> **Linda Tressel* (1868).
> *The Golden Lion of Granpère* (1872).

VIII. PSYCHOLOGICAL ANALYSES AND STORIES OF SINGLE INCIDENT

> ***He Knew He Was Right* (1869).
> *An Eye for an Eye* (1879).[7]
> **Cousin Henry* (1879).
> ****Dr. Wortle's School* (1881).
> *Kept in the Dark* (1882).
> *An Old Man's Love* (1884).

IX. FANTASIA

> *The Fixed Period* (1882).

X. SHORT STORIES

> *Tales of All Countries.* First and Second Series (1861, 1863).
> *Lotta Schmidt: and Other Stories* (1867).
> **An Editor's Tales* (1870).
> **Why Frau Frohmann Raised her Prices: and Other Stories* (1882).

NOTES

1. *Apostate*, by Forrest Reid (London, 1926).
2. George Eliot herself told Mrs. Lynn Linton that, but for Trollope, she could hardly have persevered with the extensive, patient study necessary to the completion of *Middlemarch*.
3. *A Survey of English Literature 1830–1880* (London, 1920).
4. The only strident lapse from this laudable detachment is the rather foolish reference to a descendant of the 'Sidonia' who shines flamboyantly in Disraeli's *Coningsby*. Trollope, in his role of anti-humbug,

detested Disraelian fiction for rococo unreality. His Sidonia — 'a dirty little old man, who positively refused to leave his villa till he had got a bill on Doctor Stanhope's London bankers' — is proof that he had not yet shuffled off the chains of topical prejudice.

5. Op. cit.

6. In this classification of Trollope's fiction use has been made of the grouping carried out by Mr. Spencer van Bokkelen Nichols in his valuable monograph *The Significance of Anthony Trollope* (New York, 1925). From some of Mr. Nichols' allocations I differ, but the assistance afforded by his work is gratefully acknowledged.

7. Mr. Nichols classifies this story as of the Irish series. But although the action takes place mainly in Ireland, the drama is one of human dilemma, and its protagonists could as well have played their parts in any other land.

PAUL ELMER MORE
My Debt to Trollope*

For many years I have felt a kind of obligation to write on Trollope. Through the most part of a lifetime his novels have been the chosen companions of my leisure, and, with the possible exception of Boswell's *Johnson*, have been oftener in my hands than the works of any other English author. I have not gone to them, naturally, for that which the great poets and philosophers and divines can give. But they have been like an unfailing voice of encouragement in times of joy and prosperity; they have afforded solace in hours of sickness and despondency and adversity; they have lightened the tedium of idleness and supplied refreshment after the fatigues of labour. They have been submitted to the test of reading aloud, and have passed the ordeal with more than honour. Indeed, I question whether any one has fully relished their wit and irony and their delicacy of insinuation, who has not gone through them at that slower pace demanded by such reading and with the heightened interest of participation by sympathetic listeners. I cannot boast, alas, as does that fortunate bibliophile, Mr. Newton, that 'I have every book Trollope ever wrote', much less that I possess them all in first editions; there are even eight or ten out of his six score and more volumes that I have never yet seen. But those I own spread out sufficiently over my shelves, and remind me daily of the largeness of my debt of gratitude to their author, a debt too long unpaid.

I

So it is that, released from the confinement of more exacting studies, I take the opportunity of this initial volume of a new series of essays to discharge my obligation, for my own relief if to no other end. A more particular occasion for writing is Mr. Sadleir's recently published 'Com-

* From *The Demon of the Absolute* (Princeton: Princeton University Press, 1928), abridged from pp. 89–113. Reprinted by permission of Princeton University Press.

mentary', – an excellent book in the main, broadly informative, richly documented, often finely critical, intended to be laudatory, yet with that recurrent note of apology which so frequently annoys me in those who profess themselves Trollopians [*Anthony Trollope: A Commentary*. By Michael Sadleir, with an Introduction by A. Edward Newton. Houghton Mifflin Company, 1927]. My mood is not apologetic. I see no reason why I should be niggardly of praise to one whose novels, as Hawthorne said of them, 'precisely suit my taste', whose *Orley Farm* was Cardinal Newman's favourite piece of fiction, and whose mimic world of politics enthralled the declining years of a statesman so versed in the actual ways of men as ex-President Cleveland.

Yet withal I too, like Mr. Sadleir, would wish to pay my tribute to Trollope 'soberly and without exaggeration'. I admit that 'there are novels more spiritual than his, more heroic and more beautiful'. He could not do, at any rate did not try to do, what Balzac and Dostoevsky and Turgeniev and Manzoni have done. He has his limitations. But who has not? Could Balzac or Dostoievsky or Turgeniev or Manzoni have written the chronicles of Barsetshire? Imagine the 'clumsiness' and 'awkwardness' and 'garrulity', – epithets which Mr. Sadleir bestows on Trollope, – if one of these geniuses had undertaken to fashion a society such as that in which Mrs. Proudie and Dr. Grantly and Mr. Crawley and Lily Dale and Mary Thorne play their parts. And these, I speak for myself, are the people amongst whom I am at home. Then, narrowing the field of comparison to England, I ask myself whether one ought to subscribe to the opinion of Mr. Newton: 'I do not say that Trollope is our greatest novelist; I know that he is not, but I can read him when I can't read anyone else.' Now 'great' is an ambiguous term, and it might be said that, among writers of fiction at least, he has a fair claim to be called greatest who can hold our interest when all others fail. But then I think of Thackeray, and suspend my judgement. I remember the heavy passages through which Trollope plods with leaden feet; but does Thackeray's lightness always save him from being tedious? Is there any novelist who writes largely without boring us at times with gratuitous dullness? Trollope's language lacks the sustained urbanity and the fascinating charm of Thackeray's, his constant use (to descend to trifles that are not trivial) of 'proposition' for 'proposal' and 'predicate' for 'predict', his abuse of 'commencement' for 'beginning', grate like sand between the teeth; but in the long run I wonder whether his clear, manly, straightforward style is not the most satisfactory medium after all, and whether the softness of Thackeray's overworked 'kind' and 'artlesss' and 'honest' does not end by exasperating us almost as much as Trollope's solecisms. Or shall we measure the two rivals by their great climactic scenes? I think

of the tenderness of Thackeray at his best; but is the death of Colonel
Newcome more finely imagined or more feelingly described than the
passing of Mr. Harding? I remember such revelations of character as that in
which Lady Castlewood turns upon the Duke of Hamilton and Beatrix
whispers her regrets into Henry Esmond's ear; but is the thrill of artistic
satisfaction any keener than at Mr. Crawley's ejaculation, 'Peace, woman!'
to Mrs. Proudie, which caused the bishop to jump out of his chair? . . .

II

But my concern is not to magnify Trollope at the expense of any of his
rivals, nor to complain against the caution which would season eulogy
with a proper recognition of his limitations (what writer of fiction, as I
have said, is without limitations?). My resentment, so far as I allow it, is
aroused when an admiring Trollopian, like Mr. Sadleir, thinks it necessary
to apply to Trollope, with no reservation at all, Professor Santayana's
detraction of another Victorian:

> It is remarkable, in spite of his ardent simplicity and openness of
> heart, how insensible Dickens was to the greater themes of the human
> imagination – religion, science, politics, art. . . . Perhaps, properly
> speaking, he had no *ideas* on any subject; what he had was a vast
> sympathetic participation in the daily life of mankind.

I say nothing now about Dickens, but I would maintain stoutly that so
flat a denial of all ideas whatsoever to Trollope is a slander upon the
novelist and an insult to his devoted readers.

And first of all let us distinguish. To lump politics and science and
religion and art together, as if Trollope's attitude towards all four subjects
were one of equal indifference, is not the way to get at the truth. He
himself, in one of his excursions, separates politics from the other three as
the special field in which the characters and external activities of men are
so blended that it lends itself peculiarly to the uses of fiction. And surely
it is critically unsound to accuse the author of the Parliamentary Novels,
to mention no others, of insensibility to the political doings of his people
or to the importance of politics in itself. Nor are his ideas on the subject
vague or fluctuating or doubtful. His own particular brand of liberalism is
never concealed, rather it is thrust almost too persistently upon the reader;
his distrustful antipathy to Disraeli is not only unmistakable, but goes to a
point, in my judgement, beyond reason; in one of his novels a chapter on

the theory of government and the relation of the social classes – 'The Prime Minister's Political Creed' he calls it – takes the form of a little essay barely contained within the framework of the story. Whether rightly or wrongly (rightly I think), Trollope holds the material offered by the other subjects mentioned to be less amenable to his purpose, and one suspects that, apart from this, his own private interest in them was less keen – *non omnia omnibus*. But here again it is necessary to distinguish. Science, as professedly the most impersonal of these occupations, is scarcely touched on in his novels, save perhaps in *The Fixed Period* where sociological theory takes a scientific slant; and I for my part, having in mind the exceptional flatness of that tale and the dismal consequences of such a mixture of the *genres* in certain bolder writers, can only be grateful to Trollope for his abstinence, whatever the cause of that abstinence may have been. But with religion and art the case is not quite the same.

Now in discussing Trollope's attitude to religion it is well to remember first of all that he was a novelist and dealt with the material of life accordingly. The reminder is a commonplace; but it is just the forgetting of such commonplace distinctions that causes half the confusion in criticism. . . . Trollope himself, in his *Framley Parsonage*, apologizes frankly for what might appear to be a deficiency in his account of lives devoted to worship, and at the same time shows how voluntarily he submitted to the limitations of his art:

> I have written much of clergymen, but in doing so I have endeavoured to portray them as they bear on our social life rather than to describe the mode and working of their professional careers. Had I done the latter I could hardly have steered clear of subjects on which it has not been my intention to pronounce an opinion, and I should either have laden my fiction with sermons or I should have degraded my sermons into fiction. Therefore I have said but little in my narrative of this man's feelings or doings as a clergyman. But I must protest against its being on this account considered that Mr. Robarts was indifferent to the duties of his clerical position.

With the Barsetshire novels before us, let us be glad that their creator worked contentedly within his self-imposed restrictions. . . .

So much by way of concession and explanation. But because Trollope did not compose religious tracts it by no means follows that he was insensible to religion or had no ideas on the subject. He hated, as warmly as did Dickens, a certain type of evangelical cant not uncommon in England, and he satirizes it mercilessly. His Prongs and his Slopes have a place with the most detestable hypocrites of the world, and they are not the less convincingly human because, beneath all their humbug, there is still something of genuinely righteous fervour. He could make fun of a worldly prelate like Dr. Grantly, whom yet he loves for the man's downright honesty, – as do I. But to the Church in its more majestic modesty he was loyal in his life, as to a true churchman he was always reverential in his fiction. Nor are his books wanting in hints of the deeper matters of faith. After the very defence of his reticence quoted above from *Framley Parsonage*, he permits himself to dwell for a page on the penitential qualms of the parson whose frailties as a man have been the central theme of the novel. Elsewhere (*Barchester Towers*, II, i) there is a detailed account of the 'mental struggles' and 'agony of doubt', through which the Rev. Francis Arabin fought his way to an assured conviction, that not only seems to me psychologically subtle and historically true, but satisfies my taste as a model of what can be done on such a theme within the stricter bounds of fiction. And in Arabin's apology for his own and his friends' contentious opposition to the innovating Slopes, and at the same time for the Church of his predilection, there is a quiet dignity, covering strong emotion, that only a master craftsman could attain. . . .

The clerical champion of *Barchester Towers* knew his own mind and through perseverance found the way to such peace as the world can give. In *The Bertrams* we have the sadder story of one who never, never at least until too late, grasped the full meaning of that lesson. The book as a whole is not in Trollope's best vein, but the early chapter, describing George's dedication of his life to holiness while, sitting on the hill above Jerusalem, he looks out over the scenes where the ancient drama of salvation was staged, is in its kind a veritable masterpiece of art and of delicate suggestion. It could have been conceived only by a writer who was himself deeply religious; and of its kind I know of nothing quite like it in the English language. The complications of the plot that follows do not always hold our interest; but, again, the failure of the hero to live up to his high resolve is kept finely in the background of the story, until the whole tragedy of regret breaks out in the closing sentence: 'Reader, can you remember the aspirations of George Bertram, as he sat upon the Mount of Olives, watching the stones of the temple over against him?'

III

But the element of religion which furnished not an occasional theme and moves not an exceptional character, but pervades all Trollope's fiction, is the ethical. Now and then, to be sure, he falls, like Thackeray, into the sentimentalism left over from the eighteenth century, as if morality were synonymous with a natural and undisciplined goodness of heart; but for the most part his code is of a sterner sort.

No one of our greater novelists, unless it be George Eliot, saw more clearly than he the inexorable nexus of cause and effect in the moral order, or followed more relentlessly the wide-spreading consequences of the little defalcations of will, the foolish misunderstandings of sympathy, the slight deflections from honesty, the deceptive temptations of success, the failures to make the right decision at critical moments, the ruinous corrosions of passion and egotism. It is this sense of the subtle adhesions of folly and evil that excuses the monotony of his plots turning on the entanglements of a heroine who succumbs to the baser of two loves presented to her, as in the typical story entitled *Can You Forgive Her?*, or who through mistaken pride clings to an innocent error of judgement, as in *Kept in the Dark*. . . .

I for one admire him for this integrity of mind, but I know that a man may be sturdily, even intelligently, moral, yet withal a dull writer, that the temptation to preach may invade the region of art disastrously. Morality is not art. That is a canon of criticism, out of which the Demon of the Absolute has formulated the deadly maxim that art has nothing to do with morality. And it is, doubtless, under the sway of this seductive article of faith in the autonomy of art that Mr. Sadleir defends Trollope from the ruinous charge of preaching, thus: 'In his *Autobiography* he [Trollope] speaks of the moral purpose of his fiction; but no modern reader can take this statement very seriously. It is merely another example of the influence of his period on his method of self-expression.' Now I cannot answer for the 'modern reader', being uncertain whether I should be justified in appropriating to myself so exalted a title to enlightenment. But I suspect that Mr. Sadleir, despite his modernism, has suffered some confusion of ideas between moral purpose and unmitigated preaching, and that Trollope, whatever the modern reader may say of him, was altogether serious in his claim to the former. Let us examine the passage to which Mr. Sadleir refers; it is important enough to bear quoting at length:

> The writer of stories must please, or he will be nothing. And he must teach whether he wish to teach or no. How shall he teach lessons of virtue and at the same time make himself a delight to his readers? That sermons are not in themselves often thought to be agreeable we all know. Nor are disquisitions on moral philosophy supposed to be pleasant reading for our idle hours. But the novelist, if he have a conscience, must preach his sermons with the same purpose as the clergyman,

and must have his own system of ethics. If he can do this efficiently, if he can make virtue alluring and vice ugly, while he charms his readers instead of wearying them, then I think Mr. Carlyle need not call him distressed, nor talk of that long ear of fiction, nor question whether he be or be not the most foolish of existing mortals. . . .

I believe that Trollope in this profession of his faith (which he goes out of his way to repeat several times in the course of his fiction) was as serious as was Solomon in his prayer for wisdom; I think that the critic, not to mince matters, who would defend Trollope by calling such thoughts a merely superficial blemish of the age, is simply as ignorant of the canons of art as of the laws of life. First of all, let us brush cant aside. Life is more than art: if to be true to art it were necessary to be false to life, then only a shallow dilettante would choose art; and if to seek beauty it were necessary to forget righteousness, then a whole-hearted man of experience would say, Perish the name of beauty. If there is anything more than the petulance of a spoiled child in Mr. Yeats's adoption of the 'proud words' of Villiers de L'Isle Adam, 'As for living – our servants will do that for us', then the career of a servant is more honourable than that of a poet. But these are the stale spewings of a moribund romanticism. Trollope was saying exactly this, that there is no such antinomy in the nature of things; and Trollope was right. . . .

IV

If then . . . the author aims deliberately, as Trollope says, to 'make virtue alluring and vice ugly, while he charms his readers instead of wearying them', how shall he proceed? If truth to life forbids him to do this by too open a distribution of rewards and penalties, then he must have recourse to more indirect means. He must by cunning suggestion carry our thoughts into those secret places of the heart where, beneath all the distractions of blind events and the defensive crust of vanity, our conscience dwells face to face with those everlasting laws to which the Antigone of Sophocles appealed against the tyranny of appearances:

> The unwritten statutes, ever fixed on high,
> Which none of mortal heritage can deny;
>   For not of yesterday but to all years
> Their birth, and no man knoweth whence or why.

Unless the poet or novelist, oftener by a hint than by open declamation, can centre our judgement of his characters upon those high laws and by them ultimately move and control our emotions, he is at the last, however rich his talent and refined his method otherwise, no true artist but a mountebank of letters. His upheld mirror has caught but the glancing lights, not the full face of nature. And this is the canon of poetic justice.

V

Here should be noticed a peculiarity of Trollope's attitude towards the denizens of his imaginary world which, perhaps, requires some defence. We hear a good deal about the objectivity of art and the detachment of the artist from the moral implications of his work. And there would seem to be an element of truth in this maxim. A true artist will often obliterate himself so far as to suppress any expression of opinion, letting the facts speak for themselves. I might even suspect that such alone would be the procedure of great art, were it not for the part of the chorus in Greek tragedy. But to translate this law of reticence into an obligation of indifference laid upon the writer is simply a step in the direction of a divorce between art and life which must culminate in perfect sterility. At any rate, this certainly was not the method of Trollope. As Taine, the absolutist of science in literature, complained of Dickens, so it might be said of Trollope: 'Il ne fait jamais abstraction de la morale. . . . Il n'a pas cette indifférence de l'artiste qui produit le bien ou le mal comme la nature. . . . Il n'aime pas les passions pour elles-mêmes.' On the contrary, like his own Lady Carbury, the novelist of *The Way We Live Now*, he might say: 'One becomes so absorbed in one's plot and one's characters! One loves the lovable so intensely, and hates with such fixed aversion those who are intended to be hated.' There is no indifference in Trollope, some would say no reticence. We are never at a loss to know how he feels towards his characters and their actions. For example he pursues the frigid but impeccable Lady Dumbello through several books with a kind of sullen implacability; he revels in his love of Lily Dale and Mary Lovelace; he avows his hatred of Crosbie and gloats over the rascal's discomfitures; he 'claims a tear' for Mr. Sowerby, after balancing his villainies and his sense of honour. Sometimes his practice leads him into a curious sort of double presentation, as in his reflections over the peril of his beloved Eleanor in *Barchester Towers*: 'And then it must be remembered that such a marriage as that which the archdeacon contemplated with disgust, which we who know Mr. Slope so well would regard with equal disgust, did not appear so monstrous to Mr.

Harding, because in his charity he did not hate the chaplain as the arch-deacon did, – and as we do.' That, I take it, is the sort of thing done openly and naively, which Henry James tried to accomplish by tricks of artful sophistication. The question would be whether this frank-dealing of Trollope is good or bad art; and my own answer would be that, whatever may be said of the method theoretically, its actual result is often to enhance the artistic effect. Take the story of Crosbie and Lily Dale in *The Small House at Allington*. The unconcealed vindictiveness of the author towards the villain of the piece really acts as a clever device to bring out more clearly the charm and loveliness of his heroine. Or take the case of the incomparable mistress of the bishop's palace. One day, Trollope tells us in the *Autobiography*, he was sitting in the Athenaeum Club at work on *The Last Chronicle of Barset*, and heard two clergymen abusing his novels because the same characters were reintroduced so often.

> Then one of them fell foul of Mrs. Proudie. It was impossible for me not to hear their words, and almost impossible to hear them and be quiet. I got up, and standing between them, I acknowledged myself to be the culprit. 'As to Mrs. Proudie,' I said, 'I will go home and kill her before the week is over.' And so I did.

And then Trollope adds, and this is the point of the anecdote: 'I have sometimes regretted the deed, so great was my delight in writing about Mrs. Proudie.'

That is why the lady abides in our memory also as a veritable person whom we have known in the flesh and have judged in the final court of conscience. It is for the same reason that the author's habit of interrupting the narrative to expatiate on his own feelings does not diminish but heightens the reality of his imaginary world, and that he converts his readers into accomplices with him in executing the law of poetic justice.

VI

The fact is that ethics and aesthetics are inseparable in art. Or, more precisely, just in proportion as the practice or criticism of art becomes superficial, ethics and aesthetics tend to fall apart, whereas just in proportion as such practice or criticism strikes deeper, ethics and aesthetics are more and more implicated one in the other until they lose their distinction in a common root. In this sense Keats's dictum, 'Truth beauty is etc.', may be applauded as profoundly right; though the same dictum may be turned into a mischievous fallacy when taken, as it too often is taken by the shallower aesthetes, to mean that beauty may supplant truth, or to justify the theory that art exists for its own sake in its own world, and has nothing to do with morality.

But this is not quite the view of Mr. Sadleir; and so, passing on in the chain of concessions, we are not surprised to find our encomiast of Trollope depriving him of other qualities which would lift him out of the rut of cheerful mediocrity. 'Both [Dickens and Trollope]', says Mr. Sadleir, 'lacked a lively sense for fine art, for the power of spiritual principle or for natural beauty; but both, where dramatic force in landscape or in the handiwork of man could help to illustrate a character, called it to their aid and worked it dexterously.' A strange sentence from the pen of a professed Trollopian, a sentence, I make bold to say, that contains about as much intertangled truth and error as could well be packed together in so few words. It is true that Trollope does not take art and artists for his theme, and, with the results before us of novels based on a study of the 'artistic temperament', we ought to be thankful for his abstention, or, if you will, his insensibility, in that direction. But to say that he lacked a sense for the power of spiritual principle is a sheer calumny, as I have attempted to show under the head of religion. As for natural beauty, if Mr. Sadleir means that Trollope did not sprinkle his pages with purple patches of descriptive 'fine writing' which have little or nothing to do with the plot or the characters, if he intends no more than this when he complains that 'in the finer forms of fancy he [Trollope] was deficient', then again I for one am thankful for such a deficiency. But I fear that more is intended than this. It would be tedious – though he himself is never dull – to follow Mr. Sadleir as he develops his thesis in detail. The point I would make is that the final impression left by his reservations and explanations is so exaggerated as to be fundamentally wrong. For instance Trollope's 'descriptions of country town or country house'. No doubt the prime concern of the novelist with such scenes is as they affect or indicate the life of his people, and that surely is good art. But to infer that he has no sense of the picturesque in itself, no feeling for 'the idealisms of the past', or is content before such qualities 'to parrot text-book phrases of appreciation', – that I maintain approaches the line of critical hebetude. 'In *The Small House at Allington*, Mrs. Dale's cottage and the Squire's home', says Mr. Sadleir, 'are taken so nearly for granted, that one can almost imagine Trollope glancing at any Victorian wood-engraving of the houses in a conventional English village of the time and telling himself that everyone would know the kind of cottage and the kind of manor house that Lily and her uncle must naturally inhabit.' I can only reply that, with the minute and picturesque descriptions before me in the first chapter of the book, such a statement strikes me as simply amazing. And I fail to understand how, in making his list of descriptive passages for the purpose of showing their poverty, Mr. Sadleir can have overlooked Ullathorne Court and Carbury and the country places in *Phineas Finn.* The sum of the matter is that, in making his eulogy, our lover of Trollope – and it must be remembered that I write of Mr. Sadleir as the typical Trollopian – thinks it necessary to apologize for him as intellectually without ideas and imaginatively without wings. There is for instance this quotation of a review written by Henry James and published in the *Nation* of January 4, 1866:

> Our great objection to *The Belton Estate* is that we seem to be reading a work written for children, a work prepared for minds unable to think, a work below the apprehension of the average man or woman. *The Belton Estate* is a *stupid* book . . . essentially, organically stupid. It is without a single idea. It is utterly incompetent to the primary function of a book of whatever nature – namely to suggest thought.

Now Mr. Sadleir does not exactly endorse this 'excoriation'; he quotes it rather to illustrate the beginning of the reaction against Trollope that culminated with the aesthetical insurgence of the closing century. But neither on the other hand does he totally reject it as a piece of ignorant imbecility; he compromises, and makes concessions, in a manner almost as exasperating as that of James, as thus:

> Perhaps, to those who demand of fiction what Trollope does not pretend to give, it [the novel reviewed] may be an aimless irritation – undistinguished, a waste of time and labour, incompetent (in the Jamesian sense) to suggest a single thought. Nevertheless, to a reader in sympathy with the Trollopian method and mentality [that is to say a method awkward, idealess, pedestrian, commonplace, unimaginative, narrow, etc.], the book is a delight for its smoothness, its subtlety and its faultless adjustment of character and circumstance.

Evidently Mr. Sadleir is endeavouring to be conciliatory by the fairness and balance of his judgement. More bluntly, I should say that a reader to whom no single thought is suggested by a book which is a delight for its faultless adjustment of character and circumstance has a very strange notion of what thinking really is, that such an adjustment (Matthew Arnold would call it the 'criticism of life') is precisely the method by which the novelist should display his realization of ideas. I suspect that Mr. Sadleir has fallen into the not uncommon error of identifying thought with fussy activity of mind. To me the right identification of thought is rather with the perception of truth, and there is no truth more important or profound or more difficult of attainment than that which concerns the adjustment of character and circumstance. . . .

VII

What Mr. Sadleir concedes to his favourite novelist is, in the language of Professor Santayana, 'a vast sympathetic participation in the daily life of mankind', or, in his own language, 'the inspiration of humanity and the instinct for its interpretation', – certainly a large concession and, on its positive side, eminently right. It is true that human life as it is lived in this world of ours was the dominant interest of Trollope's mind; it is true that religion and politics and art, as specific activities, were in themselves subordinate with him to this main interest, and further that in so far as he permitted them to enter into his fiction it was rather as concrete factors in the shaping of character than as the material for abstract ideas. But this, I take it, is not, properly understood, a concession so much as an appreciation of the fact that Trollope knew his business as a writer of novels. I guess that this is what Mr. Sadleir is really trying to say, and what makes him in the end a genuine Trollopian. I suspect that the tone of apology which so annoys me has crept into his 'Commentary' from the baneful influence, unacknowledged and perhaps unconscious on his part, of the current theory of the dehumanization of art. Because Trollope's tales are superlatively human, because the very warp and woof of them is woven out of the loves and hates, the joys and sorrows, the good and evil, of life, looking to the adjustment of character and circumstance, therefore, though they may be infinitely entertaining, yet they must be poor art, the product of a brain devoid of imagination and ideas. So I explain to myself why a reader so acute otherwise belittles critically what instinctively he admires, and so I am confirmed in my opinion that a theory of art which leads to such a contradiction is intrinsically false. . . .

DAVID CECIL
Anthony Trollope*

Elderly novelists, depressed by the spectacle of their waning popularity, may think of Trollope and be comforted. He was admired in his own day, though never so much as Dickens or Thackeray, but before the end of his long life his reputation had begun to decline. His books had fewer readers, and those mainly among Philistines; the pundits, led by Henry James, declared he was stupid; all serious critics agreed that he would not 'live'. Yet here we are in 1934, and if to be read is to live, Trollope is still very much alive − more alive than Thackeray, more alive than Henry James himself − and among fastidious readers. Indeed he is almost the only Victorian novelist whom our sensitive intelligentsia appear to be able to read without experiencing an intolerable sense of jar.

This is an ironical comment on the infallibility of experts; but it is not hard to understand. For Trollope is not only an admirable novelist, he is also conspicuously free from some of the most characteristic Victorian faults. Not that he is un-Victorian. On the contrary, he was in himself a more typical Victorian than any of his famous contemporaries. Dickens, Thackeray, and Charlotte Brontë were all in some degree opposed to their age − disapproved of some of its institutions, questioned some of its ideals. Trollope did nothing of the kind. He was brought up, an English gentleman *l* with an English gentleman's standards, and his experience of the world only served to confirm him in the view that they were the right ones. In his view of life, as in his bushy beard, he remained the typical mid-Victorian gentleman. Like the other mid-Victorian gentlemen he enjoyed hunting and whist and a good glass of wine, admired gentle, unaffected, modest women, industrious, unaffected, manly men, despised vulgar riches, respected good birth; like them he accepted unquestioningly the existing

* From *Victorian Novelists: Essays in Revaluation* (Chicago: University of Chicago Press, 1958), abridged from pp. 227−53. Originally published as *Early Victorian Novelists* (1934). Reprinted by permission of Constable & Co., and of the author.

state of society. Indeed his only quarrel with his age was that it questioned it too much. The only thing that ruffled his otherwise equable temper was the iconoclasm, political and intellectual, of the nineteenth-century middle-class reformer; the democratic agitations of Dickens, the Calvinist anathemas of Carlyle.

His view of the novel was as orthodox as his other views. His books are constructed within the regular Victorian convention; panoramas of character and incident, drawn more from the outside than the inside, avoiding any mention of the spiritual and animal aspects of human nature. And even more frankly than any of his contemporaries, Trollope writes to entertain – altering his plot to please his readers, rounding every story unashamedly up with a happy marriage. This, coupled with a typical Victorian carelessness, meant that his books suffered from the customary Victorian faults of form: diffuseness, repetition, incoherence, divided interest. *The Last Chronicle of Barset* is as lacking in organic unity, as full of loose ends, and irrelevant sub-plots, as *Nicholas Nickleby* itself.

All the same, in an essential aspect his novels are not typically Victorian. For, consciously or not, he approaches his material from a different angle from that of the other Victorian authors. He was a realist. . . .

For one thing he had an extraordinary power of observation. It had its limitations; it was neither subtle nor microscopic. Trollope does not discern the convoluted intricacies of human consciousness like Proust, or of human impulse like Tolstoy, nor had he that command of circumstantial detail that enabled Defoe to give his incidents their eye-deceiving verisimilitude. His observing power was a broad straightforward affair. He stood at a little distance from character and incident, and noted only their outstanding features. But these he notices all the time; and always right. He stands in a central commanding position; his view is consistently correct, clear and sensible; he never fails to see the wood for the trees.

It was a large wood too. Trollope had learned to exercise his observation over a wide experience. He was, as Dickens and Thackeray were not, a man of the world. He was accustomed to move in many societies, rich and poor, respectable and disreputable, townsmen and provincials, fashionables and foreigners. Further, he was by nature both level-headed and sympathetic. He saw human beings as they are; but he liked them and got on with them; and within the conventions of his age and class he was tolerant of their weaknesses.

All this means that his picture avoids many of the faults of Dickens' and Charlotte Brontë's. It is never so unequal; the reader is never jarred by a sudden jolt from the true to the false. Trollope is not only dependent on his imaginative force for his success. Dickens and Charlotte Brontë are;

if it fails them, or if they force it to work on a subject uncongenial to it, they come to grief. Trollope's imagination is always supported and checked by reference to actual facts. He never allows it to run away with him, and if it fails him he has the facts to fall back upon. Again, his conception of what a novel should be makes it impossible for him to write outside his range. This, like that of most authors, is confined to the world he had himself seen. But since he is concerned only to write of what he saw, he always keeps to it. His limitations surround his books, they do not cut across them. Finally, the fact that he was a man of wide experience made his range wider than those of the other Victorians. He is most at home when writing about the small gentry from which he sprang, but he gives an adequate picture of the political world of Phineas Finn, the shabby lodging-house world of Mrs. Lupex, the flashy, dubious plutocracy that produced Mr. Dobbs Broughton, the shoddy, dissipated 'bright young people' of *The Way We Live Now.* His aristocrats — Plantagenet Palliser, Lady Laura Kennedy — are the real thing; not fustian scions of a novelette noblesse, like Sir Mulberry Hawk or Lady Ingram. His comic clergymen — Mr. Slope, Mr. Quiverful — are not embodied outbursts of personal spite like the Malones and Sweetings of *Shirley*, but recognizable, credible human beings. Trollope's eye for facts, too, gave him a more varied emotional range than that of Dickens or Thackeray. There is no parallel in their works to the complex misery of Mr. Crawley, unjustly accused of theft, part wounded pride, part outraged rectitude, part self-pity; the agitation of Henry Clavering, torn between the old love and the new duty; the eating professional ambition of Phineas Finn. Trollope can describe love, too; Frank Gresham's first proposal to Mary on that sunny morning with the breeze stirring the creepers outside her window, Rachel Ray's walk in the sunset — these breathe an authentic, if gentle, note of lyrical emotion. Trollope can even — and here he is unique among Victorian novelists — describe a guilty love with understanding. His picture of Lady Glencora's passion for Burgo Fitzgerald is as convincing as his picture of Mrs. Proudie's temper. For though he disapproves of illicit passion as much as Thackeray himself, he does not allow his disapproval to distort the dispassionate accuracy with which he draws it.

Of course his description is limited by the conventions of his age; he does not describe such passion with the frank detail of D. H. Lawrence. He implies rather than describes it. But what he tells us is enough to enable us to imagine what convention forces him to omit. We believe in Lady Glencora's yearnings as fully as if they were attested by all the unprintable words of *Lady Chatterley's Lover.*

Even when he is writing of emotions within Dickens' and Thackeray's range, he does so with a more certain touch. Pathetic emotion, for instance; Trollope never spreads his pathos too thick, never tries to extract it from situations in which it is not inherent, in order the better to stir the reader's feelings. He is not concerned to stir the reader, but to tell the truth. With his eye fixed on his subject, he draws its plain facts for us; and leaves any pathos there may be in them to speak for itself. With the result that it always rings true. Mr. Harding's quiet farewell to his almsmen compels our tears; whereas Colonel Newcome's death, for all its sentimental flood-lighting, leaves us stony-hearted.

Trollope's hold on dramatic emotion is equally sure. The drama in Dickens and Charlotte Brontë is exciting, but it tends to melodrama. Its characters are either intrinsically melodramatic figures like Fagin or Mr. Rochester's wife, or they turn to melodramatic figures when their circumstances become melodramatic, like Mrs. Jonas Chuzzlewit. Trollope's characters are solid, daylight figures, the reverse of melodramatic; and for the most part they live very placid lives. But if they do by chance become involved in a dramatic situation, they do not lose their solidity. Mrs. Dobbs Broughton's reception of her husband's death is drawn with extraordinary reality. Its mixture of horror and suspense and squalor disturbs us with the discomfort that such a scene awakens in actual life. And Mrs. Broughton herself is not changed by disaster into a conventional figure of grief or heartlessness. For all her agony, we recognize her in manner and behavior as the same trivial vulgarian who roused our amusement at that dinner-party where she made her first appearance.

Indeed, Trollope's vigilant sense of reality prevents him from dividing his characters into comic and serious as his contemporaries did. Mr. Crawley has the grotesque mannerisms of a comic character part, but he is predominantly a dignified figure; there are ridiculous sides to that amiable, hapless lover Johnny Eames. People are not exclusively comic or tragic in real life, nor are they in Trollope.

They are not exclusively good or bad either. Even Trollope's worst characters have their good points. Mrs. Proudie is genuinely compassionate of Mrs. Quiverful, Lady Carberry is disinterestedly devoted to a worthless son. And if Trollope shows us no irredeemable sinner, he also shows us no impeccable saint. His heroes — Henry Clavering, wavering in ignoble uncertainty between his old love and his new, Mark Robarts, in debt from his desire to shine in society — these present a striking contrast to those faultless lifeless barbers' blocks called Nicholas Nickleby and Graham Bretton. Nor were Trollope's heroines Christmas-card angels like Agnes Wickfield. Here we come to one of his especial distinctions. Most men novelists cannot resist idealizing their heroines, using them as illustrations

of their own standards of feminine perfection. Not so Trollope. Mary
Thorne has a hasty temper, Rachel Ray is indiscreet. And these blemishes
do not make them less sympathetic. On the contrary, the fact that they
are not inhumanly faultless makes us believe in their merits. Indeed
Trollope is the first novelist of his age in describing good people. Saints
above all other types should be drawn realistically; unless presented to him
with the most careful verisimilitude, the skeptical reader doubts the reality
of exceptional virtue. But they seldom are so presented. For novelists tend
to idealise them just as they do their heroines, in order to insure the
reader's admiration. Colonel Newcome, for instance, comes before us
with every virtue haloed, every vice obscured by the rosy mists of Thackeray's sentimental admiration, so that he does not seem a human being at all,
but only the Victorian pattern of a perfect gentleman. But Trollope
presents his good people in as plain a light as his faulty ones; Mr. Harding
is drawn as unsentimentally as Mr. Slope. With the consequence that the
beauty of his character strikes us with the convincing force that it would if
we met him.

Trollope's characters are, at their worst, probable. They never undergo √
incredible conversions like Mr. Micawber or act in a manner inconsistent
with their natures like Becky Sharp; none of them are dummies. Trollope —
and here again he is exceptional among his contemporaries — can contrive
to make the most commonplace character a live person. Dickens, interested
primarily in individual idiosyncrasy, communicates life only to highly
individual types of character; Thackeray, intent to illustrate the workings
of human vanity, to characters that exhibit these workings most clearly.
But Trollope, concerned merely to draw what he sees, makes a commonplace man like Frank Gresham as living as an eccentric like Mrs. Proudie.

And his plots are as probable as his characters. They may be ill-con-
structed, he may twist them to provide a happy ending, stretch them to fit
a required length, but his unfailing grip on reality enables him to do so
without ever making them seem unlikely. Even if their development does
not seem inevitable, it never seems unnatural. The plot does not turn on
fantastic coincidences like the plot of *Villette*; it rests on no foundation of
conventional intrigue like that of *Bleak House*.

Indeed, it is at once the final effect of Trollope's realism and the
principal cause of his continued popularity that the literary conventions of
his time are to him only machinery; they do not modify his conception.
His contemporaries, concerned either to create an artistic effect or to
illustrate a view of human conduct, conceived a large part of their stories
in accordance, not with actual fact, but with some artistic or moral ideal.

And since they were of their time, their ideals were the conventional ideals of the period. . . .

No wonder some people find him easier to read than his contemporaries. No wonder even that they think him better. All the same, he is not; and it is no service to his reputation to pretend that he is. His superiority to his contemporaries is mainly negative; he did not make their mistakes. His positive superiority resolves itself into one quality – he observed the surface of life more accurately than they did. But a great novelist is not just an accurate observer. Indeed, his greatness does not depend on his accuracy. It depends on his power to use his observation to make a new world in his creative imagination. It is the characteristic merit of the other Victorians that they possessed the creative imagination in an intense degree. With its help Dickens is able to create a living world in spite of a limited power of observation, Charlotte Brontë in spite of having hardly any power of observation at all. Now Trollope – it is perhaps the briefest way of defining his talent – was, in weakness as in strength, the opposite of Charlotte Brontë. He had creative imagination – he was not a mere photographer – but it was not always active; and even at its most active it was, compared to that of the greatest writers, a relatively low power of imagination. To paraphrase Johnson on Addison, Trollope imagined truly but he imagined faintly. . . .

But it is in his style that Trollope's relative weakness of imagination shows itself most clearly. Style is the writer's power to incarnate his creative conceptions in a sensible form. And all the great writers have a very marked style. It is not necessarily a beautiful or even a competent one. Hardy's is frequently neither. But he has a style: his harshest cadence, his clumsiest phrase reveals a characteristic idiosyncrasy in the use of words. Indeed, his very harshness and clumsiness help in a way to bring out this idiosyncrasy; without them he would lose something essential to the full expression of his individuality. At their worst Hardy's words manage to convey their author's temperament; at their best they convey it with supreme force and beauty.

Now of style, in this sense, Trollope has none at all. He writes easily and unaffectedly – and his tone of voice has its own masculine friendliness. But that is all. He has no characteristic cadence, no typical unique use of image and epithet; even at his best we feel we could paraphrase him without losing anything essential to his flavor. . . .

His dialogue is better than his narrative; indeed, it is extremely good. Realistic accuracy is a far greater asset in dialogue than in narrative, and Trollope's is the most realistic dialogue of any English novelist's. No one has solved so successfully the problem of evolving a form of speech which at once furthers the action and gives the illusion of actual conversation. But his dialogue is not free from his prevailing defects. If it is true to life, it is also sometimes as dull as life. Only now and again does he manage to transmute the dross of reality into the gold of art. . . .

Trollope has an extraordinarily clear eye for the emotions of class-consciousness; pride of birth, social inferiority, the uneasy arrogance of upstarts. His snobs are among the best in our literature. They are not the most profoundly studied. Trollope cannot, as Thackeray can, penetrate the soul of the snob to expose his secret yearnings and vanities and mortifications. But, on the other hand, his power of accurate observation makes him paint their surface more truthfully. He was incapable of drawing George Osborne, but he was also incapable of that crude over-emphasis with which Thackeray draws Lady Bareacres.

This power of imagining the social scene never fails Trollope. Even if it does not show itself in individuals, it shows itself in his picture of their relation to the society of which they form part. The Duke of Omnium's dinner to his country neighbors, once read, remains in our memory forever. This is not because the individual figures in it are memorable. The duke and his guests are not among Trollope's most vivid figures. But their attitude to one another is portrayed with supreme vividness. The duke's bored contempt for his guests, the cynicism with which these guests — all but the sturdy, independent squire Frank Gresham — swallow the contempt and the excellent dinner that goes along with it, the assiduous courtesies of the duke's agent, all these go to make up one of the great comic scenes in our literature. Trollope's characters are sometimes uninteresting; their social relations to each other are always absorbing.

Indeed, that the characters are sometimes commonplace arises from the fact that he is primarily interested in people in their relation to the social structure, so that he prefers to write of those average characters that show those relations in their most universal form. He is concerned with the commonplace rule, not with the brilliant exception.

Barset is the most carefully studied of his panoramas. But it is not the only one. In *Rachel Ray*, for instance, he sketches the social structure of a small town; in *Miss Mackenzie* that of a spa; in the political novels, that of the world of fashion and affairs. Further, these different pictures are not separate, self-dependent structures without connection with one another. Trollope's novels — and this is perhaps their outstanding distinction — combine to form a picture of a national social scene. Whatever their differences, the worlds they describe share those common traditions and characteristics which proclaim them part of a larger whole. Actually he brings many of the same characters into different books, but even when they are different, they are clearly part of one civilization. Barset is a rural district in the country of which the London of Phineas Finn is the capital. Littlebath is a spa to which Barsetshire people might go for their health; Rachel Ray's home is clearly in a neighboring county to Barset; while in *The Way We Live Now* Trollope shows us the same society in the throes of corruption produced by self-indulgence and foreign penetration. He has used his experience of England to create a complete new country of his own.

It is an extraordinary achievement, and it is unique in English literature. Thackeray and George Eliot, indeed, in *Vanity Fair* and *Middlemarch*, also paint pictures of a society, and against a larger background. In *Vanity Fair* it is a specific illustration of the general moral principles governing human society; in *Middlemarch* its limitations are contrasted with the aspirations of a noble and idealistic human spirit. To Trollope it is the whole, the only world; his characters accept its conventions unquestioningly, nor do they see it in contrast to any wider moral scheme or spiritual ideal. All the same, his picture is not only more elaborate than Thackeray's or George Eliot's, it is also more certain and more convincing. He tells us everything about it, and he makes us feel that everything he tells us is true. Only Balzac succeeds in creating so intricate, so complete, and so vital a social scene. . . .

CHAUNCEY BREWSTER TINKER   Trollope*

It is natural that an essay on Trollope should begin with statistics. To forget
his voluminousness is like ignoring the extent of the ocean or the height of
Mount Everest. He, like many of the greatest authors – Shakespeare,
Boccaccio, Chaucer, Sophocles – is remarkable partly for having written
so much. In an age of great novelists, he surpassed them all in output. His
full-length novels, some forty-seven in number, exceed the total number of
Dickens's, Thackeray's and George Eliot's combined. If we reckon volumes
of short stories and books of travel, he produced twice as much as Walter
Scott. He requires, in one's library, not a capacious shelf but an entire
bookcase.

Of this fecundity the author was obviously proud. As everybody knows,
he imposed upon himself a rigorous system of daily composition with
which nothing was permitted to interfere. He never waited for inspiration.
He wrote in railway trains and on shipboard. He wrote when physically
and mentally uncomfortable, and even when seasick. At one time he
began work at 5.30 a.m., wrote with his watch on the table before him,
and exacted from himself 250 words every quarter of an hour. Henry
James, in his pleasant essay on Trollope, bears testimony to this habit:

> It was once the fortune of the author of these lines to cross the
> Atlantic in his [Trollope's] company, and he has never forgotten the
> magnificent example of plain persistence that it was in the power of
> the eminent novelist to give on that occasion. The season was unpropi-
> tious, the vessel overcrowded, the voyage detestable; but Trollope shut
> himself up in his cabin every morning.

He boasted that he could have produced three novels in three volumes
each in the course of a year, had he been so disposed. There was a smooth,

* From *The Yale Review*, n.s. 36 (March 1947), 424–34. Copyright Yale
University; reprinted by permission of *The Yale Review*.

rapid stream of publication for a quarter of a century, from 1857 to 1882, which ended only with his death, when he left behind him two complete novels — 'Mr. Scarborough's Family' (an excellent tale) and 'An Old Man's Love' — an unfinished Irish story, 'The Land Leaguers', and an Autobiography in two volumes. This amazing and unbroken productivity was not begun till the author had entered his thirty-third year, and he had no great success till he was past forty. One result of this late beginning is that he appears, even at first, in full maturity. Trollope has no *juvenilia.* 'The Macdermots of Ballycloran', his earliest novel, contains little of the charm which was later to be associated with his name; but there is no trace in it of a 'prentice hand. It is profoundly depressing, but well written and cleverly constructed. It holds the attention of the horrified reader to the end. The author rightly regarded the plot of 'The Macdermots' as the equal of any that he constructed.

But there is more significance in Trollope's inexhaustible abundance than mere quantity. Strangely enough, it contributes in a way to his popularity, for it means that those who love his work can go on reading him forever. By the time you have read forty of his stories, you are ready to begin again. Dickens, though less extensive, has for his partisans something of the same appeal.

Moreover, Trollope, like Tintoretto, requires a huge canvas. He is not given to microscopic detail, reconsideration, or altered approach. He has so much to say that he not only fills the canvas, but, like Zola, expands his novels into series. His two great examples of continued narrative, the 'cathedral series' and the 'parliamentary series', are the greatest specimens of their kind in the English language, unless, indeed, Mr. Galsworthy has surpassed them. Again, Trollope sees man in society, as an individual in a group. He seldom concerns himself with the wanderer or the solitary. There is no Barry Lyndon or Peregrine Pickle in the vast panorama of his work. Nor does he explore the hidden recesses of the mind, like Joseph Conrad, passing from chamber to inner chamber, till he reaches the very arcana of the soul. He thought George Eliot too analytical. To this general assertion, exception must be made of 'He Knew He Was Right', a story of the development of insanity out of the stubborn pride of a man unable to conceive of himself as being in the wrong.

If Trollope took a pardonable pride in his incredible fertility, he was forced to pay a penalty for being fool enough to tell about it. The Autobiography, in which his rigorous methods were disclosed to the public, appeared in 1883, and was read with consternation by a generation which had come to delight in subtler standards and a more esoteric manner. It was an age in which much was heard about the *mot juste* and the figured harmony of prose. The novelists of the new school took an obvious delight in leading the reader a chase. It became the custom to speak slightingly of the reader's concern with mere 'story', and to smile at the old-fashioned desire for a happy ending. To the newer generation Trollope was a writer who did not take his art seriously. Henry James, in his most telling fashion, remarked that 'the writing of novels had ended by becoming with him a perceptibly mechanical process'. He could turn out fiction by the yard, as though engaged in operating a machine. Even the names of his characters betrayed his superficiality. Dr. Fillgrave and Mr. Quiverful (so inferior to the more suggestive names used by Thackeray) were laughed at, and even his limpid style did not escape scorn. Had he not praised Thackeray for the wrong thing by remarking, 'The reader without labour knows what he means, and knows all he means'? Perfect communion between author and reader was no longer attempted by the former nor desired by the latter. To a generation beginning to admire Meredith, he still harped on the importance of clarity. He thought George Eliot 'struggled too hard'. 'She lacked ease', he said.

But perhaps Trollope's perfect clarity and unpretentiousness may, in his own case, prove to be a saving grace, in that this very lack of manner keeps him from becoming antiquated. His style does not 'date', like that of many of his contemporaries. It has no spot of decay, but has kept sweet as the decades have passed.

Other features of the novelist's art are dismissed by Trollope in his Autobiography with a similar unconcern. Novel-writing all seems – or is made to seem – incredibly easy. Mere plot never troubled him, and he has therefore been accused of formlessness. Although none of his works is remarkable for a classic roundness, for finish and economy of means, I cannot feel that this charge is apposite. He is guided only by what he conceives to be the reader's desire. He will not continue a story after the reader's interest has lapsed. He never leaves the reader guessing or stops the story midway because life is without clear and fixed terminations.

There are times when he overloads his novel with material that may fairly be called extraneous. The satiric passages in 'The Warden' are an ugly smear on the perfection of a story which, for once, is admirably constructed. One can forgive a failure to appreciate the buoyant, Brobdingnagian manner of Dickens, which Trollope never properly esteemed, but is at a loss to understand why he should wish to devote so many scornful paragraphs to him as 'Mr. Sentiment', and even to ridicule two of his well-known characters, Mr. Buckett and Mrs. Gamp. The attack adds nothing to the story, and the whole incident (if such it may be called) could have been excised by the stroke of a pen. The caricature of Carlyle as Dr. Pessimist Anticant, which includes a kind of parody of 'Past and Present', is even worse. It is ill-natured and long drawn out, and is, unhappily, not even clever. And there are other things in the novels that could be spared. Many readers — particularly Americans — find the chapters devoted to fox-hunting a weariness to the mind, and others are repelled by the political issues of the parliamentary series; but, considering the vast extent of Trollope's work, it is surprising how little one is tempted to skip and how little one can omit without loss.

But all these are matters of secondary importance. Trollope himself declared that the first duty of a novelist was to have a story to tell, and of this principle he was a scrupulous observer. Although he was indifferent to that smoothness and sequence of events which are found in the great masterpieces of plot, he was careful enough of the main problem, careful, that is, to lend a continuous interest to it. The presence of this feature may generally be detected by the question that is uppermost in the reader's mind, and two of Trollope's titles plainly reveal it, 'Can You Forgive Her?' and 'Is He Popenjoy?' In the latter the recurrent question, 'Is the Italian baby who was born abroad, in circumstances that cannot be investigated, the real heir to the name or is he illegitimate?' holds the entire story together and dominates the reader's attention throughout. And thus it is in other books. Can John Eames win the hand of Lily Dale? Did Lady Mason forge the codicil to her dying husband's will? Where did Mr. Crawley get the check which caused all the trouble in 'The Last Chronicle of Barset'? In 'Cousin Henry', where is the missing will? Was Mr. Scarborough's eldest son really illegitimate, and if not what was his father's motive in declaring him to be so? A single sentence on the first page of 'Mr. Scarborough's Family' initiates this interest: 'The world has not yet forgotten the intensity of the feeling which existed when old Mr. Scarborough declared that his well-known eldest son was not legitimate.' It is such questions as these that lead the reader on from chapter to thrilling chapter; and such problems may surely be said to constitute plot, if such a thing as plot there be.

Trollope never belittled the importance in fiction of exciting incidents. He defends sensationalism in his Autobiography, and contends that a good novel should be both realistic and sensational, and 'in the highest degree'. 'If a novel fail in either', he adds, 'there is a failure in art'. People who think of Trollope as drab and rather unexciting do not sufficiently reckon with this feature of his work. George Vavasor tries to kill his rival, John Grey, and comes very near doing so; Lady Mason is brought into court, and tried for perjury; the Reverend Mark Robarts's house is invaded by the sheriff's officers; Phineas Finn is tried for murder; and Sir Henry Harcourt, the successful and admired, commits suicide. Such a list could be indefinitely prolonged. But Trollope was not so foolish as to suppose that incidents like these were all-sufficient. Who cares about wills or diamonds or questions of legitimacy unless he is concerned for the persons whose lives are to be made or ruined by the disclosure of the truth? And, therefore, our author was primarily concerned with 'realism', in that he was careful first to waken the reader's sympathy for the man or woman involved. In certain stories, as, for example, in 'The Warden', the question before us is so simple as to seem almost trifling unless the reader is deeply moved for the hero's peace of mind. An elderly clergyman, precentor in Barchester Cathedral, is made to debate with himself whether his modest post as warden of Hiram's Hospital is consistent with a rigorous ideal of honesty. ✓ Can he continue to hold it undisturbed by the disquieting thought that it is a mere sinecure? His final surrender and resignation of the wardenship are made as thrilling as a shipwreck, but only because the reader has first learned to love the patient, Christian fortitude of the man. We should be equally concerned if anything were to happen to his precious violoncello. Among Trollope's countless portraits, there is no more admirable, no more appealing and lovable man than this aged musician, who has outlived all personal ambition and uneasy jealousy, and has now no other desire than to live a simple and godly life. The account of his death is one of the most moving chapters ever written by a novelist.

Or take the story of Lizzie Eustace — the fascinating and unscrupulous adventuress, who has the aims of Becky Sharp without her cleverness. I doubt whether any woman can read her story with enjoyment, but I am confident that any man will fall at moments under her spell and, for the time being, wish her well in her mean little plot. If one is not amused by her shifts and her shameful deceit, he will, of course, close the book and read no more, since all interest in what becomes of the jewels will have declined long since. I am confident that the author himself had a kind of inverted sympathy with her and her schemes. There is in her the abiding interest of the picaresque.

And yet Lizzie is but a pale creature compared with her radiant predecessor, 'Madeline Vesey Neroni, nata Stanhope'. The daughter of Dr. Stanhope, of the cathedral close (now returned to Barchester close after a long period of nonresidence) she has been reared, married, and widowed in Italy, and has devised for herself the surprising nomenclature used above. She is a cripple, condemned to pass her life lying on a sofa, but her spirit and her beauty enable her to use it as a throne, from which she proceeds to fascinate the Reverend Mr. Slope and half the men of Barchester. No reader of 'Barchester Towers' will forget her apparition at Mrs. Proudie's reception in the Bishop's palace. Her sofa is wheeled in to the crowded

assembly, and she is seen lying on her couch arrayed in white velvet –
'without any other garniture than rich white lace worked with pearls
across her bosom and the same round the armlets of her dress. Across her
brow she wore a band of red velvet, on the centre of which shone a magnificent Cupid in mosaic. . . . On the one arm which her position required her
to expose she wore three magnificent bracelets each of different stones.
Beneath her on the sofa and over the cushion and head of it was spread a
crimson silk mantle or shawl which went under her whole body and
concealed her feet. Dressed as she was and looking as she did, so beautiful
yet so motionless, . . . with that lovely head, and those large bold bright
staring eyes, it was impossible that either man or woman should do other
than look at her'.

It was on this occasion that the wheel of her sofa came in contact with
the lace train of Mrs. Proudie's gown: 'Gathers were heard to go, stitches to
crack, plaits to fly open, flounces were seen to fall, and breadths to expose
themselves; – and a long ruin of rent lace disfigured the carpet, and still
clung to the vile wheel on which the sofa moved!' But Madeline Vesey
Neroni lies in Olympian beauty gazing upon it all with a serene composure
in which one may detect a mild amusement. So might a recumbent goddess
have gazed on some earthly frivolity far beneath her. Madeline is an
impostor, but she is brilliant and indomitable, and a male reader may find
it in his heart to wish her well.

As Trollope has made the base motives of Lizzie and Madeline amusing,
so he has the power, even more remarkable, of lending an air of authenticity
and importance to the unpleasant. He wrote many unpleasant stories, but
somehow the reading of them is not unpleasant. I can, I think, read them
all with pleasure, except the horrible psychological study, remorselessly
pursued to its conclusion in madness – 'He Knew He Was Right.' Of this
novel, the author wrote in his Autobiography, 'It was my purpose to create
sympathy for the unfortunate man, who, while endeavouring to do his
duty to all around him, should be led constantly astray by his unwillingness
to submit his own judgment to the opinion of others. . . . I look upon the
story as being nearly altogether bad.' In this stricture every reader will, I
think, heartily concur.

But I do not find 'The Bertrams' unpleasant, though the author himself
did, and though the events are, in all conscience, painful enough. There are
three unhappy love-affairs, and though two of the couples are brought
together at the end, there is but little delight in the reader's heart. Youth is
revealed in its least attractive moods, harsh, sullen, proud, stubborn, and
selfish. Age is even more relentlessly depicted. Old Mr. Bertram, who has
an important part in the complication of the story, is dismissed by the

author as a bad man, whose money was his god. One could believe that at this period in his life, Trollope cherished a grudge against old age, for the disagreeable Mr. Bertram is duplicated in Lord Stapledean, a detestable ogre without a redeeming trait. Nor is the fair sex spared. Mrs. Wilkinson, widow of a vicar, is a feeble reflection of Mrs. Proudie and a pathetic fool as well, who is actually made to refer to herself as in charge of the parish of her late husband, though her son has succeeded to the post. There is, moreover, a hateful old cat, a Mrs. Reake of Rissbury, who spits venom in her every sentence; but she somehow remains credible. And there is a witch of hell who reviles her partner at whist until she drives her mad. These, and the two widows (if such they be) whom young Bertram and Wilkinson meet on their voyage from Alexandria, present a view of womankind which is by no means flattering. The story is brought to an end by the suicide of Sir Henry Harcourt, for whose degeneracy and fall no exculpatory word can be found.

All this makes the author's assertion that he should wish a serene gratification to flow from his pages seem almost ironical. Why, then, is one justified in saying that 'The Bertrams', and even 'Marion Fay' and 'Sir Harry Hotspur', may be read with a certain pleasure? What is the explanation of that vivid warming of the heart that one feels from time to time as one reads on? Is it not due to the association with the author himself, a man worldly-wise, yet kindly and, above all, fair-minded? Not even Henry Fielding associates with his readers on more agreeable terms. We do not care to lose ourselves wholly in the story, for we remember that Trollope is with us as a kind of chorus. This pleasant art he learned, it may be, from Thackeray, the god of his idolatry. But in Trollope there is none of Thackeray's pretension, no condescending to his characters, many of whom he frankly adores. He is forever saying what can be brought forward in extenuation of their actions; and at last the reader comes to feel that he would want for himself no more kindly and indulgent advocate.

Sometimes, to be sure, the author says too much. There are moments when he *will* be talking, though the reader wishes he would get on with the story. He insists on telling us about his travels. 'Can You Forgive Her?' reflects two visits to Switzerland. 'The Bertrams' is full of his travels to the Near East and the Holy Land. He must vent his feelings about Jerusalem and Alexandria, and boast that an Englishman can thrash an Arab. He confesses that he has difficulty in repressing the desire to write a book about Malta.

But when Trollope speaks to us out of the depths of his practical and kindly wisdom, no devoted reader will fail to give him a hearing. There is nothing very original or subversive in his opinions, but they are a kind of gracious common sense issuing from a warm heart and a large sympathy. In 'Framley Parsonage' he has this to say of the grief felt by Lucy Robarts on the death of her father: 'Nobody had yet spoken to her about her father since she had been at Framley. It had been as though the subject were a forbidden one. And how frequently is this the case! When those we love are dead, our friends dread to mention them, though to us who are bereaved no subject would be so pleasant as their names. But we rarely understand how to treat our own sorrow or those of others.' There is nothing profound here, only good counsel of what may be called the middle sort, but for that very reason all the more important, for we are seldom in a mood – and never in the hour of bereavement – to receive and apply truths of the sublimer kind. We have no leisure from our grief to debate their validity or meditate on their usefulness. The commonplace-ness of Trollope's opinions such as the above is the source of their value to thousands who could have given no ear to the consolations of philosophy.

In 'Orley Farm', when Lady Mason has been crushed to earth by the confession of her guilt, the words spoken by Mrs. Orme to comfort her have no originality at all, and the author himself concedes that Mrs. Orme was not strong-minded. 'This lady took her to her heart again and promised in her ear, with low sweet words of consolation, that they should still be friends. I cannot say that Mrs. Orme was right. That she was weak-minded I feel nearly certain. But perhaps this weakness of mind may never be brought against her to her injury, either in this world or in the next.'

'Sentimentality', cries the reader, and such no doubt it is, but so is Portia's speech on mercy in 'The Merchant of Venice', and so, for that matter, is the whole doctrine of forgiveness, the motive for which springs out of the emotions without any aid from ratiocination. It might be argued, I suppose, that such sentimentality is rational in some subtle respect, but that is not Trollope's way. He has none of George Eliot's habit of viewing such matters in a philosophical light. His views are set forth not as admonitions or newly discovered truths but as the natural sunshine of life. He reflects ordinary existence with such fidelity that his remarks never seem inopportune or dragged in to mend our morals or our daily conduct. Perhaps no higher praise can be given than to call him companionable. He never sets himself up as arbiter or pretends to be wiser than we; but he is charitable and broad-minded, and it is a privilege to be with him.

Trollope never used his art to promote a particular reform or to bring a current scandal to public attention. He neither interrupted nor deflected the course of fiction in his own day, for he had no revolutionary theories or mannerisms, so that of all the great Victorian novelists, he is the most ¡

engaging because of his very simplicity. He was content to be a story-teller and an entertainer, and saw no reason to blush for his profession, which he sometimes mischievously referred to as a trade. His aim was to depict life as he saw it all about him, 'enlivened by humor and sweetened by pathos', crowding his canvas with figures, and ranging with ease from the vulgar to the noble, from the commonplace to the sensational, from the street-walker to the duchess, from a tout at the race course to the chancellor on the woolsack. He had a natural love of human beings, and his novels are a radiant reflection of it. These are the qualities that made him popular in his own generation; these are the qualities, construed as weaknesses, which clouded his reputation for a quarter of a century after his death, when he was reckoned among those who, even in their own day, had written themselves out, and were doomed to oblivion. And these are the very qualities which have enabled him in our own day to renew his strength, and demonstrate once again his happy skill in entertaining a host of readers.

A. O. J. COCKSHUT
Human Nature*

What aspect does human nature bear in Trollope's work? It is not easy to
generalise about so many imaginary beings. One cannot say that on the
whole they appear either good or bad. In circumstances, wealth, occupation, social class and background, they are too various for any generalisation to be possible. Trollope is supposed by many to be the chronicler of
the rural gentry and the cathedral close. But this idea is due to a fact for
which he cannot be held responsible – that some of his books are so much
better known than others.

There is, however, one unusual omission, which can hardly be due to
accident. In all these thousands of pages there is very, very little about
children. His last unfinished book, *The Landleaguers*, does contain a ten-
year-old boy with a fairly important part in the story. Otherwise, there
are no children in all his books with any recognisable character. When they
do appear it is usually in order to illustrate some facet of adult character –
for instance, the chapter on 'Baby Worship' in *Barchester Towers*.

Interesting parallels with Dickens abound in Trollope's life and work,
and this is one of the most interesting of all. Both of them had an unhappy
boyhood, and a father who could not inspire in his children the normal
feelings of trust and security. Yet Dickens never writes better than when
his story is seen through the eyes of children, and he has perhaps a larger
proportion of children among his best-known characters than any other
novelist. I do not offer any precise explanation for this. But the difference
in social status may be a contributory cause. Dickens's origins were modest
enough for him to feel the pride of the self-made man in thinking of the
obstacles he had overcome. Trollope was more unfortunate, for he had the
added bitterness of knowing that he was the son of a gentleman, and treated
as an outcast by those who should have been his equals. One is far less

*From *Anthony Trollope: A Critical Study* (London: Collins, 1955;
rpt. New York: New York University Press, 1968), pp. 27–37. Reprinted
by permission of Collins Publishers and New York University Press.

likely to boast about that. But Dickens and Trollope had one thing in common which may well be in large measure due to their early miseries. Each could depict the ordinary pleasures and comforts of life so vividly as to make them seem like transcendent joys. No one who has always fitted easily into his environment can do that.

For all their large number and wide variety it is possible to detect a few recurring themes in Trollope's characters. The first is self-deception. He is always on the watch for it in the most unlikely places, and when he finds it he reveals it with obvious satisfaction, yet with a curious sympathy. Trollope's books abound in self-deceivers, but they contain few hypocrites. Even Mr. Slope is not a complete hypocrite in the sense that Pecksniff is. Hypocrisy is too clear-cut for Trollope's taste. He is interested more in half-shades. Indeed, he sometimes shows that what is ordinarily taken for hypocrisy is not hypocritical at all. Dorothea Ray, one might have thought, is obviously hypocritical in expressing shocked surprise at her sister's conduct, when her own is indistinguishable. But Trollope always seems eager to extend the area of self-deception, because it fascinates him. And he is prepared to demonstrate that she is unconscious of her own inconsistency. He regards complete sincerity not as an elementary moral rule, but as a most difficult achievement.

Self-deception takes many forms. For Lady Cashel (*The Kellys and the O'Kellys*) it is just a vague, warm, dreamy feeling, arising from mother-love. Told that her dissolute son is coming on one of his rare visits home, she begins to imagine that he will at last marry, live at home, and do his duty by the estate. From this her mind passes to his imaginary heir, and she discusses with her maid the merits of various rooms for her imaginary daughter-in-law's confinement. Lonely, idle, bored, fantasy comes as a pleasant relief to her. 'Visions of caudle cups, cradles, and monthly nurses, floated over Lady Cashel's brain, and gave her a kind of dreamy feel that the world was going to begin again with her.'

In *The Duke's Children* Lord Gerald Palliser's self-deception is just simple pig-headedness. He has defied the authorities of his Cambridge college in order to watch his brother's horse run in the Derby. He knows that he must catch the nine o'clock train back or he will be sent down altogether. This he and his brother are especially anxious to avoid because of the grief it would cause their father. But Lord Gerald 'knew that the special would not start until half-past nine. There were a lot of fellows who were dining about everywhere and they would never get to the station by the hour fixed.' And next morning after missing the train he says, ' "Who on earth would have thought that they'd have been so punctual? They never are punctual on the Great Eastern. It was an infernal shame." '

For others, like Major Pountney in *The Prime Minister*, self-deception is a form of defence against bitter humiliation. He is one of the extras who have managed to obtain a share in the magnificent hospitality the Duchess of Omnium is dispensing while her husband is Prime Minister. Plucking up his courage, he asks the Duke for his support in the parliamentary borough which the Duke and his ancestors have always controlled. The Duke has recently decided regretfully but out of conviction that it is his duty to give up all influence in the elections in the borough. So he turns on the major with great violence, and then sends him a letter directing him to leave the house.

After the rebuke 'the major stood for a while transfixed to the place, and, cold as was the weather, was bathed in perspiration'. But after he has had time to recover, has parried the first onslaught of ridicule from his friends at his London club, his attitude is different. 'There was a mystery; and where there is a mystery a man should never be condemned. Where there is a woman in the case a man cannot be expected to tell the truth. As for calling out or in any way punishing the Prime Minister, that of course was out of the question. And so it went on till at last the major was almost proud of what he had done, and talked about it willingly with mysterious hints, in which practice made him perfect.'

Self-deception reconciled Major Pountney to humiliation. It rendered Archie Clavering jubilant at financial loss, when his original object had been financial gain. In his desire to marry Lady Ongar, a young and rich widow, he decides to bribe her friend Sophie Gordeloup. He takes her twenty pounds and is then shocked and astonished by her greed for further payments. But he has heard that she is a Russian spy, and as he considers the transactions of the day, his mood gradually changes. 'He did venture to triumph a little when he met Doodles at the club. He had employed the Russian spy, and had paid her twenty pounds, and was enrolled in the corps of diplomatic and mysterious personages who do their work by mysterious agencies. He did not tell Doodles anything about the glove, or the way in which the money was taken from him; but he did say that he was to see the spy again to-morrow, and that he intended to take with him another present of fifty pounds.

"By George, Clavvy, you are going it!" said Doodles, in a voice that was delightfully envious to the ears of Captain Archie. When he heard that envious tone he felt that he was entitled to be triumphant.'

All these passages have an element of comedy. But self-deception can take more sinister forms than this. There is the mad obsession of Mrs. Bolton in *John Caldigate*, determined to believe her daughter's husband is a criminal. There is the crazy vanity of Mr. Gibson in *He Knew He Was Right*, enjoying the literary merits of the letter with which he has jilted his fiancée. With him and with George Hotspur, self-deception amounts to a lie in the soul. 'Then it occurred to Cousin George that perhaps he might bribe the servant; and he put his hand into his pocket. But before he had communicated the two half-crowns, it struck him that there was no possible request which he could make to the man in reference to which a bribe would be serviceable.'

How can this preoccupation be explained? It seems that Trollope's moral consciousness was dominated by the ideas of sincerity and honesty. Both his writings and his conduct suggest this. For he devoted one whole book, *Mr. Scarborough's Family*, to a searching criticism of all the current ideas of honesty, and found them all wanting, while in his dealings with publishers he was scrupulous about keeping every engagement to the day, and indignant with those who failed to do the same. But his indignation did not mean that he thought the exact fulfilment of contracts easy. The higher a man's standard the more likely he is to see the difficulty of attaining it. Conrad, for instance, was obsessed with the problem of personal honour, and regarded a man who had lost it as a maimed creature, though he recognised at the same time that it is uncomfortably easy to lose it. Trollope, thinking complete sincerity to be both very desirable and very difficult, was fascinated by all the degrees of failure. A novelist who thinks that sincerity comes easily to all decent people, is apt to write off the exceptions as obvious hypocrites of little psychological interest.

Another characteristic which consistently haunted Trollope's imagination is endurance, especially endurance in a perverse and unprofitable attitude. 'They who do not understand that a man may be brought to hope that which of all things is the most grievous to him, have not observed with sufficient closeness the perversity of the human mind', he says of Trevelyan in *He Knew He Was Right*. When a man of Trollope's nondescript style indulges in this eighteenth-century rotundity of language, it usually means that he is saying something that seems to him very important; and this sentence would have been relevant in a number of his books.

Consider the case of Dr. Harford, the old-fashioned high Tory cleric of *Rachel Ray*. Elderly male Cassandras like him are common in fiction, and surely one can guess pretty well what any of them would have said in 1863 on the question of admitting Jews to Parliament. But with Dr. Harford one is in for a surprise ' "Upon my word," said he, "I don't see the use for caring for that kind of thing any longer; I don't indeed. In the way we are going on now, and for the sort of thing we do, I don't see why Jews shouldn't serve us as well in Parliament as Christians." ' He is a man drunk with the odour of the decay of all he values.

In the same book a characteristic passage describes the attitude of the public to Luke Rowan's attempt to produce good beer in Baslehurst. 'That idea of a rival brewery was distasteful to them all. Most of them knew that the beer was almost too bad to be swallowed; but they thought that Trappit had a vested interest in the manufacture of bad beer; that as a manufacturer of bad beer he was a fairly honest and useful man; and they looked upon any change as the work, or rather the suggestion, of a charlatan.'

In a way these minor instances are more revealing because probably more spontaneous than the examples drawn from full-length characters. But there are plenty of the latter too. Will Belton and Mr. Crawley both endure to the end and both are described with the unmistakable excitement of a man investigating a quality that touches him very deeply. Mrs. Baggett in *An Old Man's Love* is an example of perversity. Proud of her position as housekeeper in a bachelor's household, she does all she can to persuade him to marry his ward. At the same time she proclaims that if he does she must go away and live miserably for the rest of her life, and that she cannot imagine why men are taken in by the facile prettiness of girls. Finally, she is very angry with the girl for presuming to resist a man's choice and refuse him. She maintains all these contradictory attitudes throughout.

Sometimes these qualities of character are so pronounced as to constitute an obsession. It may be no more than a humorous absurdity – for example, the old woman in *The American Senator* who buys a ticket on the railway for her parrot, or it may be the long drawn-out madness of Louis Trevelyan. Things of this kind, though they are commonest of all in his last books, came easy to Trollope before most of his talents were developed. In his first book, *The Macdermots*, the most memorable passages are those that deal with crazy delusions of old Larry. Speaking to his son who has accidentally killed a man in defence of his own sister and of Larry's daughter, he says, ' "Murther, who doubts but that it was murther? Of course they'll call it murther. Well, he was the only friend you'd left me, and now you've murthered him. You may go now – you may go now – but mind I tell you, they'll be sure to hang you." '

Later the old man has to give evidence in court. 'When the book was handed to Larry Macdermot, on which he was to be sworn, he at first refused it, and when it was again tendered to him, he put it in his pocket, and made the man who gave it him a bow, and was very cross when he was obliged to give it back again.' When he is questioned he begins to cry and protest his own innocence, which of course is not in question.

Writing after Thackeray's death of his affection for him, Trollope said that this was something no living man could tell another; at the close of his autobiography he said that he had not spoken of his inner life. Paradoxically for such a prolific writer, he was in some ways inarticulate, and inarticulateness in others deeply interested him. The young man, like John Eames or Lord Silverbridge, who cannot express himself, but who turns out to have plenty of sense, is one of his favourite types. It may be partly a result of his own history, too, that he so often introduces into his novels outcasts, and people who are helpless, or undecided, or despairing. He always identifies himself and the reader with his outcasts; when he is writing of such characters society assumes the aspect of an alien and indifferent power, justified perhaps (for the outcasts have often deserved their isolation), but still forbidding.

Most Victorian novelists needed to feel that their outcasts were innocent before they could place them in a sympathetic light. Usually they are simply the poor and the hungry. Even in *The New Magdalen*, where the outcast is a prostitute, Wilkie Collins contrives to prove that she has been the victim of circumstances, and is not really guilty. But Trollope, perhaps because of personal memories, can endow even Major Tifto, the crooked racing man with the pathos of 'Athanasius contra mundum.' If such a character had appeared in the work of Collins or Thackeray, he would either have been the villain of the piece or simply a joke.

One of the best of all his psychological studies is of this kind, *Cousin Henry*, the story of a weak and unpopular young man, who is apparently the heir to a large estate. After the owner's death he takes possession and accidentally finds a later will, which leaves all the property away from him. This short book is mainly a record of his mental struggle after the discovery. The struggle is of an unusual kind, for he feels no strong conflicting impulses. He is plunged into misery by his indecision, which is so heavy a burden that any decision would be a relief to him, but none is possible. It is typical of such a nature that he should fear hell as a consequence of his contemplated crime, although he has no real religious belief. Men like him only think things fully real when they become menacing. All the tenants and all his neighbours want the property to go to his cousin, a girl they have known and loved, whereas he is a stranger and his manner is repulsive. From one point of view the book is an exposure of the moral dangers of being repulsive to others; its main subject is the paralysis of the will. It is as if a brief, hardly recorded battle between conflicting desires has left his soul a no-man's land on which every landmark has been destroyed. His state of mind resembles a prolonged lull in trench warfare. The end of the story is characteristic. He is finally roused from his stupor by the sight of someone about to find the will in the place where the testator had left it. He has not hidden it on all the days on which he has half-hoped and half-feared its discovery. Only when the will is on the point of being found does he decide that he wants to destroy it, and then it is too late. This is Trollope's best study of indecision, inarticulateness, loneliness, and morbidity.

Similar in some respects, but fundamentally different nevertheless, is the case of the old lawyer, Sir Thomas Underwood, in *Ralph the Heir*. He, too, is lonely, though he has a family. He, too, is unable to decide in favour of religious belief or unbelief, and unable to summon the will-power to do what he most desires, to write the life of Bacon. He is shown dozing in his London chambers in the evening, instead of going home to his family (whom he loves in his way), and then after midnight wandering for hours alone round the Temple and Lincoln's Inn. The motives of all this behaviour are not explained until late in the book, but when they are they have all the force of a psychological explanation which is totally unexpected, yet fits all the facts. This occurs in the chapter called 'Music Has Charms'. Listening half-unconsciously to some melancholy music from the street, he yields to despair and declares to himself that everything is vanity. But as the whole chapter, and particularly its title suggest, these thoughts give him immense satisfaction. If Dr. Harford is pleased by the idea of the social fabric decaying, here is a man who takes pleasure in a despair which extends to life itself, and death and his whole soul.

> Immensita s'annega il pensier mio
> E il naufragar m'e dolce in questo mare.

Trollope himself, it would seem, had heard the siren-song of despair, and having resisted it, was able to turn it into art.

Mr. Graham Greene in his book *The Lost Childhood* has stressed similar tendencies in Dickens. Both the similarity and the contrast are instructive. For Mr. Greene is speaking, not of Dickens's subject-matter, but of an impress placed on his books by his personality. If Mr. Greene is right, and I think he is, he is speaking of something of which Dickens was not aware himself, but which the reader can deduce from his works. Trollope had not only felt but understood; and his treatment of the sweetness of despair is a deliberate study of character. So while Dickens's evocation of despair is the more vivid and compelling of the two, Trollope's study is far more revealing psychologically, revealing not so much as in the case of Dickens, the mind of the author, as the human nature he set out to draw.

To find how Trollope deals with problems of conscience, it is interesting to compare *The Warden* with Scott's *Old Mortality*. Each is a story of a man poised between conflicting loyalties. But while Mr. Harding is central, Morton seems to exist only to illustrate the principles between which he is torn. In *The Warden* the two extreme views, those of the Jupiter and of Archdeacon Grantly, are satirised and condemned. It is suggested that any fair-minded man would have been as moderate, and as uncertain of himself as Mr. Harding was. Like many moderate and liberal men, like Matthew Arnold, for instance, Trollope was apt to assume that every extreme view could merge into his own central moderation, if only people would be reasonable. But *The Warden* is an early work, and Trollope's understanding gradually widened. In the novels written after he was fifty he achieved what was bred in Scott's bones, sympathetic understanding of fanaticism, delusion, and violence. It is true, as we have seen, that from the first he was apt to dwell on obsessions. But it is only in his later works, of the type of *He Knew He Was Right*, that he was successful in showing the inner working of an obsession. In Larry Macdermot or Mrs. Proudie he simply showed how an obsession affected people's outward behaviour. His keenest psychological penetration was confined, till he was over fifty, to normal characters, which, to be fair, is a very wide field. But for Scott from the first the abnormal mind was as easy to decipher as the normal, and excited more sympathy than satire or contempt. He held the balance even between Mause, Claverton, Morton and Balfour. What little satire there is does not preclude respect. One could maintain, certainly, that old Mrs. Maclure, the blind woman who waits at the crossroads to direct the fleeing remnant of the faithful, is intended to be the moral touchstone of the book. If so, Scott's ideal is summed up by Tolstoy's description of Princess Mary. 'What had she to do with the justice or injustice of other people? She had to endure and love, and that she did.' But Mrs. Maclure is only a very minor character, and if she is the ideal by comparison with which the other characters are satirised, satire is only a small part of Scott's purpose. The interplay of religious and political ideas is what fascinates him. In *The Warden* the conflicting ideas exist mainly to exercise an old man's conscience, which is the main subject of the story. And as he shows us the innocence of the man who is so cruelly tormented, satire against the two extreme and rigid ideas becomes very marked. Compared with Scott, Trollope in 1855 seems limited in his sympathies, not because he condemns extremism, but because he does not sufficiently comprehend before he condemns.

FRANK O'CONNOR
Trollope the Realist*

I

Trollope's reputation has suffered so much from the results of his own senile fatuity that it is now almost impossible to define his proper place in English fiction with reasonable accuracy. He left behind him a posthumous autobiography in which he described his method of work and attempted to decry the element of inspiration in literature. Although he merely showed that he was incapable of recognizing it in himself, he has been taken at his word. His reputation collapsed and has never been restored. When his admirers praise the 'honesty' of the *Autobiography*, they do him little service; there is a difference between honesty and uncouthness, and as far as the business of literature is concerned, one paragraph of Flaubert's letters is worth everything that Trollope wrote.

Yet it was discovered that young men in England, leaving for the Second World War, were leaving with some novel of Trollope's in their pockets. Though a writer of no great reputation, he was, as Lord David Cecil remarks, 'almost the only Victorian novelist whom our sensitive intelligentsia appear to be able to read without experiencing an intolerable sense of jar'. Elizabeth Bowen traced the young people's interest to the stability of the world he wrote of – and, being a natural Tory, Trollope certainly wrote of the most stable part of his world and paid small attention to its firebrands and crackpots. Lord David traces his popularity to a 'realism' that has kept his work fresh while the less realistic work of his great contemporaries, filled with the burning questions and great ideals of their day, has dated. For those few kind words in favor of realism, one can forgive Lord David much, but even he will not admit Trollope among the greatest of the Victorians. He argues that Trollope's creative imagination is weak;

* From *The Mirror in the Roadway: A Study of the Modern Novel* (New York: Alfred A. Knopf, 1956), pp. 165–83. Reprinted by permission of Alfred A. Knopf. Inc.

that his characters have not the 'preternatural vitality' of Dickens's; that his style is bad by comparison with Hardy's, whose words 'at their worst . . . manage to convey their author's temperament; at their best convey it with supreme force and beauty'; and that his power of visualizing a scene – witness Johnny Eames's attack on Crosbie – is slight when we compare it with Troy's exhibiton of swordplay in *Far from the Madding Crowd*. All this is so very convincing that I almost convince myself in recording it, but there is another side to the story. Hugh Walpole, too, uses the illustration of Troy's swordplay, but it seems to me a most unfortunate example. It is a remarkable and beautiful bit of writing, which might well have strayed into Hardy's novel from some romance of Stevenson's, and might equally well have strayed out again without anyone's noticing its absence. Nor do I desire characters to have the 'preternatural vitality' of Mr. Pecksniff or Mr. Punch, for this seems to me to degrade them to the level of puppets. The only thing I am sure of is that Trollope's style is weak compared with Hardy's or Dickens's. He had little or no feeling for poetry, and, what is considerably worse from my point of view, he also had little feeling for prose; his writing at its best never rises to the level of Stendhal's or Tolstoy's, which is Continental prose without benefit of poetry. Yet I think Trollope was as great a novelist as either, and a far greater novelist than Hardy.

This is something difficult to establish because there is no one novel of his which is outstanding. *The Last Chronicle of Barset* is, to my mind, a masterpiece as great as *The Red and the Black* or *Anna Karenina*, but it is disgracefully and inconsequentially padded, and I find it necessary to ask my students to make a rough reconstruction of it before making a final judgment. But Trollope's enduring popularity is evidence that needs to be examined. Lord David, as I say, ascribes this to Trollope's 'realism', but, in spite of his careful definition, it still seems to me a vague term in this particular context. For Jane Austen is likewise a 'realist', but her popularity is of a very different kind.

If one compares the realism of the two writers, one finds, I think, the quality that has kept Trollope so popular. She writes from a preconceived idea of conduct, where he does not. She is a moralist; Trollope is whatever the opposite of a moralist may be. Though Cecil declares that his standards were those of 'the typical mid-Victorian gentleman', and though the statement could be liberally documented from the pages of the *Autobiography*, I do not for an instant think it is true.

If there is one phrase more than another which identifies a novel by Trollope it is a phrase like 'With such censures I cannot profess that I completely agree.' His favorite device is to lead his reader very gently up the garden path of his own conventions and prejudices and then to point out that the reader is wrong. This is not very like the behavior of a typical mid-Victorian gentleman. On the contrary, it is an original and personal approach to conduct, and I think it is Trollope's approach, rather than his treatment, which pleases intelligent people in our time.

I do not mean that Trollope was a revolutionary figure. In fact, he was a pernickety and crusty conservative who distrusted all new views and methods. But, unlike most English novelists, he did not start out with a cut-and-dried system of morals and try to make his characters fit it. Instead, he made the sytem fit the characters.

For instance, to take a slight example, one of the conventions of the English novel is that of 'one man, one girl', and such is the power of artistic convention that, whatever our own experience may have taught us, we never question this as we read. We could not conceive of Mr. Knightley in love with Harriet Smith as well as with Emma. We certainly could not believe that, having been rejected by Emma, Mr. Knightley would ever immediately propose to Harriet. But Trollope's characters usually behave in that way. One of his principal characters is an Irish politician, Phineas Finn, who is engaged to a very nice County Clare girl called Mary Flood-Jones. But when Phineas comes to London, he immediately forgets all about Mary and falls in love with a society woman, Lady Laura Standish. When Lady Laura rejects him for a dreary Scottish fanatic named Kennedy, Phineas at once transfers his affections to an heiress called Violet Effingham, and when she, in turn, marries a mad nobleman named Chiltern, he toys with the affections of a Jewish widow, Madame Max Goesler. Her he finally does marry, but not until he has become the widower of Mary Flood-Jones. And if the reader, forgetting his own errors, denounces Finn as a heartless rogue, Trollope, in that maddening way of his, chimes in with his pet phrase: 'With such censures I cannot profess that I completely agree.' Literature is one thing, life another.

> If it were to be asserted here that a young man may be perfectly true to a first young woman while he is falling in love with a second, the readers of this story would probably be offended. But undoubtedly many men believe themselves to be true while undergoing this process, and many young women expect nothing else from their lovers.

Not only is Trollope not a moralist in Jane Austen's sense; he even loathes the sort of moral consistency she admires. This, I feel sure, goes back to something in his own youth and early manhood. His childhood was gloomy with the desperate gloom that poverty imposes on people of gentle birth. He grew up ignorant and a bit of a waster, and was pushed into a Civil Service job for which he was not qualified. It is probably significant that he could never reconcile himself to the principle of competitive examination, for had there been such a thing in his own youth, he might never have made good. 'I was always in trouble', he says mournfully. The dun who haunts Phineas Finn's lodgings with his perpetual 'I wish you would be punctual' was the same who haunted Trollope at his office. It was in despair of his own future that the poor wretch decided to become a novelist at all, for it was the only career his miserable education seemed to have left open to him. There is something almost heartbreaking in his admission that he became a writer only in default of something better, and a novelist because the 'higher' branches of literature were closed to him.

> Poetry I did not believe to be within my grasp. The drama, too, which I would fain have chosen, I believed to be above me. For history, biography or essay writing, I had not sufficient erudition. But I thought it possible that I might write a novel.

'*Only* a novel!' one can hear Jane Austen retort. 'Only some work in which the greatest powers of the mind are displayed, in which the most thorough knowledge of human nature, the happiest delineations of its varieties, the liveliest effusions of wit and humor are conveyed to the world in the best chosen language.'

It was only after Trollope's transfer to a miserable job in Ireland — perhaps by contrast with people worse off than himself — that he acquired command of himself and finally became the model of steadiness and probity we meet in the *Autobiography*. It is more than probable that when he diverts criticism from his characters, he is really diverting it from himself. He had endured more than his share, and proved its hollowness by his ultimate success.

But, whatever the reason, he expresses again and again his dislike for men of strong character. 'The man who holds out', he says in *The Duke's Children*, 'is not the man of the firmest opinions but the man of the hardest heart.' ('Heart', incidentally, is a key word with him.) 'He has probably found himself so placed that he cannot marry without money', explains an old lady in *The Eustace Diamonds*, 'and has wanted the firmness, or perhaps you will say the hardness of heart to say so openly.' And here is the same thing in an even more striking passage:

> In social life we hardly stop to consider how much of that daring spirit which gives mastery comes from hardness of heart rather than

from high purpose or true courage. The man who succumbs to his wife, the mother who succumbs to her daughter, the master who succumbs to his servant, is as often brought to servility by the continual aversion to the giving of pain, by a softness which causes the fretfulness of others to be an agony to himself as by any actual fear which the firmness of the imperious one may have produced. There is an inner softness, a thinness of the mind's skin, an incapability of seeing or even of thinking of the troubles of others with equanimity which produces a feeling akin to fear; but which is compatible not only with courage but with absolute firmness of purpose when the demand for firmness arises so strongly as to assert itself.

There, in a paragraph, is the essential Trollope, the message of Trollope, if such a writer can be said to have a message; and there, unless I am grievously mistaken, speaks a man who had himself been badly mauled by life and who experienced an almost physical terror of doing the same to others. I suspect that this, too, is the real key to his conservatism in religion and politics. He detested reformers like Carlyle, Dickens, and Ruskin because they were men of strong principles, and strong principles were things that he associated with hard hearts.

It is not merely that Trollope sympathized with so-called 'weak' people in situations that were merely ambiguous. Though he wrote within very strict taboos and his love stories are usually as conventionalized as the plots of seventeenth-century French comedies, he had the same sort of understanding of irregular relationships. One of the most delightful characters in English fiction is Lady Glencora Palliser, yet we find her in *Can You Forgive Her?* on the point of eloping with a penniless adventurer, Burgo Fitzgerald, and hindered only by the arrival of her husband to bring her home. The two lovers are at a dance, where they are being closely watched, and the whole episode is so characteristic of Trollope that one cannot ignore it. Here, better than anywhere else, one can see what importance he attaches to what he calls the 'heart'.

The Duchess of St. Bungay saw it and shook her head sorrowing — for the Duchess was good at heart. . . . Mrs. Conway Sparkes saw it and drank it down with keen appetite . . . for Mrs. Conway Sparkes was not good at heart. Lady Hartletop saw it and just raised her eyebrows. It was nothing to her. She liked to know what was going on as such knowledge was sometimes useful; but as for heart — what she had in such matters was neither good nor bad.

This, then, rather than realism, represents Trollope's true quality as a novelist. Not merely loyalty to the facts, but loyalty to a certain attitude to the facts, to a humility and passivity in the face of life. I do not wish to suggest that artistically this is an unmixed blessing. When Trollope is not inspired by his subject, it gives his work a flabbiness and lack of energy that leave the reader feeling very flat indeed. Even on the trivial plane of 'one man, one girl', it results in a lack of incisiveness; Phineas Finn would have been as happy with Lady Laura as with Madame Max; Lord Silverbridge would have done as well with Lady Mabel as with the American girl, Isabel Boncassen. Stendhal would have been inspired by these things to some sweeping generalizations about men and women, but Trollope merely notes that they are so and that to pretend otherwise would mean being false to one's experience.

II

But it is important to remember that this very humility gives Trollope a quality not possessed to a similar degree by any other English novelist. That quality is range, and by range I do not mean merely the ability he shares with Tolstoy of handling great masses of material while keeping its elements distinct. I mean primarily the power of exploring his characters fully, of so understanding their interior perspective that by a simple change of lighting he can suddenly reveal them to us in a different way; as, for instance, in the scene in *Can You Forgive Her?* where Burgo Fitzgerald, the penniless and desperate adventurer whose only hope is to seduce Lady Glencora for her money, buys a meal for a prostitute. It is a most remarkable scene. In any other novelist of the period it would prove that Fitzgerald had a heart of gold, or, alternatively, that the prostitute had a heart of gold, or that both had hearts of gold. In Trollope it is merely one of those minor shocks by which he reminds us that life is not simple; it indicates to us that Lady Glencora is not altogether a fool, and that Fitzgerald, for all his faults, retains a capacity for spontaneous behavior which endears him to women.

But the best illustration is the wonderful scene of the death of Mrs. Proudie in *The Last Chronicle of Barset*. It is also the best example of the fatuous attitude adopted by Trollope to his own work. In the *Autobiography* he tells us that one day, sitting in the Athenaeum Club, he overheard two clergymen denounce his work, particularly the character of Mrs. Proudie.

It was impossible for me not to overhear their words and almost impossible for me to hear them and be quiet. I got up and, standing between them, I acknowledged myself to be the culprit. 'As to Mrs. Proudie,' I said, 'I will go home and kill her before the week is over.' And so I did. The two gentlemen were utterly confounded, and one of them begged me to forget his frivolous observations.

'Simple-minded' is too feeble a word to describe such a passage. Trollope fails to tell us what he could have done with Mrs. Proudie if the two clergymen had not spoken. Of course, intuitively, if not intellectually, he had already known that Mrs. Proudie had to die because Mr. Crawley, the central figure of the novel, is drawn on such a scale that she and her henpecked husband could no longer be treated as figures of fun. You cannot be merely funny at the expense of Lear, and from the opening of the book we know that Mrs. Proudie has at last met her match and that sooner or later she will be broken. She is broken, and leaves the room, knowing that her husband hates her. And then —

In spite of all her roughness and temper, Mrs. Proudie was in this like other women — that she would fain have been loved had it been possible. She had always meant to serve him. She was conscious of that: conscious also in a way that although she had been industrious, although she had been faithful, although she was clever, yet she had failed. At the bottom of her heart she knew that she had been a bad wife.

'Industrious, faithful, clever' — how subtly the woman's character has been deepened before she goes upstairs to die. Perhaps only a story-teller can realize the miracle that takes place in those chapters; the miracle of elevating two characters of low comedy to the plane of high tragedy without a single false note. Only one who understood his characters completely even in their absurdities could have changed the lighting so impressively and revealed the real perspective of their souls. The lines about Mrs. Proudie, like the passage in Jane Austen's *Emma* where the heroine denounces Mrs. Elton's vulgarity, are written on three different levels. On the conscious level, Mrs. Proudie knows that she had always meant to be a good wife. On the semi-conscious level (notice the phrasing, 'conscious also *in a way*') she knows that she has failed. But in her feelings, in her 'heart', the only ultimate tribunal that Trollope recognizes, there exists the knowledge, not yet permitted to reach consciousness, that she has been a bad wife.

But there is another sort of range which Trollope also had, and that is the power of describing extreme psychological types, types that are pathological or bordering on it. The principal character in *He Knew He Was Right* — a bad novel by Trollope's own standard — is a masterly presentation of pathological jealously. Now, Proust can describe pathological jealousy with similar mastery, but Proust was the victim of what he described, and the fact that he described it so well meant that there were scores of other psychological states that he could not describe at all. Balzac could describe a variety of extreme psychological states, but his romantic imagination made it impossible for him to treat them from the point of view of simple normality, so that ultimately they fail to impress us. Trollope, because his capacity came from the passiveness and humility with which he contemplated people, could describe scores of such types, but each one rises simple and sheer from a flat plain of normality. Mr. Kennedy, the Scotch puritan in *Phineas Finn*, is an example, as is 'the mad lord', Chiltern. But Mr. Crawley of *The Last Chronicle* is the supreme example. He rises out of the commonplace and placid plane of the story, a giant figure who, even when we are looking elsewhere, still magnetizes us like some mountain peak. And of all these characters it is almost impossible to say when they pass the limits of sanity, so closely have they been observed, so carefully has each step been recorded.

The Last Chronicle is the final volume in the Barchester series, and I do not think anyone has ever analysed the strange development in the works. This is the timetable:

1855	*The Warden*
1857	*Barchester Towers*
1858	*Dr. Thorne*
1861	*Framley Parsonage*
1864	*The Small House at Allington*
1867	*The Last Chronicle of Barset*

In the manuscript of the *Autobiography*, Trollope deliberately deleted *The Small House at Allington*. This leaves us with five novels, of which four deal almost entirely with clerical life. The fifth, *Dr. Thorne*, is a book I find extremely dull. It was written to a plot of Thomas Trollope's, and even Trollope himself thought badly of it. Leave it in, and you have a panorama of English provincial life, centered on a cathedral city; take it out, and you have a saga of clerical life, all sections of it dealing in different ways with the same problem, the problem that in Mr. Crawley is presented to us in its most complex and tragic form.

The saga begins in a very interesting way. *The Warden* deals with a contemporary controversy — that of clerical sinecures. English liberals, aiming at the abolition of feudal privileges, had exposed a succession of scandals concerning sinecures, and Trollope took advantage of this in an astute journalistic way. Trollope took a strong High Church line and satirized very cruelly and cleverly both Carlyle and Dickens, whom he disliked as reformers. He pokes fun at his own reformer, John Bold, who was so mad on the subject that he took up the cause of an old woman who had been overcharged at a turnpike by another old woman, 'rode through the gate himself, paying the toll, then brought an action against the gate-keeper and proved that all people coming up a certain by-lane and going down a certain other by-lane were toll-free'. John Bold was, in fact, another of those moralists whom Trollope disliked because their firmness of principle seemed to him to express a hardness of heart.

But Grantly, who is Bold's clerical opponent, is equally unfeeling. It is interesting to watch Grantly's development through the series. In this book he is very harshly handled. Though the son of a saintly bishop, he is a money-grubbing, success-worshipping man who reads Rabelais when he is supposed to be attending to his religious duties.

The Warden is a charming book. It has the quality of the best English novels, of entertaining in a civilized way, but it has no other outstanding quality, and I suspect that if it stood alone, it would be read only by fanatic admirers of Trollope like myself. The important thing is that it does not stand alone. For some reason, Trollope's imagination continued to linger about the cathedral close – as it was later to linger about the British House of Commons – and to ponder the problem of worldliness and sanctity in the Anglican Church. The result was *Barchester Towers*, an infinitely better book, and one that would have been outstanding, whoever had written it, even if it had had no successor. Once again, it has a background of newspaper controversy. For the cruel Whigs, who had attacked clerical sinecures, were attacking High Church bishops and re-placing them by nominees of their own who would work with the Low Church and dissenting groups that were the backbone of the Liberal party. Trollope had as great a dislike for Low Church clergymen as he had for reformers. The book opens with the death of old Bishop Grantly, and after his son the Archdeacon has failed of his hopes, there arrive a Liberal, Low Church bishop, Proudie, his preposterous wife, and his greasy chap-lain, Mr. Slope. The book is a lament for the good old days when the church was the preserve of English gentlemen.

Few things are more interesting than the sudden change of attitude we feel toward the Archdeacon in those first brilliant chapters. He is as worldly as ever; all his hopes are centered on getting the see for himself; we feel that there is little to be said in his favor, even as opposed to the Proudies and the Slopes, but suddenly Trollope pulls us up with that phrase which I have already quoted, 'With such censures I cannot profess that I completely agree.'

Our archdeacon was worldly – who among us is not so? He was ambitious – who among us is ashamed to own that 'last infirmity of noble minds'? He was avaricious, my readers will say. No – it was for no love of lucre that he wished to be bishop of Barchester. He was his father's only child, and his father had left him great wealth. . . . He would be a richer man as archdeacon than he could be as bishop. But he certainly did desire to play first fiddle; he did desire to sit in full lawn sleeves among the peers of the realm; and he did desire, if the truth must out, to be called 'My Lord' by his reverend brethren.

Even more interesting is the character of Grantly's friend, the scholar-priest Arabin, whom Grantly introduces into the diocese to gain an ally against the Low Church faction. Arabin is one of Newman's colleagues, so steeped in church history that he has already been tempted in the direction of Rome and saved from it only by the counsel of a half-crazy parson in a remote West Country village. This is the first hint we get of the character we later learn to know as Crawley, an extraordinary example of the way in which Trollope brooded over his creations.

Barchester Towers is a fine book, spoiled, as Longman's reader pointed out, by the introduction of the Stanhope family, who are an alien and jarring note. The intention is right, as showing the queer fish High Church discipline introduced into English religious life, but Trollope failed to allow for the fact that they tempt one to take a Low Church view of the whole situation. There is no such fault in *Framley Parsonage*. Once more the conflict is between piety and worldliness, but though Mark Robarts has led an irregular life and got himself badly into debt, Trollope comes out on his side in a much more outspoken way. It is all to the same tune: 'We are all the same. Life is like that. Don't be too censorious.'

It is no doubt very wrong to long after a naughty thing. But nevertheless we all do so. One may say that hankering after naughty things is the very essence of the evil into which we have been precipitated by Adam's fall. When we confess that we are all sinners, we confess that we all long after naughty things. And ambition is a great vice – as Mark Antony told us a long time ago – a great vice no doubt if the ambition of the man be with reference to his own advancement and not to the advancement of others. But then how many of us are there who are not ambitious in this vicious manner?

Sanctity in this book is represented by Mr. Crawley, whom his friend Arabin has brought to the neighborhood, but even in him the issue of worldliness in not left out. Far from it; for, whether or not he realized it, Trollope had at last found the perfect character through whom he could express the essence of the conflict. Crawley is a saint, but a saint with a wife and family and only a hundred and thirty pounds a year to keep them on. Crawley's sanctity has had to take a terrible beating from his vanity.

He had always at his heart a feeling that he and his had been ill-used, and too often solaced himself at the devil's bidding with the conviction that eternity would make equal that which life in this world had made so unequal; the last bait that with which the devil angles after those who are struggling to elude his rod and line.

There is one very curious thing about the character of Crawley on which no one has, I think, commented. His vanity is a writer's vanity, the same that Trollope described in the *Autobiography*, apparently unaware that every word he wrote could be applied with equal force to his greatest figure.

The author's poverty is, I think, harder to be borne than any other poverty. The man, whether rightly or wrongly, feels that the world is using him with extreme injustice. The more absolutely he fails, the higher, it is probable, he will reckon his own merits; and the keener will be the sense of injury in that he whose work is of so high a nature cannot get bread while they whose tasks are mean are wrapped in luxury. 'I with my well-filled mind, with my clear intellect, with all my gifts, cannot earn a poor crown a day, while that fool, who simpers in a little room behind a shop, makes his thousands every year.' The very charity to which he too often is driven, is bitterer to him than to others. While he takes it he almost spurns the hand that gives it to him, and every fibre of his heart within him is bleeding with a sense of injury.

It is Lord David Cecil who lumps Mr. Crawley with the Archdeacon, Miss Dunstable, and Mrs. Proudie as 'simple and positive, absorbed in the avocations of average human beings, devoid alike of psychological complexities and abstruse spiritual yearnings, made up of a few strongly marked qualities and idiosyncrasies'. I do not think this describes Trollope's characters very well, and I certainly do not think it describes Mr. Crawley at all. He is one of the subtlest figures in all literature, and even between *Framley Parsonage* and *The Last Chronicle* Trollope continued to make discoveries about his character, and they still continue to astonish us. All the manifestations of his stern and ill-regulated piety we are familiar with, but who would suspect the sly and brutal humor or the childish pleasures of the true scholar?

> And there was at times a lightness of heart about the man. In the course of the last winter he had translated into Greek irregular verse the very noble ballad of Lord Bateman, maintaining the rhythms and the rhyme, and had repeated it with uncouth glee till his daughter knew it by heart.

How good that 'uncouth glee' is! It is like the playfulness of a rhinoceros.

III

But the problem for the critic remains — why the Church? The answer should be in that dull *Autobiography*, but it isn't, at least on the surface. Why is Trollope so obsessed by the conflict between sanctity and worldliness? Why does he come down again and again on the side of worldliness? Is it perhaps a personal conflict that he never consciously dealt with, a relic of those bitter early days of his?

In some way, the Church in these four novels represents vocation, and Trollope seems to be fighting off the admission of his own vocation and the responsibilities it imposes. His character remains something of a mystery. He had the dual character of the perfect Civil Servant and the author, and he must frequently have wondered which was the true Anthony Trollope. The thing that hindered him from being a great writer and that makes the *Autobiography* so unrevealing was the same thing that made him the great novelist he certainly was: lack of self-consciousness. The only character this patient and humble observer could never observe was his own, and one element in that character was certainly the Reverend Josiah Crawley.

BRADFORD A. BOOTH
The Chaos of Criticism*

I know nothing in literary history to match the divided opinion on Trollope's novels. Such disputes do not occur over Dickens or Thackeray or George Eliot or Meredith. Nobody, I think, considers *Martin Chuzzlewit* Dickens's best novel, or *Philip* Thackeray's best, or *Daniel Deronda* George Eliot's best, or *One of Our Conquerors* Meredith's best. Yet among Trollope's forty-seven novels there are only a handful that someone has not called his best. One might assume from this fact that the level of Trollope's work is remarkably steady. Having found a theme, a manner, and a tone, he was able to repeat his formula so successfully and with so little deviation from the established norm of quality that readers and critics found election among them extremely difficult. On the other hand, there is the widest possible divergence of opinion on a single title. If there is someone to declare that a given novel is certainly Trollope's best, there is someone to retort that it is without the slightest doubt his worst. These disagreements can be documented at every turn, but perhaps in the discussion of individual novels readers have caught a sense of the critical disparities and little more evidence need be brought forward. It is not my purpose here, furthermore, to sketch out at length the history of Trollope's reputation, interesting and significant for literary history as that would be, but to inquire into some of the reasons for the chaos in Trollopian criticism, and to attempt a few personal judgments by way of conclusion.

It is sufficiently clear why such a novel as *The Way We Live Now* was unappreciated in 1875 and why it is today the one novel which all critics unite to praise. We do not view society as did the Victorians. Though it would be a mistake to speak of the decline of idealism in the twentieth century, it is now impossible to deceive ourselves about the nature of man and of society. The Spenglerian interpretation of history has succeeded

* From *Anthony Trollope: Aspects of His Life and Art* (Bloomington, Ind.: Indiana University Press, 1958), pp. 229–32. Reprinted by permission of Indiana University Press.

the Darwinian. So far as Trollope criticism is concerned, it is almost possible to fix the date of the change. The last critic to bring in a verdict against *The Way We Live Now* was George Saintsbury, who in 1920, reading as a Victorian, found the novel a 'dreary book'.[1]

It is not sufficiently clear, however, why *The Bertrams*, which to Walpole should be eternally and remorselessly forgotten,[2] had for Harold Laski 'all the magic of the Barchester series',[3] and is to the Stebbinses of all Trollope's novels 'the most modern in tone and the most haunting in mood'.[4] Or why *Castle Richmond*, which to Walpole is one of Trollope's six absolute failures,[5] is to the Stebbinses 'full of anxiety . . . poignant suspense . . . delicate restraint . . . without a misspent word'.[6] Or why *The Belton Estate*, thought by Henry James 'a work written for children . . . a *stupid* book . . . essentially, organically stupid',[7] should be triple-starred by Sadleir as one of Trollope's five greatest books. Or why *The Three Clerks* should be to Walpole 'a very poor novel'[8] and to Miss Curtis Brown, who discusses it at greater length than any other Trollope novel, a 'lyrical account of innocent young love'. Or why *The Claverings*, which Sadleir also three-stars, is not even mentioned by Miss Curtis Brown. One can find contrasting opinions on every one of Trollope's novels. I think there is no parallel to this situation in literary history.

What can one make of such judgments? Very little, in fact, for there *is* no rational explanation. If a novel is fresh and original, it may meet with a mixed reception, since traditionalists will resent what experimenters will applaud. But after the dust has settled for a century there should be fairly general agreement among the best qualified judges. For Trollope's novels this agreement does not exist. One would assume that the critics have been bringing to bear on these novels very different standards, but this can be true to only a limited extent and does not explain the wide discrepancies. In the face of criticism which angles off in many directions and is united only in the proposition that in some of his novels Anthony Trollope wrote perceptively and engagingly of the social life he knew, one is driven to re-examine the bases of his own opinions and come to conclusions ratified by his own studies. Perhaps one suggestion, however, can be offered.

The significance of Trollope as a novelist may appear different to various readers as one senses and another fails to sense the meaning of his stories. Superficially, he is interested only in who marries whom. He seems to be concerning himself largely with the trivia of romantic love, or otherwise dwelling on the nonessentials of life. Basically, however, his interests are much wider; and he suggests by implication the expanding circles of his microcosm. In other words, Trollope, like Jane Austen, is a synecdochist.

He is one with every artist who takes *his* corner of life as a symbol of all life.

Trollope's world is one of clergymen and sportsmen, of old politicians and young lovers. He manages very little story for these people, and he does not labor the psychology of their relationships. Yet he has an instinctive feeling for human responses that enables him to present character directly. T. S. Eliot has said, 'What a creator of character needs is not so much knowledge of motives as keen sensibility.'[9] Trollope's great gift is his sensibility. He does not spar with reasons or shadowbox with conjectures, but in his finest moments he not only transcribes what people say and do but suggests the subtleties of their association with consummate skill. Above all, he has the ability to make a casual life compelling. This is one of the rarest of all talents, one to which intellectual virtuosity and technical skill contribute very little. It comes almost entirely, I think, from the gift of sympathy. Even so simple a writer as Trollope is far too complex to be comprehended in a phrase or two, but I think one comes close to the source of his power when one recognizes the keenness of his sensibility and the warmth of his sympathy.

To be widely read in the Victorian period a novelist did not need much in the way of technical facility. A handful of colorful characters and a knack of maintaining narrative pace were often enough to assure a solid popularity. Today a slick competence in design, in construction, and in the avoidance of emotional overwriting is expected even in beginners. The contemporary novel should be, and usually is, technically excellent. But, if one may venture a prediction, no more (and very possibly fewer) twentieth-century novels will be read a hundred years hence than Victorian novels. In the long records of time the measure of fiction must ever be the mind and heart of the novelist.

Trollope's mind, though not subtle, was wide-ranging and retentive, enabling him to seize and hold what is essential in many human experiences. We do not go to him for abstract speculations; we do not expect to find in his novels a philosophical system synthesized in a pattern of coherent symbols. But for an objective report on the behavior of men and women in a situation of human interest there is no one on whom we can rely with greater confidence. Trollope is dull only to those who have no interest in people.

One who is interested in others is usually interesting himself. I have found it to be so, at any rate, of Trollope, in the company of whose ghost I have lived much during the last fifteen years. He had a positive personality. On the surface he was gruff, stentorian, and somewhat abrasive; but in his deeper emotions he was shy, tender, affectionate, and almost womanly. Superficial observers saw only the noisy extrovert. His close friends recognized the quiet introvert. One is impressed most of all, I think, with his balance, his normality, his freedom from cant, and his pervasive common sense. These are the qualities which he carried most notably into his fiction, and it is they which have preserved his work into another century. Susceptible to many of the weaknesses of Victorian fiction — its looseness of structure, its inadequacies of style, its poverty of ideas — his novels nevertheless rise above fluctuations of taste. In their genial sanity and keen-eyed wisdom they offer not only a precious documentary record of the age in which he lived but a continuing source of that enchantment which only the rarest of God's spirits can provide.

NOTES

1. George Saintsbury, 'Trollope Revisited', *Essays and Studies by Members of the English Association* (Oxford: Clarendon Press, 1920), p. 46.
2. Hugh Walpole, *Anthony Trollope* (New York: Macmillan, 1928), p. 122.
3. *Holmes-Laski Letters*, ed. Mark De Wolfe Howe, 2 vols (Cambridge, Mass.: Harvard University Press, 1953), I, 563.
4. Lucy Poate Stebbins and Richard Poate Stebbins, *The Trollopes: The Chronicle of a Writing Family* (New York: Columbia University Press, 1945), p. 160.
5. Walpole, *Anthony Trollope*, p. 122.
6. Stebbins and Stebbins, *The Trollopes*, p. 171.
7. Henry James, *Notes and Reviews* (Cambridge, Mass.: Harvard University Press, 1921), p. 128.
8. Walpole, *Anthony Trollope*, p. 143.
9. T. S. Eliot, *Selected Essays* (London: Faber & Faber, 1932), p. 132.

GERALD WARNER BRACE The World of Anthony Trollope*

A hundred years is usually time enough to settle a writer's reputation, but Anthony Trollope has not yet come into his own; much of his worth is still to be discovered. In his day, he was overshadowed by Dickens and Thackeray and George Eliot. A few months after his death late in 1882, when long familiarity with his books had bred a kindly contempt in the critics, Henry James published the valedictory essay which has been the starting point of nearly all Trollopian commentary. When the *Autobiography* appeared still later in 1883, under the editorship of Trollope's son Henry, it was at once taken as confirmation of the charge that he sacrificed quality for quantity, that he was deficient in imagination, that he regarded novel writing as merely an industry, and that he had no adequate 'views' on the serious questions of the day.

In the last decades of the century, new artistic ideas, amounting to cults and factions, came to the fore, Pater proclaimed the *mystique* of beauty. Zola and his *roman expérimental* broke through the native English defenses. Pessimism and doubt took hold. Revolt mounted and spread, and Victorianism became a bad word. By the twentieth century, Trollope was looked upon as a symbol of the discredited genteel tradition. His world, it was said by critics who knew little or nothing about him, was made up of kid gloves and teacups and well-fed clergymen. He wrote about ladies and gentlemen without apology. Worse than this, by his own naive admission, he wrote his novels to 'teach lessons of virtue' as well as to be a 'delight to his readers'.

It may seem that these prejudices are receding and that our view of Trollope is at last coming clearer. There is no doubt that a private following of faithful readers has sustained itself from generation to generation,

* From *The Texas Quarterly*, 4 (Autumn 1961), 180–9. Copyright the University of Texas at Austin; reprinted by permission of the publisher and Mrs Gerald W. Brace.

regardless of cults and factions, and is now larger than ever. Trollope is actually the sort of writer who will never need formal critical endorsement; his hold over the future is as sure as Chaucer's. But it must be recorded that the old Jamesian assumptions are still prevalent in many of our current literary histories. James actually admired Trollope's art with a combination of intelligence and warmth that makes his essay a classic appraisal, but he could not resist — he seemed almost compelled to utter — the faint damns that have haunted the textbooks ever since. He said that Trollope published 'too much', that his fertility was 'gross', that he displayed 'a certain infusion of the common', a 'heavy-footed prose' [sic!] and 'those flatnesses which kept him from standing on quite the same level as the masters'. In *The English Novel* (1954) Walter Allen expresses similar views: he thinks highly of Trollope but adds that he had little skill in plot construction, that his style is commonplace ('as a prose writer, Thackeray makes Trollope look a bumbling, clodhopping amateur'), and that his inferiority to Fielding and Jane Austen as an artist 'is so obvious as not to need stating'.

The habit of ranking writers like tennis players is endemic among critics and professors. It provides pleasant arguments and a sort of sporting-page attitude toward literature which gives entertainment to all. It rests partly on the truth that values are known only by comparisons: when stacked up against Dickens, Bulwer-Lytton is seen to be inferior, and it may be that Trollope's inferiority to Fielding is equally obvious. But there are areas where the game becomes unplayable. To argue that Chaucer is less 'great' than Milton, or vice versa, though it has the sanction of Matthew Arnold behind it, seems to me like arguing on the merits of the oak and the elm as trees: a comparison is enlightening, but the notion that one must be graded A and the other B makes little sense. The great writer is one who has earned the right to be considered in a class by himself: Trollope is unquestionably such a writer. He may be inferior to Fielding on Fielding's ground, or to Austen on hers: if he is an elm he can't be expected to produce acorns; but on his own ground he is uniquely and perfectly himself, and no one is his superior.

The question is, what is his 'ground'? Does he actually have a uniqueness that sets him apart from his predecessors and competitors? Mr. Allen, whom I quoted above, suggests that he does not — that he is akin to Jane Austen and Fielding, and must be given a lower ranking.

The first category of Trollope's special genius that I cite is one so simple that it is usually overlooked — a familiar problem in Trollope criticism, incidentally: his fertility of invention. That he could spin out his stories in such endless webs seemed almost indecent to the fastidious

James, but I see no reason for not admiring it for what it is – a miraculous gift. I think no other English writer can match it. The places, people, family trees, complications of property and inheritance, the clerical and political minutia, the very fabric and texture of innumerable lives, the infinite illusion of a people caught in the very act of life, 'as if', in Hawthorne's famous phrases, 'some giant had hewn a great lump out of the earth and put it under a glass case' – all this flowed into his fifty or so novels with tireless vitality. The quantity is vast, but what counts most for us is the life-giving freshness which runs through the whole creation from the somber *Macdermots of Ballycloran* in 1847 to the matchless *Mr. Scarborough's Family* in 1883. In this respect only Scott and Dickens can come within sight of him in England; perhaps a better measure of his creative achievement can be given by naming as his true peers the French Dumas and Balzac.

Inventiveness in a novelist inevitably leads to the question of plots and plotting, and the critical assumption has been that Trollope is indifferent or slovenly in this area. James objected that he 'never troubled his head with theories about the nature of his business'. Others have objected, with some point, that he repeats again and again the familiar theme of true love thwarted by family opposition – though it is hard to see how the Victorian novel may be otherwise written. But I think critical opinion has been somewhat beguiled by Trollope's own candor: he always made fun of the plotters like Wilkie Collins, and he let it be known that he was often as surprised as his readers at what happened in his books – witness his decision to kill off Mrs. Proudie after he overheard two clergymen abusing her in his club reading room. His methods were undoubtedly casual, but they were seldom unskillful and never unprofessional, as a close reading of the *Autobiography* should make clear.

James was quite mistaken in saying that he had no views on the subject of novel writing or that he never took himself seriously as an artist. In his valuable biographical commentary, Mr. Michael Sadleir cites 'the sensational perfection' of *Doctor Thorne*, which he considers one of Trollope's five technically faultless books. It is certainly a great deal to say of any novelist. Fielding has achieved immortality with one such performance (which I believe has always been overpraised), Jane Austen with possibly four (a very high average), and Scott and Dickens with none.

But of course technical perfection is not the main thing in Trollope, any more than it is in Fielding or Scott or Dickens. The great thing about his manipulation of material is that he can maintain forty or fifty characters, as he does in *The Last Chronicle of Barset*, in a state of living suspension, as it were, yet with such vitality and relevance that we believe in them and follow them from moment to moment and share their destinies. He creates too an illusion of wholeness, of large interrelationships — often awkward and tenuous, but in the main sufficient for the aesthetic adventure that a long novel proposes.

I have been speaking of Trollope's distinctive fertility, the unique flow of his human material; certainly no English novelist has matched his ability to sustain the same characters and themes through so many volumes, so many novels, so many generations. An endlessly continued story has no aesthetic validity: it dwindles into the sort of frustrating experience we have learned to call soap opera — a phrase that has been mistakenly used against Trollope. His problem was to give form and point to his separate novels, so that each exists as a finite drama with its own motive and resolution, and at the same time to build the overarching *comédie humaine* which included all the units in a satisfactory whole. It may be questioned whether he achieved such a finished monument, in any architectural sense, at least; but in his hit-or-miss way he produced a cultural masterwork whose significance is still too slightly regarded.

'There is sadness', James wrote, 'in the thought that this enormous mass does not present itself in very portable form to posterity.' Partly because the books are not available, partly because there are so many, our view of the work is imperfect, but as centuries pass and perspectives grow clear it will be found that the life of a great nation at almost the peak of its greatness appears more truthfully and richly in Trollope than it does anywhere else. One hesitates to call his work epic because he so carefully avoided the heroic or the pretentious, but in such a character as Plantagenet Palliser in the political novels we have a deliberately created national figure of classic stature, a stubborn, slow-thinking, exasperating, supremely just and conscientious English gentleman, member of the House of Commons, Chancellor of the Exchequer, Prime Minister, Duke of Omnium, and long-suffering husband and father. He stands more firmly on the ground, Trollope said, than any other personage he created, and if he is not a perfect gentleman, 'then I am unable to describe a gentleman'.

Truthfulness is said to be one of the distinguishing marks of genius, but truth is of such infinite variety that it destroys logic. Twentieth-century realists denounced Trollope because he did not tell the truth, by which they meant that he dealt too little in evil, too much in virtue: their facts of life differed from his, their hatred of gentility opposed his love. Under these conditions truth is hardly worth talking about. But none the less there is a sense in which Trollope's truth-telling is one of his unique talents. He is not committed to a satiric bias, as Fielding was — or even Jane Austen, whose attitude toward her world has been defined as 'regulated hatred'.

As far as any man's mind can be free, his was free. It is a condition that baffles critics, who delight in bias or commitment or any sign of personal or social warfare. Trollope's freedom is a little like the freedom of air or water: they are both life-giving elements but there is nothing much to be said about them. Volumes may be written on the diffusions and refractions of Dickens or Melville or Joyce, but why spend critical energy on the clarity of Trollope? One of the phenomena of human history is that Trollope's boyhood was spent in utter hopeless misery; he was psychologically conditioned for catastrophe, and by all the signs and portents accepted by modern critics his work should have represented the compensations and frustrations of a tortured psyche. Yet what we have from beginning to end is balance, clarity, and candor.

Actually he seems to have achieved this grace by intelligent and deliberate choice. Again and again in his novels we can see him consciously cleaving to the truth as a matter of policy. He is tempted into satire: conceive what Fielding would have done with Archdeacon Grantly, for example; and Trollope perceives the satiric potential of the Archdeason with equal clearness – but no, the man is a man after all, a many-sided creature of pompous snobbishness and Christian kindness. Consider all the girls Trollope created with love – did he ever once allow himself to be beguiled as Fielding was beguiled by Sophia or Dickens by any number? Lily Dale, Alice Vavasor, Glencora Palliser, to name three, are all beautiful and charming and gentle, but not one is a 'heroine' in any conventional Victorian sense; each is an imperfect and accurate individual. The Reverend Mr. Crawley has all the makings of a martyr on whom great sympathy might be spent: in outline he is a saint – but in fact he is vain and cantankerous. The whole complex 'truth' of his character is beyond the range of any of Trollope's peers with the one exception of George Eliot, and the fact that commentators have described him as a Victorian Lear rightly suggests the quality of this truth.

There are times, of course, when Trollope loses his clarity, when he is not faithful to his own 'moral consciousness', as he called it. For a man of such overwhelming talent he seems to have been possessed by some curious timidities. His almost compulsive fox hunting was a continuing demonstration that he possessed requisite courage and sportsmanship; his plunge into London club life gave him a needed sense of his own worth – as he candidly said (he was always candid). But here and there in his novels one finds values which are obviously un-Trollopian and which spring from a momentary distrust of his native genius. He greatly admired Fielding, but the lethal edge of Fielding's satiric humor is not for him. Yet I think such abortive caricatures as Dr. Pessimist Anticant and Mr. Popular Sentiment in *The Warden*, as well as Mr. Quiverful and Sir Abraham Haphazard and many others, represent simply his vain desire to be counted among the satirists. He not only admired Thackeray, he almost worshiped him, and inevitably allowed himself to deviate here and there into cynicism. But there is no doubt whatever that his own genius was a genius for the wise and compassionate acceptance of the conditions of life.

Near the close of his life he wrote to a friend, 'What is needed in writing, as in other work, is honesty: – honesty to see that the work given is as good as can be sent out.' Ordinarily it might be said that one who favors honesty is in the same category as the clergyman who opposes sin, but with Trollope the evidence is that he strongly and deliberately meant it. The pages of his *Autobiography* are surely the most nakedly 'honest' self-record that the age produced – and what seems to us today a priceless revelation of the truth of a great career seemed to the world of the eighties too candid to be respectable or admirable. His very style, which has been deprecated by James and Mr. Allen and others, was molded and shaped into an instrument of his honesty, and though it indeed lacks the grace of Thackeray's, in its own way it may be said to have the strength of ten.

There is a small climactic scene in *The Last Chronicle of Barset* that is worth quoting. Mr. Crawley has been existing on the very edge of despair and disaster and has clutched his woes to his breast with an arrogant vanity that exasperates the reader and almost destroys his infinitely long-suffering wife. And no matter what hell he endures or causes, he must go through with his duty – which on this occasion is the giving of a Greek lesson to his daughter Jane. She reads from *The Odyssey* a passage describing the agonies of the blind giant.

'The same story is always coming up,' he said, stopping the girl in her reading. 'We have it in various versions because it is so true to life.

Ask for this great deliverer now, and find
him Eyeless in Gaza, at the mill with slaves.

It is the same story. Great power reduced to impotence, great glory to misery, by the hand of fate, – Necessity, as the Greeks called her; the goddess that will not be shunned! At the mill with slaves! People, when they read it, do not appreciate the horror of the picture. Go on, my dear. It may be a question whether Polyphemus had mind enough to suffer; but, from the description of his power, I should think that he had. "At the mill with the slaves!" Can any picture be more dreadful than that? Go on, my dear. Of course you remember Milton's *Samson Agonistes.* Agonistes indeed!' His wife was sitting stitching at the other side of the room; but she heard his words, – heard and understood them; and before Jane could again get herself into the swing of the Greek verse, she was over at her husband's side, with her arms round his neck. 'My love!' she said. 'My love!'

Style, I believe, can do no more than is done in this passage, and to use such words against it as 'heavy-footed' or 'bumbling' and 'clodhopping' is a blindness indeed. It would not be easy to find this side of Shakespeare such a scene of controlled and exquisite dramatic art.

There are of course many great scenes in Trollope; he was in fact a master of 'scene', and arranged and set his stage, moved his actors, controlled every gesture and inflection, with superb generalship. Witness in *The Last Chronicle* the great confrontation of Mr. Crawley and Mrs. Proudie in the Bishop's drawing room – one of the decisive battles of literature; or the many lesser scenes: Major Grantly consulting with the genteel Miss Prettyman (who 'played her fish cautiously'), Grace Crawley breaking down the defenses of that old curmudgeon the Archdeacon, Johnny Eames calling out of the window to a passing policeman to save him from Madalina and her dragon mother, and that culminating moment when the Bishop says to his wife, 'I do not want to speak to you at all.' If such art is achieved by a bumbling amateur we can do with less of what usually passes as professional and admirable.

Trollope's brother Tom complained in his memoirs that 'the world in general dislikes accuracy of speaking'. It seems to have been a peculiarly Trollopian problem, for the world disliked Anthony's accuracy of speaking – and we remember how America reacted to the accuracies of Mrs. Frances Trollope. But the accuracy of one era becomes the classic of the next. The fact that Anthony's manner of writing sustains itself with such strength through the almost countless volumes of his fiction and travels is a result partly of his plainness. 'I fear,' he writes, 'that it may now be too late for me to excite much sympathy in the mind of any reader on behalf of Mrs. Proudie. I shall never be able to make her virtues popular. But she had virtues, and their existence now made her unhappy.'

Plainness such as this offended Henry James, yet it is one of Trollope's peculiar marks and it does him no harm. He knew Mrs. Proudie as well as he knew his own mother and was quite free to say what he believed about her – and of course the fact that she had virtues is the sort of truth he insisted on, and the fact that they made her unhappy is the sort of irony he delighted in. His candor could spoil the dramatic illusion – and perhaps here and there it does – but never with Mrs. Proudie, who is a creature no less substantial than her queen.

The *Autobiography* contains the most reliable advice to writers that I know of: no textbook on the subject can equal it – and the most remarkable fact about it is that such an opinion can be soberly offered almost a century after it was written. It may be 'dated' in its views on moral teaching, but I believe it is in no important sense invalid. In it, Trollope gives us a good many clues as to his success as an artist. He stresses spontaneity, for example, in somewhat the same way Robert Frost does in his famous credo, 'The Figure a Poem Makes'. He endorses clearness and harmony, as one might expect ('pleasant words', he calls it). And he says, 'Every sentence and every word used should tend to the telling of the story.' Like his approval of honesty this may seem to be merely what every writer tells himself, but we see by now that Trollope means exactly and conscientiously what he says. One of the secrets of his art is relevance. Every sentence, every word – it is a large commitment in a novel designed to fill three volumes; but there is no doubt that his best work reflects the success of his method. There is slowness, deliberation, leisure, but once the motion has started there is no interruption – not by a single word. Everything 'tends'; motion is constant.

When occasionally the method breaks down – as it does in the latter part of *Orley Farm*, for example – the resulting effect of dullness is quite flagrant. Can this be Trollope, we say? We take his mastery of dramatic movements so for granted that only when it falters do we notice it. With all his vast extensiveness, I believe readers are less apt to skip in Trollope than in any of his great contemporaries. Can anyone read the graceful Thackeray today without skipping? Even Dickens, whose brilliance is unique, advances through his novels in a series of fits and starts that make sustained attention almost impossible. But with Trollope the steady progress of the fable wholly controls the reader's imagination: what seems at first like the most casual sort of garrulity slowly acquires function and inevitability so that even the characteristic Trollopian reflections on such topics as croquet and love-making, or the exact social value of a footman with a little greased flour rubbed in his hair, become essential to the unfolding of the drama.

It is to be remembered that Trollope spent sixteen years of his young manhood in Ireland; his first novels dealt with Irish life, and excellent novels they are. I don't know any better of their kind. But I think his Irish experience in some subtle way accounts for his extraordinary success in writing dramatic dialogue. It is a fact that the dialogue in his novels is more pungent than it is in other 'standard' novels of the English tradition. All his speakers project themselves with vitality and self-revelation, as though their personalities had a right to be heard and would be heard.

'Curates indeed!' the Archdeacon cries out when it is proposed that he share his precious '20 port. 'It's too good for a bishop, unless one of the right sort.' It has always seemed to me that the cultivated Irish have a power of dramatic speech that the English deny to themselves – which doubtless accounts for the fact that the best English dramatists are usually Irish. And perhaps Trollope acquired some of that pungency during those sixteen years; it is said that at his London clubs, later on, he was known as one who spoke loudly and irascibly. Whatever the cause, his use of dialogue in the drama of his novels is nearly always masterly.

It may seem gratuitous to ask, after the comedy and pathos and human insights of his novels, what they are all 'about', but criticism has too often suggested that while they are pleasant entertainments they lack the serious stuff of important art. It is noted that Dickens attacked social evil, and George Eliot proclaimed the need of social responsibility, and Meredith had misty ideas about Nature, and Hardy took God to task – but Trollope simply went on writing about the troubled course of true love. One explanation for this view may be that many of Trollope's best books have been unavailable or unread.

His sardonic criticism of modern materialism in *The Way We Live Now* can stand comparison with Dickens' *Little Dorrit* – but of course it is said that *The Way We Live Now* is not typically Trollopian, brilliant as it may otherwise be. The observation is just; the book does present a sharper cutting edge than seems natural to him. But a similar theme is implicit in *Mr. Scarborough's Family*, which is not only 'Trollopian' in every favorable sense of the word but comes close to being the best novel he ever wrote. Our century has hardly discovered it yet, but when the ultimate judgment of the Victorian world is rendered, *Mr. Scarborough* will have been one of the major exhibits. And not far behind in evidence will be *Is He Popenjoy?* and *Rachel Ray*. A recent history of English fiction dismisses Trollope with the sort of language that has become almost a refrain. He was no thinker. He did not criticize the world he depicted. He was a snob. He was, finally, 'an industrious Philistine'.

Another theory, promoted by commentators who I can only assume have never read him, is that he dealt only in the placid and amusing amenities of the governing class. 'All that was tranquil in Victorian England preened itself in his pages.' True – up to a point. But *An Eye for an Eye* is a tragedy of betrayal, murder, and unsoftened disaster. *Sir Harry Hotspur of Humblethwaite* is similar. Trollope's compassionate understanding of the Irish tragedy led to his first novel, *The Macdermots of Ballycloran*. If he had not based his sympathies on a recognition of the whole human complex, his gentle Barsetshire comedies might be open to a charge of

Philistinism. He clearly enjoyed the placid and the amusing as much as most of us do. He delighted in well-tended gardens, well-run households, and well-mannered people. But the roster of his unhappy and ill-adjusted and even tragic characters is remarkable. One thinks of that handsome and prosperous gentleman Louis Trevelyan of *He Knew He Was Right*, who gradually destroyed himself by jealousy; or Laura Kennedy, whose love for Phineas Finn drove her to the edge of madness; or George Vavasor who relieved his frustrations by riding to hounds in a suicidal frenzy in *Can You Forgive Her?*; or the wicked Marquis in *Is He Popenjoy?*; or even Carry Brattle in *The Vicar of Bullhampton*, who so far as I know is the first 'fallen woman' in Victorian fiction to be restored to ordinary social decency.

In any analysis of what Trollope's novels are 'about', that long and brilliant comedy *The American Senator* is an essential document. Like all English writers, Trollope took a dubious view of the American character, and his senator, Elias Gotobed, hardly emerges as anything more than a crude caricature: but because Trollope uses him as the well-intentioned outsider who comes to observe and study English life, the effect of contrasting attitudes is nicely realized. The senator's opinion of English institutions is wholly reasonable: they simply don't make sense. He observes with growing bewilderment the rituals of a fox hunt, he asks shrewd and realistic questions about the protection of foxes and how farmers feel when the gentry gallop over their fields, and of course to a practical mind the whole thing is preposterous. He asks the same sort of questions about the church – or the Establishment, to use the more formidable term – and obviously he gets the same answers. After a struggle to explain sinecures, preferments, curacies, and all the rest, his advisers give up in confusion. To all except literal-minded Mr. Gotobed it is clear that the best things in life aren't meant to make sense – at least not in any such practical and utilitarian fashion as his elementary logic demands.

In *Hard Times*, Dickens promoted the same thesis. But of course the word 'thesis' is not suitable for Trollope – not, at least, for the large bulk of his work. Yet always, first and last, he had a grand vision of man and society. In Shakespeare's *Henry IV* the ideal of honor is splendidly represented by word and deed – until Falstaff reduces the whole thing to nonsense: there is certainly no thesis, pro or con, nor is there any thesis anywhere in Shakespeare – except the 'grand vision'. Man is what he is, a creature often preposterous, irrational, vain, sometimes wicked, sometimes like a god. Trollope's intensities and insights are not as great, but his view is similar. He cared little about institutions of state or church because he saw all things as reflections of human nature: to him the ideal government was merely the lengthened shadow of Plantagenet Palliser, the supremely conscientious — if slightly absurd — English gentleman.

There has always been some laughter at the expense of Margaret Fuller because she so solemnly 'accepted the universe'. I don't know exactly what universe she had in her mind, but none the less some sort of acceptance must be the aim of wisdom. At what point the treaty is made, and upon what terms, are the variables that may be argued — and of course it has been argued that Trollope accepted too much too easily. There is a heroic merit, we sometimes think, in being unreconciled. But certainly, as great writers go, he was among the reconciled. Of all his peers the one who comes closest to him in talent and temperament is Geoffrey Chaucer, who lived five hundred years earlier but who shared with him the 'large, free, simple, clear yet kindly view of human life' that Matthew Arnold admired. They both made the best of humanity without distorting it. They both made the best of the virtues of their native culture.

GORDON N. RAY
Trollope at Full Length*

I

It is not surprising . . . that the most salient aspect of Trollope's work, compared with that of other novelists, is its enormous bulk. In addition to his short stories, his travel books, and his miscellaneous prose, of which I shall say nothing, he wrote 47 novels extending to more than nine million words. As early as 1858 reviewers of *Doctor Thorne* were expressing wonder at his productiveness, all unconscious of the flood that was to engulf them during the quarter-century that followed. His contemporaries came gradually to accept Trollope's fertility as a marvellous fact of nature, yet in a way it has had an unfortunate effect on his reputation. With a few honorable exceptions, critics have hardly tried to comment on his total achievement. They have limited themselves instead either to individual books or to chosen groups of novels. The well-known essay which Henry James wrote after Trollope's death is a case in point. It takes little account of what Trollope published after 1869, thus in effect omitting the latter half of his career as an active novelist,[1] and is indeed the 'partial portrait' that the ever scrupulous James declared it to be.

If we seek guidelines by which to measure Trollope's achievement in its entirety, we cannot do better than inquire what broad discriminations he himself made among his novels. Though most of them appeared initially in magazine installments or independent part issues, it is evident that Trollope planned them primarily in terms of book publication. In 1876 he drew up a list of his writings and the sums that they had brought him for inclusion in his *Autobiography*. This manuscript list, which was given to me by his granddaughter, Muriel Trollope, a good many years ago, includes

* From *The Huntington Library Quarterly*, 31 (Aug. 1968), 317–34. Originally an address delivered on 26 February 1967 at the Henry E. Huntington Library and Art Gallery. Reprinted by permission of the author.

a column of figures not printed in that book. At first glance this column seems merely to record the number of volumes in which each title initially appeared. *The Macdermots of Ballycloran*, three; *The Kellys and the O'Kellys*, three; *La Vendée*, three; etc. Then one notes that the number for *Orley Farm* is five and the number for *The Small House at Allington* is four, though both originally appeared in two volumes. On further scrutiny it becomes evident that Trollope thought of his novels in terms of units equal to volumes of a 'three-decker' like *Framley Parsonage*, the book which brought him his first great success, each of which runs to about 330 well-leaded pages of large type averaging about 215 words, for a total of about 70,000 words. A letter of 1869 concerning a serial for *Once a Week* confirms this surmise. There he speaks of *The Claverings* (210,000 words) as 'a novel in 3 volumes' and of *The Small House at Allington* (283,000 words) and *Phineas Finn* (267,000 words) as novels 'equal in amount to 4 volumes',[2] though each of these novels was first published in two volumes. And a passage in the *Autobiography* nails the matter down. There he writes of 'being paid . . . £600 for the quantity contained in an ordinary novel volume, or £3,000 for a long tale published in twenty parts, which is equal in length to five such volumes'.[3] I suggest that all this amounts to a somewhat breathtaking discovery. Trollope's motto can clearly be summed up in the old-time French music-hall pun: *'Vive l'ampleur!'* There is a grandeur of conception in thinking of one's stories in terms of multiple units of about 70,000 words to which few novelists have aspired.

Regarded in this light, Trollope's novels may be readily divided into three categories. Twenty are standard 'three-deckers', that is, stories published in three small octavo volumes. Since some Victorian publishers gave better measure than others, their length runs from 155,000 to 280,000 words. Most were assigned three units by Trollope, but *The Belton Estate* (155,000 words) is alloted two and *The Eustace Diamonds* (276,000 words) four. Ten of these 'three-deckers' came early in Trollope's career, most of the others late. Between the eighteen-fifties and eighteen-seventies the 'three-decker' was rivaled for a time as the standard vehicle for popular novelists by two large octavo volumes with lightly leaded pages of small type. Nine of Trollope's novels appeared in this format, beginning with *Orley Farm* in 1862 and ending with *The Way We Live Now* in 1875. Their length runs from 210,000 to 387,000 words, and Trollope assigns them from three to five units each. Finally, there are sixteen short novels which appeared in one or two small octavo volumes. These extend from 52,000 to 150,000 words and are assigned one or two units each. They are dotted throughout Trollope's career. Two novels fall outside these categories because their book publication reflects unusual exigencies imposed by initial part issue. To avoid resetting, the 240,000 words of *The Vicar of Bulhampton* were published in a single large octavo volume and the 418,000 words of *The Prime Minister*, the longest of Trollope's novels, in four medium octavo volumes. Nonetheless, the affinities of *The Vicar of Bullhampton* are clearly with 'three-deckers', just as those of *The Prime Minister* are clearly with the two-volume large octavos.[4]

These figures have interesting implications. It is evident that Trollope's major energies throughout his career were directed to his big books, and that it is among them that we should seek his major accomplishments. The landmarks in his work are such early 'three-deckers' as *Barchester Towers*, *Doctor Thorne*, and *Framley Parsonage*, such later 'three-deckers' as *The Eustace Diamonds, The Duke's Children*, and *Mr. Scarborough's Family*, and above all the splendid pairs of large octavos that began with *Orley Farm* and ended with *The Way We Live Now*, including along the way *The Small House at Allington, The Last Chronicle of Barset, The Claverings*, and *Phineas Redux*. To this *massif central* of Trollope's fiction I shall shortly return.

Meantime, let me briefly survey Trollope's sixteen[5] one- and two-volume novels. As a rule, these were written very rapidly. *Harry Heathcote of Gangoil, An Eye for an Eye*, and *Doctor Wortle's School* required less than a month each, *Linda Tressel, Sir Harry Hotspur of Humblethwaite, The Golden Lion of Granpère*, and *Cousin Henry* less than two months. Trollope expected to be paid for these stories only a fourth or fifth as much as he was paid for his big novels, and in writing them he felt himself to have a freedom for experiment denied him in his longer books. He accordingly used them for departures from his established norm, and as time went by these departures became puckish, even almost perverse, as he searched for ways of keeping himself amused and interested in what he was doing.

The Warden (1855), which really belongs outside the series since it was written before Trollope established his characteristic manner of procedure, saw him tentatively exploring the Barsetshire setting. In *The Struggles of Brown, Jones, and Robinson* (*Cornhill Magazine*, 1861–62), *Rachel Ray* (1863), and *Miss Mackenzie* (1865), Trollope shifted his attention from Barsetshire gentlefolk to the lower middle classes. He was in effect inquiring how much of his success lay in the charm of good society, as he had depicted it in *Barchester Towers* and *Framley Parsonage*. The answer can hardly have pleased him. *Brown, Jones, and Robinson*, 'a satire on the ways of trade',[6] was judged to be coarse and pointless as it took its disastrous way through the *Cornhill Magazine*. Trollope's faithful presentation of a small Devon community in *Rachel Ray*, though replete with clergymen, did not sufficiently compensate his readers for a story which centered, as a whimsical reviewer put it, on 'a young woman whose unhappiness is caused by her lover not setting up a brewery fast enough'.[7] As for *Miss Mackenzie*, the general response was: surely even Mr. Trollope cannot expect us to take any interest in how a homely spinster of thirty-six comes finally to marry a bald-headed widower of fifty with nine children?

Both in person and through books, Trollope was a 'tireless traveller', and during his travels he found much that was to his purpose as a novelist. But his public wished him to stay in England. As one reviewer remarked: 'It is fatiguing to be obliged to travel when one wants to remain at home, and a reader generally turns sulky if he is called upon to go farther than Paris, or Brussels at the utmost.'[8] Trollope laid four of his novels in foreign lands, but in each case he hedged his bet by making the story a short one. In *Nina Balatka* (1867) and *Linda Tressel* (1868), set in Prague and Nuremberg respectively, he also attempted to determine whether 'a name once earned carried with it too much favor'[9] by publishing anonymously. As might have been expected, the answer to this quixotic question turned out to be 'yes', much to his financial disadvantage. *The Golden Lion of Granpère* (1872) and *Harry Heathcote of Gangoil* (1874), set in Lorraine and Australia, were hardly more successful, though published over Trollope's name.

In his last years Trollope used short novels primarily for a series of virtuoso explorations of unlikely, difficult, unpopular subjects. Three of these stories are demonstrations of the art of making bricks without straw. In *Cousin Henry* (1879) the feeble Henry Jones vacillates through two volumes over the question of whether or not he should reveal the existence of a will unfavorable to his interests. *Kept in the Dark* (1882) is the equally trivial tale of a marriage which nearly founders because a wife fails to tell her husband of a former engagement. And *An Old Man's Love* (1884) relates how a bachelor of fifty falls in love with his adopted daughter, but after much soul-searching gives her up to a younger suitor. Far more interesting is *Sir Harry Hotspur of Humblethwaite* (1871), a kind of rural *Washington Square* which sturdily sustains comparison with James's novel. This moving account of how Sir Harry destroys his daughter and himself in preserving her from the wastrel with whom she has fallen in love is Trollope's 'saddest story'. *Lady Anna* (1874) caused a stir by its account of a tailor's successful wooing of a titled lady. Given the current ascendancy of Carnaby Street, any surprise that such an event would cause in today's England might well derive from the tailor's willingness to marry the lady, but to Trollope's first readers its implications seemed to threaten the social fabric. *An Eye for an Eye* (1879) is a dour and powerful study of obsessive family pride, that sweeps to an almost operatic climax. In *Doctor Wortle's School* (1881), another of his notable successes, Trollope explores the repercussions of the revelation that a schoolmaster has unwittingly entered into a bigamous marriage, a subject which he would hardly have dared to undertake earlier in his career.

Almost the last of Trollope's novels was *The Fixed Period* (1882). This characteristically pedestrian Utopia, written when Trollope was sixty-five, has old age as its center of interest. Holding that 'men should arrange for their own departure, so as to fall into no senile weakness, no ugly whinings of undefined want, before they shall go hence and be no more thought of', Trollope posits that by 1980 men will withdraw from active life at the age of sixty-seven and be put painlessly to death at sixty-eight. Told by a friend that his endorsement of euthanasia was 'a somewhat grim jest', Trollope is said to have replied: 'It's all true – I *mean* every word of it.'[10]

II

Before we embark on a similar survey of Trollope's big novels, let us see how he overcame 'the burden of many pages' through his technique of 'writing for lengths', perhaps the most important of what he disparagingly called his 'mechanic tricks'.[11] A novel of three, four, or five Trollopean units, extending from 200,000 to 400,000 words, obviously made heavy demands on the inventiveness and power of organization of its author. Beginning with *Framley Parsonage*, Trollope gradually evolved as a means of meeting these demands what might be called the expanding novel. This form of fiction explores a truism of which *Rosencrantz and Guildenstern are Dead* has recently reminded us, that every exit is an entrance somewhere else. Instead of concentrating on a narrowly limited group of characters and a single narrative line, Trollope filled his vast canvases with several related sets of characters, all with their independent though intersecting narrative lines, thus conveying something like the movement of life itself. By the time Trollope's hand was fairly in, he had become extraordinarily deft in managing this technique of amplification in breadth. He knew exactly how to assign each set of characters its proper part in the story, to time his shifts from one plot to another so as to obtain maximum emphasis, contrast, and change of pace, and to bring the whole to a smooth conclusion within the space allotted. Trollope, in fact, made himself a great master of the contrapuntal novel long before anyone had thought of the term.

Critics used to a different kind of fiction, when they have written about

Trollope at all, have tended to lump his longer novels with the 'large, loose, baggy monsters' denounced by Henry James. In doing so they have altogether missed his achievement as a craftsman, quite literally failing to see the wood for the trees. Not individual destiny but life in society was Trollope's primary subject. His aim was the faithful representation of a segment of the Victorian world, rather than the unwinding of a single human coil. The point has never been more vividly put than by Hawthorne in the famous tribute which Trollope himself so treasured:

> Have you ever read the novels of Anthony Trollope? They precisely suit my taste, — solid and substantial, written on the strength of beef and through the inspiration of ale, and just as real as if some giant had hewn a great lump out of the earth, and put it under a glass case, with all its inhabitants going about their daily business, and not suspecting that they were being made a show of.[12]

So each of Trollope's longer novels, as [Richard Holt] Hutton wrote of *Orley Farm*, has its 'host of living men and women who scatter themselves in the loose grouping of real life'.[13]

Let me illustrate Trollope's method from one of his best yet least familiar novels, *Mr. Scarborough's Family*, published posthumously in 1883. Mr. Scarborough is among Trollope's most remarkable creations. This wealthy landowner is a *grand seigneur, méchant homme* who sets conventional morality at defiance. Of all things he hates most the entail on his estate; he hates it, indeed, with the sheer animal hatred of a Texas millionaire for the Internal Revenue Service. He has two sons. The elder, Captain Mountjoy, is an incorrigible gambler who has borrowed extensively from moneylenders on the expectation of his inheritance, and the younger, Augustus, is a cold-blooded, cynical opportunist. But Mr. Scarborough, determined to do what he will with his own, has prepared himself early in life for all contingencies. He has gone through two ceremonies of marriage with his wife, the first before Mountjoy's birth, the second after. When the need arises, therefore, he is able by suppressing evidence of his first marriage to persuade the world that his older son is illegitimate. Then, after Mountjoy's notes of hand have been recovered from the moneylenders for no more than he received for them, and after Augustus has shown how selfish and hateful he really is, Mr. Scarborough produces testimony to his first marriage which effectively reestablishes Mountjoy as his heir. All the while that he is carrying out these complicated machinations, he is a dying man, subject to painful, recurring surgery. His energy, his pagan delight in the dexterity with which he gets round the law and outwits those who administer it, and his terrible candor, make him a character of whom any novelist would be proud.

But all this is only a small part of Trollope's novel. He had three volumes to fill, and by the time he wrote *Mr. Scarborough's Family* he was a past master at filling them. So Mr. Scarborough is provided with a niece beloved by Mountjoy, but in love with Harry Annesley. To discourage the latter's attentions, her mother takes her to Brussels, where the reader is made at home in English diplomatic society as the niece repels a pair of unwanted suitors. Meanwhile, Harry finds himself quite innocently ostracized through Augustus' slanders, and we are amused with the futile efforts of his bachelor uncle to marry in order to produce an heir and cut Harry off from the family property. Still a third subplot concerns Mr. Scarborough's lawyer, whose honorable devotion to his profession makes him an admirable foil to his unscrupulous principal. At last he retires prematurely from practice, utterly dispirited and exhausted by the ingenuity with which Mr. Scarborough has made him the agent for his illicit maneuvers. The lawyer in turn is sustained by his daughter, who is reconciled to spinsterhood by her devotion to her father; and we learn at length how this pair are tormented by the demands of the lawyer's sister, her vulgar children, and her worthless husband.

So it goes. Each subplot necessitates the depiction of several new settings. Each new figure brings with him two or three more. All are presented in a leisurely fashion, described at length, located as to social position, identified as to character and habits, and allowed to speak for themselves in extended scenes. Mr. Scarborough and his sons sometimes disappear for five or six chapters at a time. Yet the action does advance, and when crucial events occur, their impression is all the more forceful for the long, slow, almost imperceptible preparation that has gone before them. A whole society has been created, and the figures of the main plot gain salience and reality from being seen in relation to so many other characters and against a background so comprehensively depicted.

Yet I have still not described the book's full impression on the reader. Trollope's formula for writing fiction allowed him to find room for many 'fine isolated verisimilitudes' which stricter standards of relevance would peremptorily have excluded. In another of his novels, for example, we find him alluding to a certain Miss Stanbury, 'to whom had come considerable wealth in a manner most romantic', and he goes on immediately to assure his readers that 'the little tale shall be told before this larger tale is completed' [*He Knew He Was Right*, chap. iv]. His novels are full of such 'little tales'. So it is that in *Mr. Scarborough's Family* one recalls not only the principal characters, who stamp themselves on the memory with varying degrees of vividness, but also many quite incidental details, such as Miss Thoroughbung's fondness for 'despatched crab', and transient characters, such as the odd but winning Mr. Harkaway, M.F.H.

When Harry descended from the gig he found himself close to old Mr. Harkaway, the master of the hounds. Mr. Harkaway was a gentleman who had been master of these hounds for more than forty years, and had given as much satisfaction as the county could produce. His hounds, which were his hobby, were perfect. His horses were good enough for the Hertfordshire lanes and Hertfordshire hedges. His object was not so much to run a fox as to kill him in obedience to certain rules of the game. Ever so many hindrances have been created to bar the killing of a fox, – as for instance that you shouldn't knock him on the head with a brickbat, – all of which had to Mr. Harkaway the force of a religion. The laws of hunting are so many, that most men who hunt cannot know them all. But no law had ever been written, or had become a law by the strength of tradition, which he did not know. To break them was to him treason. When a young man broke them he pitied the young man's ignorance, and endeavoured to instruct him after some rough fashion. When an old man broke them, he regarded him as a fool who should stay at home, or as a traitor, who should be dealt with as such. And with such men he could deal very hardly. Forty years of reigning had taught him to believe himself to be omnipotent, and he was so in his own hunt. He was a man who had never much affected social habits. The company of one or two brother sportsmen to drink a glass of port wine with him and then to go early to bed, was the most of it. He had a small library, but a book never came off the shelf unless it referred to farriers or the 'Res Venatica.' He was unmarried. The time which other men gave to their wives and families he bestowed upon his hounds. To his stables he never went, looking on a horse as a necessary adjunct to hunting, expensive, disagreeable, and prone to get you into danger. When anyone flattered him about his horse he would only grunt, and turn his head on one side. No one in these latter years had seen him jump any fence. But yet he was always with his hounds, and when anyone said a kind word as to their doings, that he would take as a compliment. It was they who were there to do the work of the day, which horses and men could only look at. He was a sincere, honest, taciturn, and withal, affectionate man, who could on occasion be very angry with those who offended him. He knew very well what he could do, and never attempted that which was beyond his power. (Chap. xxviii)

Mr. Harkaway counts for nothing in the story; he is encountered briefly for a chapter halfway through the book and then disappears. Yet he is presented with entire authenticity, he is interesting and characteristic in himself, and he thereby adds his mite to the total effect of Trollope's expanding novel. So much for *Mr. Scarborough's Family*. But let me remind you that this is only one of thirty-one such novels, all as fully elaborated as is this vast construction – indeed, with respect to the nine in two large octavo volumes, still more fully elaborated.

If we turn from the structure of Trollope's novels to their texture, we again find that amplification is the key to his best and most individual effects. Each of his principal figures is seen in many changing situations, and it is out of the impressions that accumulate from these varied scenes that our understanding of his character emerges. It should be noted, moreover, that Trollope has his distinctive way of imparting dramatic interest to these scenes. When Luke Rowan visits Bragg's End to propose to Rachel Ray, Trollope has his heroine pretend not to understand her suitor's purpose. After inquiring, 'Why did she thus falsely talk of his waiting a long time?' he explains: 'Dogs fight with their teeth, and horses with their heels; swans with their wings, and cats with their claws, – so also do women use such weapons as nature has provided them' [*Rachel Ray*, I, xiv]. Thus one of the humblest and most unworldly of Trollope's young ladies sees even the moment in which she accepts her lover as an occasion for asserting her dignity as a human being. Near the other end of the social scale the tragic dilemma of Louis and Emily Trevelyan illustrates the same preoccupation. Each is obstinately bent on vindication at the expense of the other's self-esteem. If Trevelyan knows he is right (as Trollope emphasizes in his title), his wife knows she isn't wrong, and it is she who conquers in the end. But even when there is no practical issue at stake in these encounters, we find one character struggling to achieve or maintain an ascendancy over the other, thus keeping in practice, so to speak, for the more significant confrontations that are sure to come.

It was Hutton who first presented this view of Trollope's characters as 'social combatants' in his notice of *The Small House at Allington*. Throughout this novel, he observed, Trollope displays his remarkable 'intellectual grasp of his characters . . . almost exclusively in the hold they get or fail to get over other characters, and in the hold they yield to other characters over them. It is in his command of what we may call the moral "hooks and eyes" of life that Mr. Trollope's greatest power lies.' When he reviewed *Miss Mackenzie* the following year, Hutton drew an important conclusion from his theory. Since Trollope 'occupies himself with turning the social kaleidoscope in which the individual characters are always taking new relations to each other', since his 'creative effort is chiefly spent on the construction of little circumstances, the variation of the angles of the little mental and moral reflectors in which we catch a new glimpse of his characters' nature and essence', it follows that he 'requires space to bring out his conceptions to their full perfection; his longest novels are as a rule his best'.[14]

III

We may turn to Trollope's big novels, then, in the confident conviction that they provide the proper material for a survey of the broad pattern of his career. Trollope's first three books, apprentice works published between 1847 and 1850, attracted little attention. Nor was this neglect unjustified, except perhaps with regard to *The Macdermots of Ballycloran*. In 1851 he remarked wryly to his mother, who at the age of 70 remained herself a prolific and popular novelist, that he intended 'to exhibit four 4 vol. novels − all failures!' at the Crystal Palace.[15] His career really began with *The Warden* in 1855, and during the next five years he wrote five more novels in the same vein. These early books bear the marks of their origin in the tradition of slapdash, helter-skelter narrative which dominated English fiction during the eighteen-thirties and eighteen-forties. Proportion and consistency of taste are hardly envisioned as objectives. There is a good deal of topical satire and many caricature portraits, usually heavy-handed and incongruous. So Dickens and Carlyle are attacked in *The Warden*, the Low Church party in *Barchester Towers*, and the new system of competitive civil service examinations in *The Three Clerks*. Facetious names are everywhere, a trick about which Henry James's comment concerning Mr. Quiverful and his fourteen children in *Barchester Towers* is definitive: 'We can believe in the name and we can believe in the children; but we cannot manage the combination'.[16] Authorial asides of an insistent intrusiveness provide a recurring distraction from the narrative. Two of these six novels, *Barchester Towers* and *Doctor Thorne*, are nonetheless among Trollope's very best. Indeed, with regard to its position in his work, *Barchester Towers* may fairly be called his *Pride and Prejudice*. Yet it is a pity that casual readers usually know Trollope only by *The Warden* and *Barchester Towers*. For all their vigor, dash, and brilliance, these early books lack the easy narrative mastery, the nice balance of judgment, and the harmony of tone that Trollope was shortly to make a habitual part of his equipment.

In 1860 the selection of *Framley Parsonage* as the leading serial in Thackeray's newly founded *Cornhill Magazine* gave Trollope an opportunity to rise to the top of his profession. He seized it not only by 'toning down the sharpness' of his 'smarter style', as a critic in the *Saturday Review* had advised, but also by fixing his attention on the aspects of English life and character most likely to interest his respectable readers. Here too he was following the counsel of the *Saturday Review*, which had taken approving note of his 'talent for drawing what may be called the second-class of good people – characters not noble, superior, or perfect, after the standard of human perfection, but still good and honest, with a fundamental basis of sincerity, kindliness, and religious principle, yet with a considerable proneness to temptation, and a strong consciousness that they live, and like to live, in a struggling, party-giving, comfort-seeking world'.[17]

So successfully did Trollope establish himself as the chronicler of this element in English society that when a writer in the *National Review* desired in January 1863 to refute the contention of the French critic E. D. Forgues that English morality was becoming lax, a contention based on the examination of a dozen recent novels, he turned naturally to Trollope for his illustrations. 'Mr. Trollope has become almost a national institution,' read habitually by 'more than a million people,' he asserted, and 'if the popularity of the portrait is the result of its truthfulness, and English life is at all what Mr. Trollope paints it, whatever its other failings may be, it is at any rate a very correct affair. . . . There are occasional villains [in *Orley Farm*] of course, but they seem to belong to an outer world, with which the audience has so little in common that it can afford to treat their crimes as a matter of mere curiosity. . . . The real interest of the story is concentrated upon well-to-do, decorous, and deservedly prosperous people, who solve, with a good deal of contentment and self-satisfaction, the difficult problem of making the most both of this world and the next.'

Here we see in the very process of formulation that sense of belonging to the charmed circle of an inner world which is undoubtedly part of the pleasure of reading Trollope's novels of the early and middle eighteen-sixties. The notion that Trollope is an author who appeals to comfortable people who want to stay comfortable, and perhaps equally to uncomfortable people who want at least temporarily to become comfortable, derives particularly from the novels which he wrote between *Framley Parsonage* and *The Last Chronicle of Barset. Orley Farm, The Claverings*, and *The Belton Estate* are all books of this reassuring sort, but of course it is the Barsetshire novels, with their recurring characters and settings, that provide its epitome. When Trollope abandoned good society for the lower middle class in *Rachel Ray* and *Miss Mackenzie*, without otherwise departing from his established formula, his readers were not pleased. 'A great deal of Mr. Trollope's popularity is perhaps attributable to the care he has generally taken to fill his stories with nice people', remarked one reviewer of *Miss Mackenzie*, going on to chide Trollope for disappointing him in this regard.[18]

The special relationship which Trollope had established with his readers in *Framley Parsonage, The Small House at Allington*, and *The Last Chronicle of Barset*, is underlined in the contemporary notices of *The Last Chronicle*, in which he took formal leave of Barsetshire. The *Spectator's* critic tells of an acquaintance's response: 'What am I to do without ever meeting Archdeacon Grantly? . . . he was one of my best and most intimate friends, and the mere prospect of never hearing his "Good heavens!" again when any proposition is made touching the dignity of Church and State, is a bewilderment and pain. It was bad enough to lose the Old Warden, Mr. Septimus Harding, but that was a natural death, and we must all bow to blows of the kind. But to lose the Archdeacon and Mrs. Grantly in the prime of their life is more than I can bear. Life has lost one of its principal alleviations. Mr. Trollope has no right to break old ties in this cruel and reckless way.' As for the reviewer himself, he confesses that he 'has indulged some rash thoughts of leaving England for ever'. 'What are we to do — what *are* we to do without the Archdeacon?'[19]

But triumphant as was Trollope's success between 1860 and 1867, it was not complete. Even *Framley Parsonage* had been dismissed in the *Dublin University Magazine* in April 1862 as 'a book well suited to invalids, and all who cannot bear much intellectual or emotional rousing'; and even Hutton, to whom Trollope listened with careful attention, at last began to urge him to show what he could do in depth of characterization as well as in breadth of coverage. To satisfy himself, as well as to meet this critical undercurrent of complaint, Trollope determined to alter the focus and tone of his work. With his farewell to Barsetshire in *The Last Chronicle*, he in effect crossed a great divide. Henceforth his readers were not to expect that he would be primarily the chronicler of nice people, that young ladies and clergymen would predominate in his books, and that his stories would be altogether wholesome.

The new phase in his work began with *Phineas Finn* (1869), the first of his parliamentary novels, though it had been foreshadowed four years earlier in *Can You Forgive Her?*, the book which introduces the chief figures of the parliamentary series. Discerning critics of the latter novel were agreed that Trollope must originally have intended Lady Glencora to elope with the deplorable Burgo Fitzgerald. By failing to provide such a conclusion, Hutton argued, Trollope was 'shrinking from a province of his art'.[20] As for George Vavasor, Fitzgerald's companion wastrel, it was Henry James's contention that 'the wretched man should have killed himself'.[21] Whether or not Trollope took such specific criticisms to heart, from *Phineas Finn* on he no longer shrank from analyzing the darker aspects of life and character. Henceforth unhappy women in his novels sometimes do leave their husbands (Laura Kennedy, Emily Trevelyan) and hard-pressed scoundrels sometimes do kill themselves (Lopez, Melmotte). Indeed, even madness (Robert Kennedy, Lucinda Roanoke) and murder (Farmer Trumbull, Mr. Bonteen) are henceforth not absent from his scene.

Nor were Trollope's elaborate studies of disappointment and frustration, of figures who are unable to assimilate and overcome defeat and humiliation (Laura Kennedy, Louis Trevelyan), isolated pictures in a generally cheerful panorama. Even for characters less profoundly tested, life became a more complex affair. The treatment accorded his heroines is a case in point. They are no longer at the center of things, as in the Barsetshire novels. Take fresh, innocent Mary Flood Jones, for example. Neglected even as the *pro forma* heroine of *Phineas Finn*, she is killed off in the middle of a paragraph at the beginning of *Phineas Redux*, in order to make room for the experienced and worldly Mme. Max Goesler. Elsewhere simplicity and innocence may eventually triumph, but Trollope devotes most of his attention to the passionate, rootless, dissatisfied women of the world, whom he finally dismisses empty-handed.

Trollope's new mode occasioned mounting protest among his readers. The 'glad, confident morning' of the Barsetshire period was gone forever. As they read his major books of the early eighteen-seventies, *The Vicar of Bullhampton, The Eustace Diamonds*, and *Phineas Redux*, they complained again and again that his tone was no longer wholesome, his characters no longer nice, his attitude toward them no longer affectionate. Yet they faithfully followed Trollope into the new country that he was exploring. Something of the same feeling began to emerge for the recurring figures of the parliamentary novels – Plantagenet Palliser, Lady Glencora, Mme. Max, and the rest – as had prevailed so generally regarding his Barsetshire creations. Then *The Way We Live Now* (1875) provided a severer test of fidelity. Five years before, Trollope had told Alfred Austin that 'Satyre runs ever into exaggeration, leaving the conviction that not justice but revenge is desired.' But by the time that he began this novel, he was ready, as he put it, 'to take the whip of the satirist into my hand', and *The Way We Live Now* was avowedly written for 'revenge' against the aspects of English life which Trollope most deplored.[22] Though reviewers complained that he had 'surrounded his characters with an atmosphere of sordid baseness which prevents enjoyment like an effluvium',[23] they nonetheless found *The Way We Live Now* too powerful a book not to be admired. Yet Trollope had won a Pyrrhic victory. Knives were out for his next novel, *The Prime Minister* (1876), which, like *Framley Parsonage* and *The Last Chronicle of Barset*, marked a turning point in his career. Here was a major work both somber and tedious. It failed, and with its failure his time of great popularity was over. References to the 'decadence in Mr. Trollope's powers' became common in the increasingly perfunctory notices that were still accorded his novels. 'Mr. Anthony Trollope rarely writes a bad book', runs a characteristically condescending review, 'and almost as rarely now writes one which may be distinctively called good.'[24] He was one more old favorite of whom the public had grown tired.

Trollope required a little time to accustom himself to his diminished status, but once he had done so, the effect upon him was liberating. He put his quarrel with society aside and in effect went on holiday. The acridity of atmosphere which had blighted his books for some readers was largely dissipated. Young love, a subject subordinated since Barsetshire days, again appeared in the forefront of his fiction; indeed, a manual of Victorian courtship might readily be compiled from *Ayala's Angel* and *Mr. Scarborough's Family*, which must contain twenty proposal scenes between them. The latter novel, a variant on the *Volpone* theme, as we have seen, could have been as scarifying as *The Way We Live Now*. It is, in fact, a cheerful book.

Reviewers were soon congratulating Trollope on 'reverting to his characteristic manner',[25] but these final novels are really written in a new spirit. In them Trollope is not only pleasant and agreeable, but also a little irresponsible. He is no longer fettered by the careful realism that had hitherto been so characteristic of his work; indeed, it is apparent from time to time that he is teasing his readers, playing with their stock expectations. His attitude is exampled in Chapters ix and x of *The Duke's Children*, where he provides a neat lecture-demonstration of his narrative method, or in that passage in *Ayala's Angel* where he has his hero compare his behavior with that expected of heroes of novels, the novels in question obviously being Trollope's own (Chapter xxxvii). Telling a friend: 'my real mission is to make young ladies talk',[26] Trollope filled *The Duke's Children* and *Ayala's Angel* with some of his sprightliest dialogue, conversation which is all the livelier because he no longer limited himself to what young ladies probably would say, but allowed his imagination to enlarge on what they just possibly might say. *The Duke's Children*, *Ayala's Angel*, and *Mr. Scarborough's Family* are carelessly organized. They are marred by many little errors and inconsistencies that Trollope would not have tolerated

earlier in his career. But these relatively serene novels of his old age are
nonetheless among his most delightful books.

IV

In my account of the pattern of Trollope's career, as illustrated in his
long novels, I have tried to suggest that he is a novelist of wide and diverse
interest. But admittedly this interest arises most readily if he is approached
on his own terms as a faithful recorder of mid-Victorian life. His contemporaries did not hesitate to honor such a claim on their attention. In his
obituary article, Hutton made it a chief ground of praise that 'without a
familiar knowledge of [Trollope's] works no historian who emulated the
style of Macaulay would even attempt to delineate English society in the
third quarter of the present century'. 'He depicted the society of our day
with a fidelity with which society has never been pictured before in the
history of the world.'[27] This judgment was confirmed by Bernard Shaw,
who grew up during Trollope's heyday as a novelist. After remarking that
his early views of English 'county, clerical, and West End Society' were
derived in part from his intensive reading of Trollope's fiction, Shaw told
Ashley Dukes:

> I used to feel that Trollope's pictures of English society were good just
> as you feel that a portrait is a good likeness without knowing the original;
> and now that I do know the original I am confirmed in my good opinion.
> If Trollope had gone an inch deeper he would have come to the universal
> epic humanity that is common to all classes and periods; as it was, he
> just got deep enough to make his people lifelike without getting out of
> the *specific* stratum that gives historical value to his work.[28]

. . . Trollope's fiction fell out of critical favor during the decades in
which most things Victorian were generally disregarded. In 1921 W. B.
Yeats found unexpected satisfaction in going through a course of Trollope's
novels. Endeavouring to explain this phenomenon to himself, he surmised
that they had 'gained with time and not with any merit of their own like
Frith's Derby Day and his Railway Station'.[29] This sort of grudging
recognition was all that it was fashionable to accord to Trollope until the
Second World War, when a renewed appetite for his novels swept them
from the shelves of second-hand bookstores both in England and the
United States. Since 1945 there has been a Victorian revival of major
proportions in all fields. If Trollope still attracts relatively little attention

from literary critics, he has kept his wartime audience of common readers, and he is benefiting as well from the recent vogue of Victorian microhistory. As each new study in depth appears, whether it be Mr. F. M. L. Thompson's *English Landed Society in the Nineteenth Century* (1963) or Part One of Professor Owen Chadwick's history of *The Victorian Church* (1966), we see how nicely the findings of modern scholarship accord with the record of his fiction. All this has resulted in the emergence once again of a public receptive of Trollope's novels.

In his review of *Can You Forgive Her?*, Henry James protested that 'It is too much to be called upon to take cognizance in novels of sins against convention, of improprieties. We can have charity and pity only for real sin and real misery. We trust to novels to maintain us in the practice of great indignations and great generosities.'[30] When he wrote this in the eighteen-sixties, James was living a quiet existence and looked to fiction for his excitement. In the nineteen-sixties, on the contrary, we live an excited existence and are apt to look to fiction for our quiet. We desire to escape from 'great indignations', particularly since they are rarely accompanied any longer by 'great generosities'. We prefer short views of limited subjects to long views of large issues. In sum, we don't want always to be on the stretch, and this is the perfect frame of mind in which to read Trollope's novels.

A signal advantage in thus viewing Trollope as a mid-Victorian master who by and large took what Walter Bagehot called 'the optional view of life' is that we are content to go to him for what he did best, not for his occasional deviations and eccentricities. We need feel under no compulsion to follow Mr. A. O. J. Cockshut in preferring a mediocre 'dark' novel like *He Knew He Was Right* to superior sunny novels like *Barchester Towers* and *Doctor Thorne*.[31] We can make bold to disagree with Michael Sadleir, who in 1927 ranked *The Belton Estate* above *Barchester Towers* and *The Last Chronicle of Barset*, because, despite the former's relative insipidity, its simplicity and shapeliness made it easier to defend at a time when Trollope's more characteristic merits were not appreciated.[32] Critical neglect does not usually afford reason for rejoicing, but perhaps we should even feel grateful that Trollope's novels have rarely been exposed to that relentless preoccupation with symbolism, irony, and depth psychology which since the war has so distorted our reading of the fiction of those other mid-Victorian masters, Dickens and George Eliot.

Yet in the last analysis it is not fair to Trollope to present him as primarily a sedative author whose novels allow us to return for a time to a more comprehensible and reassuring world. Like Chaucer in Blake's fine tribute, he 'numbered the classes of men'.[33] A novelist pure and simple, he allows us through his books to cultivate our feeling for the nuances of behavior, our sense of what people are like, in a way that modern fiction hardly permits. And occasionally in a novel like *The Last Chronicle of Barset* he attains the epic level that Shaw denied him through the affectionate understanding that he brought to his seemingly ordinary characters. In fact, Trollope was a great, truthful, varied artist, who wrote better than he or his contemporaries realized, and who left behind him more novels of lasting value than any other writer in English.

NOTES

1. Dating its beginning from *The Warden* (1855).
2. *Letters of Anthony Trollope*, ed. Bradford Allen Booth (London, 1951), p. 235.
3. Anthony Trollope, *An Autobiography*, 2 vols (London, 1883), I, 244. A comprehensive study of the 'number' and 'volume' divisions in Trollope's manuscripts, which often differ from the divisions in the novels as published, would prove interesting.
4. Three of the 36 books covered depart widely from the formula I have proposed: *The Bertrams*, 280,000 words, 3 units; *Ralph the Heir*, 210,000 words, 4 units; *The Prime Minister*, 418,000 words, 4 units. I can explain the first two deviations only by assuming that even Trollope occasionally nodded. The last is perhaps to be attributed to the fact that *The Prime Minister* had just been published in four volumes at the time Trollope drew up his list.
5. I exclude *The Vicar of Bullhampton* for reasons already given.
6. *Autobiography*, I, 214.
7. *Saturday Review*, Oct. 24, 1863.
8. *Athenaeum*, Mar. 26, 1859.
9. *Autobiography*, II, 10.
10. W. L. Collins, 'The Autobiography of Anthony Trollope', *Blackwood's Magazine*, CXXXIV (1883), 594.
11. *Letters*, p. 387.
12. Quoted by Trollope in *Autobiography*, I, 193.
13. *Spectator*, Oct. 11, 1862.
14. *Spectator*, Apr. 9, 1864, Mar. 4, 1865. In one of the brilliant but wrongheaded reviews of Trollope's fiction which James wrote for the *Nation*, he deplored 'the three different plots' of *Can You Forgive Her?*, 'if the word can be applied to Mr. Trollope's simple machinations' (Sep. 28, 1865), and in another he remarked that *The Belton Estate* 'has the advantage of being a single story, unencumbered by any subordinate or co-ordinate plot' (Jan. 4, 1866). For Hutton, on the other hand, there were 'scarcely figures *enough* [in *The Belton Estate*] to bring out Mr. Trollope's special talents. The mutual influence of different social groups on each other is a department of his work in which he always excels. In this tale there is no room for any

such influence' (*Spectator*, Jan. 27, 1866). Therefore, though its design is shapely and its outlines of character perfectly drawn, *The Belton Estate* is in his view an insipid book in comparison with Trollope's longer novels.

15. *Letters*, p. 9.
16. *Partial Portraits* (London, 1888), p. 118.
17. Dec. 5 and May 30, 1857.
18. *Saturday Review*, Mar. 4, 1865.
19. July 13, 1867.
20. *Spectator*, Sep. 2, 1865.
21. *Nation*, Sep. 28, 1865.
22. *Letters*, pp. 266, 321. *The American Senator* was also written from an avowedly satirical perspective (the same, p. 359).
23. *Spectator*, June 26, 1875.
24. *Saturday Review*, Oct. 4, 1876; *Spectator*, Aug. 31, 1878.
25. *Saturday Review*, July 8, 1882.
26. *Graphic*, Dec. 23, 1882.
27. *Spectator*, Dec. 9. 1882.
28. An undated letter, quoted in Sotheby's catalog of Feb. 4, 1952, lot 120.
29. Joseph Hone, *W. B. Yeats 1865–1939* (New York, 1943), p. 359.
30. *Nation*, Sep. 28, 1865.
31. See *Anthony Trollope: A Critical Study* (London, 1955), pp. 9–10. It should be mentioned that the gloominess of *He Knew He Was Right* is easily exaggerated. The Exeter chapters centring around Miss Stanbury, whose cross-grainedness is amusing rather than sinister, are cheerful enough: indeed, they would not be out of place in the Barsetshire novels.
32. Sadleir gives *The Belton Estate* two asterisks in his 'Baedeker fashion' rankings, the other two novels only one (*Trollope: A Commentary* [London, 1927], pp. 415–19). In the 1933 edition, *The Last Chronicle of Barset* gets a second asterisk.
33. Quoted by Geoffrey Keynes (*William Blake's Engravings* [London, 1950], p. 13) from Blake's *Descriptive Catalogue* for his engraving of Chaucer's *Canterbury Pilgrims*.

J. HILLIS MILLER
Self and Community*

Like George Eliot's fiction, Trollope's novels reveal the covert structure of society by the indirect means of exploring individual quests for self-fulfillment. His fiction concentrates with admirable consistency on the question of what constitutes authentic selfhood. Each novel is a variation on this theme and brings another aspect of it to light. If the narrator is a genial giant who has hewn out a solid piece of English earth and speaks as the collective mind of the community, much of the texture of each novel is made up of passages in which the narrator enters into the mind of one member of this community and represents with perfect tact each nuance of his thought.

For Trollope no individual can fulfill himself in isolation. A man comes into existence in his relations to other people. The person and his social role are identical. This role, however, is not given with birth. It does not coincide with the person's inherited place in a family or in a social class. It is created only in the fundamental decisions of the self. These are made in the context of the initially given place in society, but may change the character's relation to that context. In any case they determine more exactly that relation, place the character once and for all as involved in a certain way in the community.

For Trollope the most important example of this commitment of the self is falling in love. Almost any of Trollope's novels would provide an example of this theme, but a late novel, *Ayala's Angel*, is one of the subtlest as well as one of the most characteristically Trollopean in the beguiling willfulness of its heroine and in the attractive tang of irony, so typical of Trollope, which lies in the discrepancy between the heroine's uncertainty

*From *The Form of Victorian Fiction* (Notre Dame, Ind. and London: University of Notre Dame Press, 1968), pp. 123–39. Originally part of an address delivered on 14 April 1967 at the University of Notre Dame. Reprinted by permission of the University of Notre Dame Press and of the author.

about her future and the reader's certainty, guided by the narrator's equanimity, that all will end happily.

At the center of this novel, as of so many others by Trollope, is the idea that a man's substance is his love for another person. I am my love for the other. My selfhood is outside myself and can move from possibility to actuality only when my love is returned. It must be embodied in marriage and in assimilation into the community's structure of roles and relationships. My falling in love is not, however, governed by the collective wisdom of society. A man cannot choose to love or not to love someone, nor can any other person or group exert the least effective pressure to determine authentic loving. Falling in love is a spontaneous commitment of one self to another, a commitment in which the person comes into existence as himself once and for all.

Falling in love is for Trollope an absolute. It cannot be explained in terms of any cause or ground which precedes it and which supports it in existence — neither the personality of the lover, nor the personality of the loved one, nor any social criteria of choice, nor any divine impetus which says I can become myself by loving such and such a person. Falling in love is uncaused and unfounded, a gratuitous flowing out of the self toward another person. Moreover, the man or woman who falls in love gives himself entirely to the person he loves, as in *Dr. Wortle's School* (1881), Mrs. Peacocke describes the moment when, without needing to speak at all, she gave herself forever to the man who became her husband: 'He had never said a word. He tried not to look it. But I knew that I had his heart and that he had mine. From that moment I have thought of him day and night. When I gave him my hand then as he parted from me, I gave it him as his own. It has been his to do what he liked with it ever since, let who might live or who might die.' (II, vii).

Trollope often emphasizes what is spontaneous, irrational, and uncontrollable about falling in love. In *Ayala's Angel*, for example, Ayala asks: 'How can I help it? One does not fall in love by trying, — nor by trying to prevent it' (Chap. xliii) or in *An Old Man's Love*, published posthumously in 1884, the heroine, Mary Lawrie, is unable to love Mr. Whittlestaff however hard she tries, and unable not to love John Gordon:

'But I accepted you;' [she says to Mr. Whittlestaff,] 'and I determined to love you with all my heart, — with all my heart.'

'And,' [he replies,] 'you knew that you would love him without any determination. . . . No; you cannot love two men. You would have tried to love me and have failed. You would have tried not to love him, and have failed then also.' (Chap. xxiii)

Trollope's characters do not justify their loving in any rational or theoretical terms. They speak rather with a wholesome vagueness about having a 'sort of feeling' that they love someone.they are unwilling to seek reasons for this feeling, to uncover its grounds, or to clarify it. To clarify it would be to falsify it, for it is no more than a feeling. When the characters delay in committing themselves to another person, this is not so that they can make up their minds, but in order to allow their spontaneous feelings to became manifest. Such a commitment of the self cannot be hurried by taking thought, and a decision which is made on abstract grounds or on grounds of social prudence is shallow and insubstantial. Once Trollope's characters have become aware of the direction in which their feeling has moved, they become extraordinarily tenacious in sticking to this commitment against all opposition or difficulty, even when sticking to it is most disadvantageous from a worldly point of view. They hold to it because it is what they are. It is all they have, as Adelaide Palliser, in *Phineas Redux*, explains in justification of her love for Gerard Maule:

> 'You ask me why I got into his boat,' [she says to Lady Chiltern.] 'Why does any girl get into a man's boat? Why did you get into Lord Chiltern's?'
> 'I promised to marry him when I was seven years old; – so he says.'
> 'But you wouldn't have done it, if you hadn't had a sort of feeling that you were born to be his wife. I haven't got into this man's boat yet; but I never can be happy unless I do, simply because–'
> 'You love him.'
> 'Yes;–just that. I have a feeling that I should like to be in his boat, and I shouldn't like to be anywhere else. After you have come to feel like that about a man I don't suppose it makes any difference whether you think him perfect or imperfect. He's just my own, – at least I hope so; – the one thing that I've got. If I wear a stuff frock, I'm not going to despise it because it's not silk.' (II, i)

Being in love is as substantial a fact as having one garment rather than another. But though it is not in control of conscious choosing, it is nonetheless an act of the will. For Trollope the self is an energy of volition which is the focusing of the whole self on another person. Eventually Trollope's good characters become aware that their spontaneous wills have chosen for them, that they now exist as a force of loving so fundamental to them that they cannot betray their love without betraying themselves. The good characters then ratify their involuntary wills with an act of voluntary willing which puts the rational and irrational levels of the self in harmony. Such a choice is usually in conflict with the obvious social good of the lover. All his friends, family, and the community generally advise him to do otherwise than he does, as, for example, in *Mr. Scarborough's Family* everyone tells Florence Mountjoy to give up Harry Annesley. Usually, as in this case, the issue is money. The lovers will not have enough income to live in a way proper for ladies and gentlemen in English society. This conflict between self-fulfillment and social obligation recurs again and again in Trollope's fiction. While the conflict persists there is an incompatibility between the commitment of the self in loving and the absorption of the person into the community of ladies and gentlemen. At the same time, however, Trollope sees clearly that a person cannot fulfill himself in isolation either from the one individual he loves or from society as a whole. The lover's problem is to get his love made real in its acceptance by the loved one and by the community. Until this happens he is incomplete.

The character who gives her name to *Ayala's Angel* is an admirable example of this. Ayala's 'Angel' is her subjective image of the man who will be worthy of her love. He will be an 'Angel of Light', divine in his beauty and in his superiority to ordinary mankind. 'If there was any law of right and wrong fixed absolutely in her bosom, it was this, – that no question of happiness or unhappiness, of suffering or joy, would affect her duty to the Angel of Light. She owed herself to him should he come to seek her. She owed herself to him no less, even should he fail to come. And she owed herself equally whether he should be rich or poor' (Chap. xxvi). Measuring the men who propose marriage to her by this theoretical model, she obstinately refuses them one by one, rejecting firmly the counsels of her uncles and aunts, her friends, and the collective judgment of society, saying to each suitor, by her refusal rather than by her words, for she keeps her image of the Angel a jealous secret hidden in her heart: 'You are not he, – not he, not that Angel of Light, which must come to me, radiant with poetry, beautiful to the eye, full of all excellences of art, lifted above the earth by the qualities of his mind, – such a one as must come to me if it be that I am ever to confess that I love. You are not he, and I cannot love you' (Chap. xxv).

Ayala's obstinacy is a defense of her selfhood from the pressures of the community. To accept someone she does not love would be to deny herself any authenticity as a person. The narrator therefore fully approves of her stubbornness. It is, like the stubbornness of so many of Trollope's girls, the doubling of the first involuntary will by a second voluntary choice, the will as free decision ratifying the will as spontaneous power of loving. Or rather, it is a negative version of this theme. As long as Ayala is not conscious of having fallen in love she is right to refuse all offers for her hand. 'How is a girl to love a man if she does not love him?' she asks (Chap. xxvii). At the same time, however, the narrator deplores Ayala's isolation from the community. This isolation is defined by the fact that she does not tell anyone of her secret expectation that an Angel of Light will appear to love her. Such an isolation is commitment to a romantic invention. It is a kind of insanity. A subjective idea not embodied in relationships to others is always dangerously akin to madness for Trollope, as, for example, in the central story of Louis Trevelyan in *He Knew He was Right* (1868–1869), or in the parallel story of Robert Kennedy in *Phineas Redux*. As long as Ayala has not found a real man who incarnates the qualities she has imagined for her angel she is in a dangerous state of solitude and incompleteness, for all her beauty and charm. In the same way, poor Tom Tringle, hopelessly in love with Ayala, will end in the insane asylum, as his father foresees, if he remains the prisoner of a love which cannot ever be fulfilled.

Here the subplots of *Ayala's Angel*, according to a paralleling usual in Trollope's fiction, are analogous to the main plot and act as a commentary on it. Ayala's sister Lucy commits herself wholly to her lover, Isadore Hamel. Like Mrs. Peacocke in *Dr. Wortle's School*, she says she belongs to her lover and will do whatever he says. Lucy serves as an example of authentic love against which Ayala's prolonged failure to know that she is in love may be measured. The relationship of Frank Houston and Imogene Docimer is another kind of commentary on the main story. It is a good demonstration of the way Trollope's lovers, like Johnny Eames in *The Last Chronicle of Barset*, or Frank Greystock in *The Eustace Diamonds* (1873), or Lady Laura Kennedy in *Phineas Redux*, may choose wilfully to betray their love for another person without permanently damaging the integrity of their identities. It is not in their power to cease loving, but it is in their power to act in ways which temporarily or even permanently deny that love fulfillment. Since Frank Houston thinks he does not have money enough to marry Imogene honorably, he attempts to make a cynical marriage for money to Gertrude Tringle. When he escapes from this entanglement and comes back to Imogene in spite of his poverty, he can say truthfully that this is no renewal of his affections. It is an act of voluntary willing at last in accord with the orientation his spontaneous will has maintained all along: 'It is no return', he says. 'There has never been a moment in which my affections have not been the same' (Chap. xli).

In the same way, when Ayala finally comes to accept Jonathan Stubbs, after a series of gradual approaches toward a recognition that she loves him, Trollope has her reiterate her knowledge that she has loved him from the instant she first met him. 'I think I fell in love with him the first moment I saw him', she says at last (Chap. lv). It was love at first sight, that fundamental allegiance of the whole substance of the self in an outward movement of the involuntary will which constitutes true selfhood for Trollope. Ayala is for a long time, however, unaware of what has happened to her. Her abstract fidelity to the idea that an Angel of Light will come to her keeps her from understanding herself and leads her to refuse Jonathan Stubbs' proposals repeatedly. The central sequence of the novel focuses not on her gradual change, for she does not change, but on her gradual discovery of who she is. Her obstinate allegiance to what Trollope calls 'the theory of her life' (Chap xlix) keeps her from being immediately transparent to herself. The same phrase had been used to describe Frank Houston's decision not to marry Imogene. 'The whole theory of his life,' says the narrator when Frank returns to Imogene, 'had, − with a vengeance, − been thrown to the winds' (Chap. xli). Ayala can finally bring theory and spontaneous feeling into harmony when she discovers that Jonathan Stubbs is in fact that Angel of Light for whom she has longed:

It was of him she had always dreamed even long before she had seen him. He was the man, perfect in all good things, who was to come and take her with him; − if ever man should come and take her. . . . In the fulness of her dreams there had never been more than the conviction that such a being, and none other, could be worthy of her love. There had never been faith in the hope that such a one would come to her, − never even though she would tell herself that angels had come down from heaven and had sought in marriage the hands of the daughters of men. Her dreams had been to her a barrier against love rather than an encouragement. But now he that she had in truth dreamed of had come for her (Chaps lii and lv).

The way in which interpersonal relations replace religious experience for Trollope is particularly clear in this text, with its explicit echo of Genesis 6:2: ' . . . the sons of God saw the daughters of men that they were fair; and they took them wives of all which they chose'. Ayala's Angel of Light is a specifically religious concept, the idea of a superhuman figure who will transform her life by loving her and on whom her self-fulfillment depends as that of a Christian does on being chosen by God. She discovers finally that the part of herself which is outside herself, the ground of her selfhood, is Jonathan Stubbs: ' . . . he was in truth the very "Angel of Light" ' (Chap lv). Until she finds a real person to embody the subjective image she has cherished within her imagination, she remains only an insubstantial image of unfulfilled desire, but such a person does come to her. Trollope's novels, unlike those of Hardy, can end happily because one person can, for Trollope, stand in the place of God to another and be the foundation and support of his selfhood.

If the self, for Trollope, affirms itself in terms of the other, this means that the willing reiteration of the deepest involuntary energy of the self is the origin of society. Society is constantly renewed in acts of self-affirmation which sustain the community and keep it from becoming an empty framework of conventions, habits, rules, judgments, and institutions. Trollope's view of society is like those cosmological theories which suppose the continuous creation of matter and energy. According to such theories, new matter and energy are constantly flowing in from some ubiquitous creative source, perhaps at innumerable points in the universe. So for Trollope, each duplication of spontaneous choice by voluntary choice, a choice often made in denial of the particular role in the community the individual has inherited, sustains the community and is its source.

In *Dr. Wortle's School*, for example, it is right that Mr. and Mrs. Peacocke should continue to live together as man and wife, even though they discover that they are not married in the eyes of the law. She has become bone of his bone and flesh of his flesh. This extra-social union is more important than the abstract convention of marriage. Marriage as an institution within the community has its source and validity in the unsponsored commitments of one person to another. The marriage bond is descriptive rather than prescriptive. Authentic relations between persons are self-creating.

The fundamental revelation of Trollope's novels is the dependence of the general mind on particular minds. The collective mind exists only in individuals as they are related to one another. It is generated only by them and sustained only by them. The narrator, who speaks for the general mind, has therefore been brought into existence by the characters, so that it may be said that the narrator is made by his world rather than that he makes the world of the story he tells. He has risen magically into being out of the interchanges between person and person and is kept in being only so long as those interchanges continue.

The collective consciousness is like each individual consciousness in that it exists as the spontaneous will to sustain itself as continuous with itself. Like the individual self, it is sustained by nothing outside mankind. It is for this reason that Trollope puts such a high value on the unbroken historical continuity of English society, and, like Walter Bagehot, whom he much resembles in sensibility and in outlook,[1] has such distaste for sudden changes in society and such faith in open discussion among gentlemen and ladies as capable of maintaining the unbroken flow of the community through time. The fact that a culture is a collective game, the shared will to go on living by certain rules of action and judgment, is not seen by those living within the culture and accepting its rules as absolutely valid. The action of a novel by Trollope is a temporary whirlpool in the midst of the surrounding mind of the community. This local disturbance reveals the fact that society is a structure which organizes itself according to its own immanent laws and without the intervention of any superhuman law-giving power.

In *Ayala's Angel*, as in most of Trollope's novels, the whirlpool in the end vanishes, the characters fulfill themselves and melt into the collective mind for which the older characters, happily settled into a place in society, have spoken throughout the story. During the prolonged period of uncertainty which takes up most of the novel, however, this coincidence of private self and social self is for the protagonists held open as unfulfilled possibility. The main characters, Ayala, Lucy, Tom Tringle, Frank Houston, Imogene Docimer, still exist as unassuaged desire. Their continuation in this state reveals the fact that society transcends its individuals and yet exists only in terms of its individuals, as a game transcends its players, but exists only in the individual actions of each player. The player brings something irreplaceable to the game, his strength of willing, and yet he exists only in terms of his relations to others. By choosing a story which puts the game in question, *Ayala's Angel*, like *Henry Esmond, Our Mutual Friend*, or *Middlemarch*, allows the reader to glimpse during the time before it closes in on itself, the secret presence which sustains the whole. This presence disappears if one tries to fix it in a single person. It exists only in the intercourse between persons. In the same way, the source of meaning which makes language possible can be located in no single word, but only in the interaction of words in syntactical patterns. The power of structures of words to create meaning is usually taken for granted. It becomes visible in language turned back on itself, for example, in poetry. The novel, to follow out this analogy, might be defined as the poetry of interpersonal relations.

Victorian fiction raises for the twentieth-century reader the dark question of whether the assimilation of the protagonists into the community by way of a happy relation to another person is a valid resolution, or whether, to our deeper insight, it should appear as a covering over and forgetting of the fundamental fact of human existence so persuasively dramatized in the body of the book — in the desire for some 'illimitable satisfaction' of Dorothea in *Middlemarch*, for example, or in Ayala's grandiose dreams in *Ayala's Angel*. This is the question, to continue my analogy between language and interpersonal relations, of whether the perfected sentence brings into the open the latent principle of meaning which makes language possible, or whether it hides it. Perhaps the power behind language is only brought to the surface in the gaps between words, in the failures of language, not in its completed articulations. Correspondingly, human beings, it may be, are characterized by unappeasable desire and consequently by permanent alienation from their deepest selves. Any replacement of desire by fulfillment is only temporary and illusory. For the Victorian novelists, on the other hand, the existence of an authentic satisfaction of desire makes the happy ending possible, though by no means inevitable.

In Trollope's case, for example, the happy ending is reached in spite of many opportunities for failure. Along with those characters like Ayala who obtain a final happiness, there are those, like Lily Dale in *The Small House at Allington* and *The Last Chronicle of Barset*, who remain in unfulfillment, or those, like Johnny Eames in the same novels or Lady Laura Kennedy in *Phineas Redux*, who commit themselves in love to another person, but never, for one reason or another, attain possession of that person, or those, like Louis Trevelyan in *He Knew He Was Right* or Robert Kennedy in *Phineas Redux*, whose conscious wills have in some strange way lost contact with their spontaneous wills. The obstinacy of such characters gradually so alienates them from themselves that they are led step by step to destroy their own lives. Nevertheless, most of Trollope's novels end for the main characters in a happy coincidence of private self and social role.

Hardy's difference, perhaps his 'modernity', lies in the fact that the desire of his protagonists — Eustacia, Henchard, or Jude — remains illimitable, and so his most characteristic novels must end unhappily. Whenever Hardy's characters attain what have seemed their goals, their longings are magically constituted anew and reoriented toward something or someone they do not yet possess. In Trollope's fiction, on the contrary, the angelic ideal may be incarnated in another person, and possession of that person brings peace. Even so, Trollope has a strong sense that the life of the individual and of the community is a continuing process. A certain openness to new involvements remains even in those who appear to be most settled into a role in society and to have obtained the fixed self which accompanies it. The most obvious evidence of the open-endedness of Trollope's novels is the persistence of the same characters from novel to novel as persons who may still have new experiences involving the deepest reality of the self. Examples of characters who appear in this way in more than one novel are Septimus Harding, Mrs. Proudie, Lily Dale, Lady Glencora, and Phineas

Finn. For Trollope, each man or woman depends on others, who depend in turn on others, in an endless round of encounters forming a constant interplay of wills. The process of mutual dependence suggests covertly, however, that there is a hidden foundation within the social game. This foundation is revealed by Trollope's work in one of its most important manifestations: the power of willing which is intrinsic to each man and woman. The individual will, for Trollope, is the ground of everything else in society.

NOTE

1. For a discussion of some aspects of this relationship, see Asa Briggs, 'Trollope, Bagehot, and the English Constitution', *Victorian People: A Reassessment of Persons and Themes, 1851–1867*, Harper Colophon Books (New York and Evanston: Harper & Row, 1963), pp. 87–115.

RUTH apROBERTS
The Shaping Principle*

'You must look to the circumstances.'

The Last Chronicle of Barset

How can we, then, talk about Trollope as an *artist*? − a man quite insouciant as to point of view, intruding himself without shame or compunction, quite as ready to tell as to show, naively faithful to chronological order − if he does give us a flashback it seems to be because there is something he forgot to tell − not concerned with elegance or intricacy of plot, innocent of symbol, ritual and myth. *Are* these novels anything other than random colloquies, histories, rambles? Of course they are. Mere rambles, mere history, mere photography could not conceivably hold us as these novels do. What then *can be* the controlling element, what *is* the non-random, shaping principle?

To begin at the beginning is to begin with *The Warden*, which is, as generally agreed, the start of his *oeuvre*. It has been more commented on than Trollope's other work, but I beg, nevertheless, attention for another close look at it. Or rather, let us stand back from it a little. For I believe the significance of its shape has been missed. This novel especially has suffered from our tendency to categorise: because it deals with a contemporary issue, it has been hard for us to think of it in terms other than those of the *Tendenzroman*, the novel of social purpose.

The trouble with this is that the purpose is not very clear. As propaganda, *The Warden* seems to fail. We are, in fact, puzzled to find what side Trollope is on. Is he in favour of reform or not? Apparently he does not

*From *Trollope: Artist and Moralist* (London: Chatto & Windus, 1971). abridged from pp. 34−54. Published in the US as *The Moral Trollope* (Athens, Ohio: Ohio University Press, 1971). Reprinted by permission of Chatto & Windus and of the author.

quite know his own mind, and he suffers from a terrible indecision. A recent critic, with quick pity and ready diagnosis, finds the novel a symptom of Trollope's illness: which is the Divided Mind.[1] This is called his *plight*, and it is also the *plight* of the mid-Victorian Liberal-Conservatives. Trollope is interesting, I suppose, just because he had it worse than the others. And while so far as I know no one has found Trollope *alienated*, he nevertheless achieves chic when it is discovered that he has a 'late, dark period'.[2] So strong blow the winds of criticism.

This is the result of the persistent tradition that Trollope is a naive writer, that *he* has no control over his material, and that his material serves to give *him* away. And then Trollope's characters seem so 'free' to develop themselves along their own lines that some critics talk as though these characters are somehow smarter than Trollope, and know more than he about motivation and morals. I think we ought to make a declaration that an author cannot be more naive than his characters. Trollope must be at least as capable of subtle rhetoric as his dazzling lawyer Mr. Chaffanbrass, or the wily Prime Minister Mr. Daubeny; he must have at least the terrible acquaintance with the human demonic that oppresses Josiah Crawley; he must have at least the wit of Glencora Palliser, and at least her rueful understanding and love for that very trying and very admirable man her husband. Nor need we pretend to be naive when we read Trollope's novels; as someone said of Thackeray, he really has very little appeal for the illiterate charwoman.

So, then, let us look at *The Warden* as our literate selves. We know that sinecures are by definition immoral and must be reformed. We — or Trollope's contemporaries — know, too, that the Ecclesiastical Commission is in session, and that reform is in process, and that the process will be à *l'anglaise*, that is, slow, and by degrees. Trollope is not trying to expose an abuse, nor is he trying to demonstrate the beauties of the *status quo*. His art lies in his carefulness to do neither, to avoid the *partis pris*. For it is his delight to regard the juxtaposition of the two *partis*. He has a Divided Mind, and it is no *plight*, but rather a distinct artistic advantage. *The Warden* involves both sides in a beautifully ironic demonstration of incongruities. It is a case that is richly funny in itself, and it also has a certain instructive value. Trollope exploits this case, both for its humour and for its value as enlightenment. And because of the humour, the enlightenment proceeds with as little pain to the reader as may be. Look at this case: here is a palpable abuse. The money left by Hiram's will for the benefit of twelve aged paupers has increased many fold, and it now yields chiefly a fat income for the Warden of Hiram's Hospital. But: the Warden, the instrument of this abuse, is as beneficent a man as we can imagine. Here is the *donnee*, as James would say. Here is the germ of the book. But this *donnée* is not merely the starting-point for working out an idea for a story. It *is* the book. The shape of this case is the shape of the novel. Consider *The Warden*, by contrast, in the more usual way, as a sequential line of events. A reformer, John Bold, draws attention to an abuse: Mr. Harding, the Warden of Hiram's Hospital, is in receipt of an income far greater than intended by the original endowment. Mr. Harding gradually realises he is indeed party to an abuse, and he resigns the post. John Bold gives up the prosecution and marries Mr. Harding's daughter. Nobody wins. The only excitement at the end is not an action but a non-action: the Bishop decides to do – nothing. Surely this is a remarkably inconclusive story, and the narrative is hardly of much interest. Very early we suspect Eleanor Harding will marry John Bold, and we are not surprised when Harding resigns or when Bold gives up the case. There is not enough story-line to hold anybody.

The potency of the work is simply not in its story. It is, rather, within this situation that Trollope has taken, and in the way he exploits it. What he does, is to insist on the incongruities, by sharp juxtaposition of different perspectives. What is called his 'realism' functions to this end, and it functions like this: Not only are we told that Mr. Harding is a good man, and not only do we see him and know him as virtuous – and his virtue can only be as real as it is because he is highly individuated – not only is all this so, but further, we *love* Mr. Harding. We are involved. We know he accepted the sinecure innocently, and he performs his duties with the greatest devotion and success; he is not one to stick by the Letter of the Law – he supplies the old men with extra allowances out of his own income. He glorifies God in the excellent sweetness of his music, and the corresponding excellent sweetness of his life. But then we are involved with John Bold, too, the young idealist who devotes his labour, his medical skill, and his money to the public good, and we must love him for his principles. Readers sometimes observe that Bold is not a very sympathetic character, as though to imply that Trollope somehow fails there. But surely the limits of his charm are part of Trollope's scheme: Bold *is* in the right, and so the balance must be shifted away from him; Harding is in the wrong, and so must be made as attractive as all the novelist's virtuoso powers can make him. Nevertheless, we suffer with John Bold when Eleanor's logic of the heart has won out over his larger social logic, and he gives up his cause. He has then to face the dread Archdeacon who pounces on him with a loud 'Aha', saying, 'You, Bold, are giving up your cause because you haven't a leg to stand on.' Bold – and we – know his cause was good. He has also to face Tom Towers of the *Times*, and be accused of knuckling under to the forces of reaction, of 'vested wrong'. In such a way do subsidiary situations develop out of the main one. It is only by casting off the demands of conventional 'plot' that Trollope is free to exploit his situation so thoroughly. He wrings his *donnée* with the sort of relentless exuberance that characterises distinguished art. By making us take cognisance of the incongruous perspectives of this case, he makes us laugh at the absurdities into which principle and precept can lead men. And he thereby catches us and leads us directly into the difficult ethical problems of the variance between seems and is, between the motive of an action and its results, between ends and means, into some understanding of the paradoxical quality of life itself.

Trollope's contemporary, Bishop Connop Thirlwall, in his important essay on the irony of Sophocles, describes the kind of situation that obliges us to reconsider our moral biases. He moves from this into his main subject, Greek tragedy and its great moral meaning. But if we stop with him at an early point in his essay, he can help us to understand the Trollopian structure. In real life, Thirlwall says,

> Our attention [will be] anxiously fixed on a struggle in which right and wrong, truth and falsehood, virtue and vice, are manifestly arrayed in deliberate opposition against each other. But still this case, if it ever occurs, is not that on which the mind dwells with the most intense anxiety. For it seems to carry its own final decision in itself. But the liveliest interest arises when by inevitable circumstances, characters, motives, and principles are brought into hostile collision, in which good and evil are so inextricably blended on each side, that we are compelled to give an equal share of our sympathy to each while we perceive that no earthly power can reconcile them.... What makes the contrast interesting is, that the right and truth lie on neither side exclusively: that there is no fraudulent purpose, no gross imbecility of intellect: but both have plausible claims and specious reasons to allege.[3]

Fiction uses both kinds of situations, of course. Stories that use the first kind, where 'right and wrong, truth and falsehood, virtue and vice, are manifestly arrayed in deliberate opposition', draw our interest to the narrative itself. The interest of narrative in itself can be very great, and is, of course, perfectly legitimate. Fairy tales charm us; stories of a mystery, of a chase, of a pilgrim's progress, all can draw us from our work, our play, or our chimney corners. Or our interest may go beyond the mere narrative into some symbolic meaning or ritual usefulness that the narrative bodies forth. But the other kind of case, 'in which right and truth lie on neither side exclusively', is compellingly interesting in itself. In art that presents this kind of case, we do not care much about narrative *per se*. In fact, the *ficta nota* works better than the mystery; Chaucer's *Troilus*, and Shakespeare's *Julius Caesar* have always been the richer for the fact that everyone knows how they are going to turn out. Narrative is not the essential, because the two sides cannot be reconciled, and there can be no real resolution. Nobody wins. This kind of art lives on realism; for the more real we feel both sides of the case to be, the more interesting and demanding the case is. Symbolic significance or ritual elements are absolutely out of place here, because they would distract from the insistent actuality of the ambivalent case which is the centre of the work, and the point of it. Sequence of events in such a work is valuable for the new and shifting perspectives it enables the author to throw on his central situation. He catches us first, perhaps by amusing us with a case in which the moral ambivalence is striking, and then he may give us pause; for we realise some theory, some precept, some generalisation is being invalidated. And there are in this, implications of very great importance. May it be that *any* theory or precept can be invalidated, in *some* case? Any case, we realise, *may* be the insistent exception, and therefore the case demands our utmost honest – and realistic – consideration. We are ethically obliged to be, then, casuists. Casuistry is a way of dealing with the practical exigencies of real life, but I should like to propose that in Trollope's work, casuistry is also a way of art. Trollope's carefully selected and significant cases constitute his content, and they also constitute the significant form of his novels.

Let us stay yet a little with *The Warden*, for it offers not only what seems to me the supremely definitive unit of Trollopian structure, but also an extra, corroborative definition of method. At this point in his career, when he has at last discovered his bent, he seems, as it were, anxious to define it for himself. I refer to the parodies of Dickens and Carlyle. Some readers find them offensive artistically, and so proceed in kindness to assess the non-offensive parts of the book, thereby missing a point. Whether these parodies succeed or not – whether they are good as parodies and whether they are decorous – they are altogether functional. Trollope is defining, by negatives, what he himself would do.

His Carlyle, Dr. Pessimist Anticant, writes a pamphlet with the heavy-handed title 'Modern Charity', where he shows Hiram, the founder of the Hospital, as a walking angel, for he lived in the time of Abbot Samson, when all things were well; and the Warden is the typical clergyman of the present day, characterised chiefly by 'the magnitude of his appetite'. Certainly Trollope had good reason to revere the early Carlyle, and even now cannot forgo all praise; but he is chiefly anxious here to indicate Carlyle's main limitation: 'We all of us could, and many of us did, learn much from the doctor when he chose to remain vague, mysterious and cloudy; but when he became practical, the charm was gone.' Or we may say that when he got down to cases his theories did not hold. He would not recognise a certain 'fact' – 'the fact, that in this world no good is unalloyed, and that there is but little evil that has not some seed in it of what is goodly' (Chap. xv). Of course, this is still the valid objection to Carlyle: he overstates his position, and then is accordingly obliged to let the end justify the means. Trollope would be a sort of watch-dog, careful to sound the alarm if precept or principle threatens to become a tyrant. He will not let ends tyrannise over means, he insists on the significance of the exception to the generality, and he would protect the minority from the majority.

The novelist, Mr. Popular Sentiment, has, like Dr. Anticant, found in the news items from Barchester a theme for a Message. In his novel, *The Almshouse*, the Warden has become a demon:

> A man well stricken in years, but still strong to do evil: he was one who looked passionately out of a hot, passionate bloodshot eye; who had a huge red nose with a carbuncle, thick lips, and a great double, flabby chin,

and so on. On the other hand, the inmates of the hospital are wonderfully good. Such is the beauty of the sentiment in their conversation that it is

> really a pity that these eight old men could not be sent through the country as moral missionaries, instead of being immured and starved in that wretched almshouse. . . . The artist who paints for the million must use glaring colours, as no one knew better than Mr. Sentiment . . . his good poor people are so very good; his hard rich people so very hard; and the genuinely honest so very honest (Chap. xv).

Both Carlyle and Dickens, Trollope would say, work by simplifications. Carlyle, to preach his sermon, has to rely on a division of phenomena into the ideal and the fallen-off from the ideal; he 'instituted himself censor of things in general', and issued a 'monthly pamphlet on the decay of the world'. Carlyle's Sermon posits a simplistic philosophy, and Dickens' Message does the same. Accordingly, Dickens' characters are caricatures and fall into classes of Bad or Good; his ethics is caricature, too, the simplified ethics that virtue will win and vice will lose. We need not here go into the advantages and limitations of an art of simplifcation: all we need note here and now is that Trollope is declaring simplification is not his way. He has found in Barchester that single situation which demonstrates the complexities of moral problems, and this situation in itself is a refutation of the simplistic views of such as Carlyle and such as Dickens. Trollope is everywhere a complicator. Even in his *North America*, when he is trying to elucidate the issues of the Civil War for his English readers, he explains how the views current in England are false simplifications; he demonstrates the pros and cons on each side. His recurrent theme in the novels is that motives are never simple.

Wayne Booth, in his careful and tentative way, almost proposes that it is a special forte of the novel 'to give form to moral complexities'.[4] I think this should be proposed quite loudly. Morals *are* complex; and the only form they can take is that of the complicated, unique case. Because the novel is the loosest and potentially the longest of literary genres, the most permissive, it can take the shape of the unique case, no matter how involved or ambivalent or paradoxical, and no matter how unshapely the narrative that gives rise to it. Surely it is this forte of the novel that Trollope makes his own. This is, I think, what Geoffrey Tillotson indicates when he says Trollope 'masters complexity'.[5] The situation Trollope chooses is in itself a concrete diagram of a moral complexity; if the problem was put in abstract terms it might well escape us, but the problem of *The Warden* is — one might say — proved on our pulses. With dialogue and drama, along with clear and easy commentary (or 'intrusion'), Trollope can communicate the most tenuous nuances in a psychological state, or the most extreme subtleties in a social situation. He is like James in this, but he so 'masters complexity' that we hardly realise how complicated the things are that he has made us apprehend easily.

Trollope's interest in complex cases is thoroughly and frankly and insistently ethical. His tender casuistry demands the most careful, detailed consideration of the circumstances, even those of a 'crime', and it is remarkable how often circumstances tend to be condoning circumstances. There are gounds in philosophy for this circumstantiality of the novel. Bertrand Russell, for instance, taking the premise that all morality must be based on immediate moral intuitions — and I suppose we must accept the premise — has this to say:

> Circumstances are apt to generate perfectly concrete convictions: this or that, now present to me, is good or bad; and from a defect of imagination, it is impossible to judge beforehand what our moral opinions of a fact will be.

A novelist like Trollope, we may say, can remedy that 'defect of imagination'. Russell continues:

> The notion that general maxims are to be found in conscience seems to me to be a mistake fostered by the Decalogue. I should rather regard the true method of Ethics as inference from empirically ascertained facts, to be obtained in that moral laboratory which life offers to those whose eyes are open to it.[6]

Or that laboratory which, we may add, the novelist can offer. And he can offer it better than life because he can select the cases that, by invalidating general maxims, extend our understanding. The kind of novel that does this has links with various strains of nineteenth-century thought. Theorists as disparate as Emile Zola in France and George Henry Lewes in England both reprobated the separation of science and art. Science and art can both serve, it was felt, in our researches in psychology and sociology.

And there can be something like the experimental method in the novel, if it is realistic. A failure in realism is in this sense an unethical manipulation of data. Conventional plot is out of place for it may distort life processes. Once a character is established in a situation the writer must not let him act uncharacteristically for the sake of a Fourth Act crisis or a To-Be-Continued-in-the-Next-Issue cliffhanger, or a drumroll conclusion. There must be no mysteries; we must be put in command of all relevant information as soon as possible. Trollope, of all the Victorians, is the most faithful on all these counts. He will not mystify us: time and again he tells us who did the murder or whatever. He will not let Lily Dale marry Johnny Eames, because she wouldn't have. He *says* he killed Mrs. Proudie because he overheard some clubmen saying they were sick of her. But a few sentences later he tells us the truth: 'As her tyranny increased so did the bitterness of the moments of repentance increase, in that she knew herself to be a tyrant, – till *that bitterness killed her* [my italics].'[7] It is often said in deprecation that Trollope's commonest 'plot' is the ordinary courtship plot ending in a marriage. But then, one should say in the interests of scientific accuracy, that people often do marry; and one should say in the interests of ethical research that a marriage is often the shifting of a situation in which 'the right and the truth lie on neither side exclusively'; and one might say in the interests of life that courtship and marriage are rather engaging in themselves. Trollope's last chapter marriages are generally quite probable, and though they seem like conclusions they do not necessarily make a conclusive end to a novel. It is because his endings are not generally 'conclusive', that his characters can turn up in sequels, still breathing, aged to the proper degree, still unmistakably themselves. They had not been 'killed' by some sentimental change of heart, nor by some exigency of an elegant plot, nor by some pandering to a fictitious sensationalism. Life is

sensational enough. Trollope will not suppress a murder, a suicide, a mis-
carriage of justice, a seduction, a bastard, a case of sexual frigidity, a case
of syphilis, nor a neurosis or psychosis. Nor will he suppress a shabby
motive for a 'noble' action, nor the fact that a man can be 'in love' with
two women at once. Nor will he suppress the occasional emergence of
what seems very like disinterested virtue.

Trollope is as realistic or as 'scientific' as conceivable, all in the interests
of determining an ethics more serviceable than the simplistic ones of the
abstract philosophers, and of the Sunday schools. In this he is close to
George Henry Lewes, and George Eliot, but he is even closer to an older
humanism. It is not enough known that he was a good Latinist, and
especially devoted to Cicero. Of all Cicero's works he most reveres the
De Officiis, which is Cicero's closest study of ethics and which reveals a
strain that speaks to the Victorian, a sense of duty as strong as George
Eliot's: 'Duty! How peremptory and absolute!' Cicero's mode of presentation is more urbane than hers, of course, and then so is Trollope's. In the
De Officiis, Cicero himself is highly specific: he refers principle to particular cases, and for his particular cases he chooses those that are difficult —
Thirlwallian cases or moral dilemmas — where there is much to be said on
both sides. Trollope repeatedly acclaims Cicero for this, and for his consonant rejection of systematic philosophy. He says that Cicero's great achievement is that he brings us 'out of dead intellectuality into moral perception'.
And this is precisely what Trollope would do with his cases. In *The Last
Chronicle of Barset*, there is a painful situation where Josiah Crawley
seems to have betrayed his clerical calling by a base and petty crime. The
good-hearted Robarts tries to deflect those who would impose civil law or
ordinary moral maxims. 'You must look to the circumstances', he insists.
And 'You must look to the circumstances', Trollope is always insisting, in
every one of his novels. In the case of *Orley Farm*, we know that Lady
Mason has committed forgery. Sir Peregrine Orme has been her *preux che-
valier*, outraged that anybody might think it possible she might commit
such a crime. Now he knows she has, and, heart-broken, feels he must reject
her. His daughter-in-law, Mrs. Orme, pleads for her. 'In this case, though
the mind of Sir Peregrine might be the more logical, the purpose of his
daughter-in-law was stronger.' *She* leads Sir Peregrine 'out of dead intellectuality into moral perception'; she resolves that friendship will withstand
this evil.

> 'Do you mean,' said Sir Peregrine, 'that no crime would separate you
> from a friend?' 'I have not said that. *There are circumstances always*
> [my italics] . . . . I cannot bring myself to desert her' (II, vi).

The case, in all its peculiar individuated circumstances, must assert itself. This case, of a forger whom we cannot bring ourselves to condemn, constitutes the structure of *Orley Farm*.

Professor Gordon Ray in his illuminating and useful survey 'Trollope at Full Length'[8] has declared that Trollope's excellence is exercised most characteristically in his long novels. This is indubitably so; he needs the vast expanse of the three-decker filled with people and multiplying contingencies to demonstrate the circumstantiality of life and its ethical problems. But I think the short novels, having, of course, their own minor charms and interests, as Ray would agree, have also a special usefulness to the critic. . . .To see these short novels as demonstrating the Trollopian unit is to help us toward understanding the structure of the long, three-volume, multi-plotted panoramic books; they are, I propose, elaborations of this unit. The parts can be seen as congruent to each other and to the whole. *Barchester Towers*, for instance, expands the ironic case of *The Warden* into variations on the theme of Reform. In the ecclesiastical scene, the Proudies and Mr. Slope, although repulsive in themselves, are nevertheless the agents through whom will be purified the sons of Levi. The love passages comment on this theme of church reform: Eleanor's three suitors correspond to the three church parties, Arabin to the old High Church with all its traditions of decorum and learning; Slope to the new low evangelical party, even if he is merely riding the bandwagon of Reform for his own selfish ends; and Bertie Stanhope, the walking spirit of ecumenicism, scion of the Broad Church – so broad, spread so thin, that it is *no* church. In the sphere of the laity, it is the Thornes who stand for the beauty of the Old, and its absurdity, too. In religion, you recall, Miss Thorne was really a Druidess, and the Church of England as reformed by Elizabeth I was quite modernist enough for her. The Ullathorne Games are an attempt to reassert, however gently, the old social hierarchy, and they are, naturally, a gently ridiculous flop. Mrs. Proudie's Reception and the Ullathorne Games are both great climaxes in the structure of the novel, for in each there is the maximum juxtaposition of incongruities: Thirlwallian situations exfoliating and contrasting with one another in algebraic progressions of absurdity. These climactic collections of situations are the centres, the *raisons d'être* of the book, much more important than how the story turns out. At the end, with Eleanor's marriage to Arabin, the focus narrows down again to Church reform, the conflict between High and Low.

If it be essentially and absolutely necessary to choose between the two, we are inclined to agree with Mrs. Grantly that the bell, book and candle are the lesser evil of the two. *Let it however be understood* [and let me underscore this] *that no such necessity is admitted in these pages* (III, xix).

The right and truth lie on neither side exclusively.

To move with Trollope from the micro-state of Barchester to the macro-state of Whitehall, is to move from the earlier novels that falter occasionally, to the later ones where he proceeds with a greater economy, a greater sophistication, and a more delicate wit. One of his finest situations is that one in *Phineas Redux* where we find the Tory Prime Minister bringing in a bill for the Disestablishment of the Church. The situation is just possible enough: it exaggerates only a *little* the audacity of Disraeli, and the ironic fact that the most radical reforms of the nineteenth century were effected under Conservative administrations. The mature Trollope exploits this situation with elegant economy and a wonderfully witty inventiveness. First: it is in a routine election speech to his constituency that Daubeny (Disraeli) makes the proposal, a speech so beautifully obscure in its rhetoric that the electors of East Barsetshire have no idea what he is saying. They take 'more actual enjoyment from the music of his periods than from the strength of his argument'. They enjoy the references to clerical matters; the word *mitre* 'sounds pleasantly in their ears as appertaining to good old gracious times' (I, v). It is only as a double-take that the newspapers and public discover Disestablishment has been proposed. And then we have grand general consternation everywhere. London swarms with the buzz of activated and anxious clergymen. The Tory party is in an agony of strained loyalties: shall the Tory member vote to support the party he loves, and thereby support this flashy 'Cagliostro' whom he inclines to distrust even though he keeps the party in power? And shall he thereby vote against the Establishment he stands for? And then there is the suffering Opposition, absolutely dished by this cruel move which takes Reform out of the hands of those whose proprietary interest it is. Shall the Liberal member vote against this bill, in loyalty to his party and in the hopes of turning out the Tory administration so that *his* party will then be in power and proceed with Reform? And shall he thereby vote against a measure which takes a grand step toward the ideal society he strives for? The wily Daubeny asks: is it not best that reform of the church be by our means who best revere her? And, of course, he can accuse the Opposition of a great lack of principle and an unseemly lust for power. Trollope delays the narrative and explores the repercussions of this pregnant situation, thereby exploring the nature of man as political animal. He discovers in actualities those truths Walter Bagehot discovers in theory in *The English Constitution*: that there must, for instance, be a degree of party loyalty or parliament simply cannot achieve anything; and whenever there is a degree of party loyalty there is a degree of personal integrity sacrificed. This is the abiding great problem of the relation of truth to politics that Hannah Arendt has recently reappraised.[9] Trollope's service is that he demonstrates the relationship so dynamically, in terms of such a variety of irresistibly interesting people, that we cannot help but grow in political understanding.

The two *Phineas Finn* novels are that part of Trollope's work which might be classified structurally as a loose sort of *Bildungsroman*. And yet I think that they too, like the other novels, are best considered as situation-structured. So considered, they are really not very loose. For this grand situation of the Tory bill for Disestablishment is the extension of Phineas' own problem of adjusting his honesty to political usefulness. One minor but related situation, for example, finds Phineas standing for a rotten borough so that he can get into Parliament so that he can effect the abolition of rotten boroughs. And then, in his complicated love-life, we see him so obstinately and contrarily honest as to demand from one discarded sweetheart the warm sympathy and help he wants to win the new one. All these related anomalous situations comment on one another and together constitute a cogent form for the novel.[10]

The ethical ends of Trollope's art appear to be best served by his situation-structure. His concern is always moral, and he is always recommending, by means of his cases, a more flexible morality. His stance is that of what we now call Situation Ethics, and I propose that he has a corresponding Situation Aesthetics. His ethics and his aesthetics, that is, are functions of each other, both turning on casuistry. The art of it makes us see the uniqueness of character in circumstances, and the end of it is moral perception. It is a very satisfactory thing that the means to this end is so delightful that we can take the means for end, and the end still achieves itself.

One of the incidental pleasures of the novels is Trollope's postively virtuoso display of a variety of lawyers in action. His interest in lawyers and the law, however, is not really incidental, but a significanct aspect of his Situation Ethics. The lawyer is on principle dedicated to the uniqueness of cases. Trollope shares with Cicero a sense of the law as the imperfect but best human effort to implement the excellent idea of Justice, which Cicero saw as though innate and as the omen that man is, after all, worth troubling with. There is in both Cicero and Trollope a consequent ultimate optimism about human destiny, in spite of all appearances. Appearances were bad enough in Cicero's time, as Trollope points out, when everything of the old republican tradition and everything of political honesty was doomed. For Trollope, the vision of society in *The Way We Live Now* is bad enough: he sees how prevalent is our willingness to come to terms with evil, if there is something in it for us. And yet it is his idea that even the worst of us has a right to an advocate, and his legal cases are only more technically casuistic than his other cases. In *Orley Farm*, Lady Mason commits forgery out of love for her son. In her worst agonies of guilt, she pleads (or Trollope does) that she has put her son ahead of the safety of her soul. Trollope displays at least twenty perspectives on the relation of law to justice in this case, each one viable because each one is in terms of the view of an actualised character. The later novel *Mr. Scarborough's Family* is a marvellously manoeuvred case where law and justice run quite at odds. And yet Mr. Scarborough who so deliberately and cleverly perverts the law to his own ends is not all bad, is admirable in his *virtù*, and is motivated by a kind of extra-legal sense of justice. We follow the touching disillusionment of lawyer Grey, who had dedicated himself to the law in the faith that it does indeed march with justice. In *Phineas Redux*, there is what Harold Laski called the best murder trial in modern literature. Phineas, whom we know to be not only innocent but a man who is the least liable to commit a crime, is accused of a vengeful and brutal murder. The great criminal lawyer, Chaffanbrass, manipulates the Court, and ourselves, with such eloquence that we cannot believe anyone there present could any longer have any doubt whatsoever as to Phineas' innocence; and then we see Chaffanbrass retired to a little room, exhausted and old in the service of the law, brooding on what he thinks to be the 'fact' of Phineas' guilt. So curious are the processes of this man-made institution the law; such may be the wisdom in the odd principle that the lawyer's belief in his client's innocence is irrelevant to his duty as advocate. We see justice done: Phineas is released and exonerated. But we see him far from joyful. The bitterness of his ordeal has left him in a depression, incapacitated for a while at least. Justice at best is not enough to alleviate the soreness of man's cruelty to man.

Trollope and the law is a subject that has been studied closely and lovingly by those distinguished lawyers who have been Trollopians. For us, the point of it might be put this way: it is Trollope's art to be advocate for each one of his characters; he makes the best case possible for one, and then juxtaposes this with the demands of the other, defended with a similar passionate sympathy. His art is distinguished by largeness of view, encompassing the conflicting claims of all his people and of society. His great achievement, often just called being 'good at characterisation', may be really that he communicates his characters' sense of self. It is his own lively sense of the uniqueness of personality that not only makes him a great artist of character but also leads him to his Situation Ethics. And this is really another name for the old humanistic idea of man as the measure of things. So it is that Trollope presents life always in terms of human beings all with claims nearly as valid as one's own. His art is responsible to society; his novels, being organised according to specific challenging cases, do in fact implement a casuistic ethics. The old idea of Trollope as a purveyor of escape will hardly do; if there is a logical opposite to *escape*, that is what Trollope's novels are. He takes us into the centre of life, obliging us to recognise incongruities, forcing the appreciation of the dilemma. The novels are, in a way, more demanding than life itself generally is, and in reading them one as it were flexes one's moral entity and exercises one's humanity.

NOTES

1. John H. Hagan, 'The Divided Mind of Anthony Trollope', *Nineteenth-Century Fiction*, XIII (June 1959) 1–26.
2. A. O. J. Cockshut, *Anthony Trollope: A Critical Study* (London, Wm. Collins Sons, 1955; New York, New York University Press, 1968).
3. 'On the Irony of Sophocles', *The Philological Museum*, II 1833 483–537.
4. *The Rhetoric of Fiction* (Chicago, 1961), p. 188.
5. 'Trollope's Style', *Mid-Victorian Studies*, pp. 56–61.
6. *Autobiography* (Boston, Little, Brown, 1967), p. 253
7. *Autobiography* (London, Allen & Unwin, 1967), pp. 230–1.
8. *Huntington Library Quarterly*, XXXI (August 1968), 313–40.
9. 'Reflections: Truth and Politics', *New Yorker*, February 25, 1967, pp. 49–88.
10. Jerome Thale, in 'The Problem of Structure in Trollope', *Nineteenth-Century Fiction*, XIV (Sep., 1960), 147–57, demonstrates unity by theme and variation. He is especially acute when he asseses the effect of the novels as 'reminding us of the complexity of human affairs, of urging tolerance, of making us wary of simple views and monisms' (p. 157). As Thale says, however, mere thematic unity can hardly explain such an effect (note p. 156). Only when it is supplemented by a grasp of case-structure can one see the connection between technique and effect.

JAMES GINDIN
Trollope*

The principal problem in almost all Trollope's later work, from *The Last Chronicle of Barset* (1867) to *Ayala's Angel* is that of judgment, of learning to understand and evaluate the worth of all the varying issues and individuals one sees around him. Sometimes, as in *The Way We Live Now*, the questions of judgment are posed for the reader, leaving him skeptical and wondering if any clear guides for conduct can be extrapolated from the experience of the novel. At other times, Trollope (fairly early in the novels) gives the reader the standards on which the characters are to be judged, establishes a kind of ideal, but then depicts a world in which no one understands the issues as the author does, in which everyone, at least for a time, misjudges a central character or situation. This latter kind of novel, less completely skeptical than the other, still underlines the tremendous difficulty involved in establishing any applicable guide for ethical conduct. In *The Prime Minister*, for example, Trollope plants sufficient clues concerning Lopez' unprincipled exploitation of others early in the novel, but we gradually discover how and when the rest of society will see through him. The interest is in the process of coming to know, rather than in the suspense of what is to be known. Captain Marrable in *The Vicar of Bullhampton* is also a shadowy figure for rather a long period of time. Are his complaints about his father justified or is he really a character dominated by indolent self-pity? Is he really worth all the devotion Mary Lowther is willing to grant him? In this instance, the reader has no guide, knows no more than the several different characters through whose perspective he sees Marrable, until Trollope finally focuses on the essential worth of the man. Similarly, in the same novel, Trollope allows us to wonder foɪ a long time about young Carry Brattle, to ask whether her 'sin' was a single and understandable event or a symptom of callous rebellion against family

* From *Harvest of a Quiet Eye: The Novel of Compassion* (Bloomington, Ind. and London: Indiana University Press, 1971), pp. 47–57. Reprinted by permission of Indiana University Press and of the author.

and society, before he finally demonstrates his conviction that her flaw
has been minute in comparison with the kind of inhumanity man gets
away with every day. The whole texture of *The Way We Live Now* is one
of misjudgment, and emphasizes our inability to use any known gauge to
measure the worth of the characters in the novel. Financial and social
reputations are governed by rumor and half-apprehended hint; the origins
and principles of Melmotte are unknown; trusted people in responsible
positions suddenly vanish with other people's money; Mrs. Hurtle has been
violent and scheming, but we wonder if she really did kill a man and, more
significantly, could kill another if provoked sufficiently. Even the kind of
character supposedly easy to peg, the spoiled and indolent young aristocrat,
is hard to judge, for the two principal examples in the novel, Adolphus
Longestaff and young Lord Nidderdale, turn out to be very different from
each other and Lord Nidderdale is far from the original cliché. In a novel
in which almost everyone changes character, shifts opinions and convictions,
only gradually discovers what he is and what his motives are, the dominant
impression is that of the great difficulty and loneliness the sensible person
undergoes in trying to find his way through contemporary experience.

Ayala's Angel, which depicts an apparently more ordered world than
does *The Way We Live Now*, also deals primarily with the problems of
judging character. Ayala is always looking for an 'Angel of Light', rejecting
mundane young men who do not fit her romantic preconceptions. For a
long time, Trollope satirizes her, pointing out that a spirited horse she has
been given to ride comes closer than any man to her idea of the 'Angel of
Light'. Her preconception is also shallow, for she initially rejects Jonathan
Stubbs because he is physically unattractive, even though she acknowledges
that he has the wit and intelligence she associates with her romantic dream
figure. Yet Ayala does learn, and eventually realizes that an 'Angel of
Light' can wear bristling red whiskers. In this instance Trollope lampoons
exaggerated romanticism, although he defends the basic assumption of the
romantic heroine that the young lady should wait for the truly superior
young man who will stir her soul. Ayala waits and is rewarded. Yet, in
other instances in the same novel, the whole attitude of the romantic
heroine seems dubious. Ayala is frequently played off against her rather
unattractive cousin, Gertrude Tringle. Gertrude suggests to her first lover,
Frank Houston, that he overcome her family's objection by eloping with
her to Ostend. When Frank refuses (as he also ignores her instructions to
address all letters to her by unnecessarily mysterious means), Gertrude
makes the elopement to Ostend the central issue of the relationship with
her next suitor, Captain Batsby. She is more interested in the romantic
fiction than in the man himself, and Trollope points out Gertrude's pathetic

folly, that she simply isn't attractive enough or clever enough to afford the romantic role. The romantic attitude is a luxury in a world that grants graces and wisdom in unequal portions. Gertrude, like her brother, Tom, is the victim of both nature and an unwise mother, and must finally settle for a relationship in which her romantic assumptions are bound to be demolished repeatedly. Yet formulating the final judgment on Ayala and Gertrude takes time, consumes a major portion of the novel. In ways, *Ayala's Angel* is an elaborate and extensive treatment of a central question: under what conditions is fidelity to romantic attitudes possible and desirable? With his acute sense of the way the world operates, his recognition that justice seldom exists in society but that people do have a limited control over their own fortunes, and his genuine compassion for the people he describes, Trollope concentrates far more on the possible than on the desirable.

Trollope, in the later novels, places far more emphasis on man's accepting what he has to accept than on his establishing ethical principles that apply universally. And because man, half-ignorant and prone to mistakes, has to accept his world out of necessity, Trollope maintains a sense of compassion toward most human creatures. Especially toward the end of his career, the compassion dominates the novels, dominates them in direct proportion to the recognition that a meaningful code of virtue cannot be followed and applied within the unjust world. Compassion is a matter of emphasis, an attitude that fills the void left by all the codes, guides, and formulae that are inadequate for human experience. In the perspective of Trollope's later novels, only the very wise and the very fortunate could make their way successfully through a world that offered unequal possibilities. Man had no power to change his world, and, even if he had, he had no assurance that the changes would not involve inequities at least as great, or conditions that would destroy just as many individuals. He could only accept, follow whatever forms of order he could see and apply, remain resilient, and sympathize.

This kind of compassion was not entirely new with Trollope, for English poetry and drama have particularized it as far back as Chaucer's attitude toward those of his pilgrims whose characters did not fit their occupations in the highly stratified and schematized medieval society, or Shakespeare's feeling toward the historically doomed Trojans in *Troilus and Cressida*, or the humanity toward Shylock which leaks through and saturates the structure of *The Merchant of Venice*. Even in the early novel, generally molded more by the instructive lesson than was the drama, writers like Jane Austen had substituted compassion for what they could not justify as truth. Yet, in Trollope's world, the emphasis on compassion

increased, accelerated, as the attempt to provide lessons or guides for
conduct became increasingly difficult to sustain.

The novel of compassion frequently relies on a density of social characterization, a completeness in describing man and his environment, both to
demonstrate the world's complexity and to fill the space left by the lack
of a universal truth. In addition, Trollope, like other novelists of compassion, is often at his best in developing an extended relationship between
people, another fictional richness appropriate to the novel that conveys no
abstract message. If there is little discernible 'truth' about man, little that
can be labeled his fundamental nature, the novelist is likely to study his
characters in combinations in order to demonstrate their variety and
complexity. The self, since it expresses little essential truth, can be known
only in its actions and combinations. Trollope writes most skillfully and
profoundly when describing his characters interacting with one another,
each helping to define and illuminate the other. The relationship between
the Duke of Omnium and his Duchess, Lady Glencora, for example, is
rich, complex, and humane. Lady Glencora had originally stayed with the
Duke, in defiance of her love for Burgo Fitzgerald, because of the pressure
of society and propriety. The pressure, in part, made the marriage work,
and the constant memory of this makes the Duke, after Lady Glencora has
died, apply so much pressure on his daughter to try to force her to follow
his will. Yet Trollope deliberately avoids the generalization. The kind of
pressure that is desirable and that works in one instance is both undesirable
and ineffective in another; people and circumstances differ. This realization
of complexity allows Trollope to trace the constant shuttling, the constant
turns of position and attitude that go on within a marriage. He carefully
develops the marriage of the Duke and the Duchess from its arranged
beginnings in *Can You Forgive Her?*, through storms and the establishment
of mutual although distant respect, to the genuine love and concern in
The Prime Minister. By the time of *The Prime Minister*, the last novel in
which the Duchess appears, each partner feels and acts as almost part of
the other, absorbing the other's reactions to a given situation or person
into his own. They incorporate each other's attitude toward the Duke's
becoming Prime Minister, switching sides several times as the Duchess
develops some of the Duke's reticence and desire for quiet while he adopts
something of her zest (although in entirely different terms) for pursuing a
job to its conclusion. The Fenwicks, the principal couple of *The Vicar of
Bullhampton*, comprise another of Trollope's close marriages in which
each partner adopts something of the other and learns, in part, to think
through the other's perspective. Man, in Trollope's world, is both more
visible and more humane in combination with others.

Human connections are, of course, not confined simply to those involved in marriage. *Ayala's Angel*, for example, also depicts along with numerous marriages, other familial relationships, such as that of two orphaned sisters. Lucy and Ayala Dormer are constantly defined through each other and against each other, and easy polarities of the differences between the sisters frequently change. The supposedly quiet sister (Lucy) is less happy in and less adjusted to the quiet life of the Dosetts; the more vivacious and social sister (Ayala) is really, at first, less sure of herself in society. Man's connections with institutions and conventions also change constantly, frequently in ironic and unexpected ways. Lord Silverbridge is originally provided with good reasons for deserting his father's Liberal allegiances and becoming a Conservative, even if the young lord does not fully understand the reasons he announces. When he later returns to the Liberal party, he is unable to offer any reasons, although, as a person, he has become far more forceful and independent. In an ironic way, he has become enough a man not to insist on having his own political opinion.

In *Ayala's Angel*, Lady Tringle, Lucy Dormer's aunt, objects to Lucy's connection with Isadore Hamel, the improvident young sculptor. And Isadore's father, also a sculptor, objects to the connection equally. Were the son willing to live a Bohemian life in Rome, the father would gladly support him, but the elder Hamel refuses to grant a penny to a son anxious to engage in a conventional and respectable marriage. Sir Thomas Tringle, superficially more vulgar and more interested in money than is his social-climbing wife, is at first willing to take a more generous view of young Hamel and his art, willing to try to help the young couple. A benevolent Philistine, Sir Thomas tries to work out ways in which Isadore's art might become commercially profitable. Yet, Isadore is intransigent, refusing to consider a change from vast allegorical figures to busts of people who will pay for them. Furthermore, he even refuses to defend his ideas or explain them to Sir Thomas. As Trollope brilliantly delineates the situation, the businessman's Philistine attitudes are exactly matched by the artist's priggishness. Each has, in his own terms, relevant motives for his own attitudes, yet no understanding or communication is possible. As the novel develops, Isadore's intransigence gradually lessens and he becomes more tolerant of conventional attitudes toward art. He does not become corrupt (again, Trollope always guards against the possibility of sweeping judgments) and he still under any circumstances would marry the girl he loves, but he does voluntarily turn from his allegorical Bacchus to more mundane and marketable forms of sculpture. Ideas, in Trollope never fixed or dominant, are always used to explain the motives or the attitudes of complex and changing characters.

Trollope's novels despite occasional prescriptive insertions are generally descriptive, emphasizing what man is and calling for compassion because man is not other than he is. Often Trollope and Dickens seem to be subscribing to the same values: love, humanity, genuine emotions, the importance of the individual in contrast to an indifferent or hostile society, values that can be connected with the Romantic movement. But they express these values in very different ways.

For Dickens, humanity or the importance of emotion is a truth, an essence, an idea, and the whole novel is bent to the structure of the reigning truth, molded to demonstrate the idea. In *Bleak House*, Esther represents the 'truth' — Richard Carstone, Lady Dedlock, Horace Skimpole, various different errors. Appropriately, Esther gains a happy ending — relief from her suffering and the perfect mate — while the other three are shunted off to the death or disaster they have earned. We are left with a feeling of justice, no matter how difficult for man the terms may be.

In Trollope's fiction, on the other hand, the humanity or the importance of emotion is part of a point of view that may or may not work out in the world of the novel; the characters who represent the point of view may win or lose, may be justified or not, may be defeated and have to accept defeat for all the wrong reasons, like Marie Melmotte or Mrs. Hurtle. Dickens does, at times, portray victims of injustice with whom we sympathize; almost always, however, these are children crippled, twisted, or otherwise determined by the forces that surround them. Only children living out the destiny others' mistakes have established for them can be the victims in a world in which following the 'truth' in the author's terms can enable grown men and women to survive. Trollope, unlike Dickens, has almost no interest in children as such, no fictional purpose for the creature who cannot possibly make meaningful choices. In Trollope's world, everyone can make ethical choices, can try to determine his own end, although the connection between the freely made choice and the result may well be far from anything the individual intended or anticipated. Trollope's world is more free and flexible than Dickens', but it is ultimately more mysterious, more chaotic, less amenable to human understanding or control.

Another way of stating the difference between the two authors is to point out that Dickens, despite all his objections to the church and other institutions, is a Christian writer. His perspective becomes a world view, a morality, a kind of guiding principle, although that principle is not necessarily in agreement with the hierarchical and organized principles of much conventional nineteenth century English Christianity. In addition, in Dickens' world, 'the sins of the fathers are visited upon the children', actions have invariable consequences, and the world seems to operate on a fixed principle behind all the visible complexity. Trollope's world is far more accidental. He often prefers the very same virtues, the same emotion and human responsiveness, but these are seldom made into principles or guiding forces in the non-metaphysical universe he depicts. Despite all his piety, Trollope finally does not establish a world that operates on any principle beyond itself, does not develop a Christian universe. Compassion becomes an attitude in the fictional world that is unsystematized and unregulated, becomes a substitute for the metaphysical assurance man seeks without finding.

The prose techniques of the two authors also reflect the difference in their perspectives. Dickens frequently takes an image – the fog in *Bleak House* or the empty wind in *Martin Chuzzlewit* – and makes it dominant in the novel, repeating, developing, inventing, until the image comes to organize the life of the entire novel. For Trollope, imagery is momentary and never structural, used to explain an idea, or, at most, encapsulate a scene the point of which is likely to be reversed in a subsequent scene. Trollope's imagery is certainly less interesting than Dickens', is far closer to the cliché or the little moralistic proverb, and it never extends, never proliferates to explain anything further than itself. Dickens' language, like his thematic principle, coheres to provide an intricate but ordered cosmos which man can know. Trollope's language is bits and pieces, separate facts, conversations, points like tiny individual men in a cosmos never really knowable.

This is consistent with Trollope's concentration on men and women, on character, on depicting human beings the way he saw them, for he claimed in *An Autobiography* that drawing character was his greatest skill, although he attempted to provide models for behavior. *An Autobiography* recognized the contrast with Dickens, for Trollope, after complaining that Dickens' characters were not human beings (and Trollope's criticism was always sufficiently unsophisticated to make this his major reason for devaluing Dickens), went on to say, 'It has been the peculiarity and the marvel of this man's power, that he has invested his puppets with a charm that has enabled him to dispense with human nature.' Trollope did not see that the charm is partly that of having established a system, a coherent world in terms of which all experience can be explained and understood. Lacking such a system himself, Trollope concentrated on the individual, the particular, the man within a society that had no consistent guides for conduct, no justice, no God beyond itself.

In the later novels, Trollope's satire is seldom that of the elevated point of view looking down on all the follies and errors of the world, of the

positive answer scoring off the negative examples. Rather, his comic point
of view embodies frequent switches of character and perspective, develop-
ments of one side of human nature until that hardens and can then be
turned to demonstrate the other side, and juxtapositions that indicate
man is not the wise, purposeful creature he likes to think himself. Trollope,
describing the human being within the hypocritical society he has himself
created, concentrated on the difference between man's aspirations and his
achievements, between his illusions and his nature. With all the comedy,
all the development of the sometimes ludicrous differences in human
behavior, the tone remained almost always gentle, sympathetic, aware that
man would be much more than he is, never militant or strident, because
Trollope recognized that saying 'man would be more than he is' is different
from saying 'man should be more than he is'. Comedy works on such
differences, on inconsistency, on the juxtaposition between unlike people
or events. Some comic writers, Swift for example, or Evelyn Waugh, fill
the space between the differences with mockery, with a sharp and bitter
sense of human inadequacy. Other comic writers, like Trollope, fill the
spaces with a gentle version of the attitude of compassion.

Trollope's kind of compassion, particularly in the work of his last fifteen
years, seldom degenerates into sentimentality, is seldom shallow or superficially comforting. Rather, the later work gives an extensive and profound
description of man as he relates to and operates in his social setting. The
acute problems of man himself and man in society are depicted, despite all
the gentle comedy and some of the apparently smooth resolutions. If, at
times, the acceptance of society seems shallow or the conviction that it is
impossible to change man and society seems shoddily developed or senti-
mentally conservative, still Trollope's acceptances and resolutions never
obscure the relevance of the questions he poses, as well as the fact that
the questions have no complete or fully satisfactory answer. As in a
great deal of fiction, from Jane Austen's to that of numerous twentieth
century contemporaries, the questions are far more memorable than
the resolutions. And, in Trollope's fiction, the range of the questions,
the skepticism, prevents sentimentality. The resolutions become the graceful and compassionate means of emphasizing that, for most people, for all
save the accidentally fortunate, the difficult questions – the social and
personal displacements, the injustices – really have no answer.

DAVID SKILTON
Trollopian Realism*

Any description of Trollopian realism must account for a central paradox
in his novels: that of all novels they are the most 'social', in the sense of
depending on the interaction of sets of persons, and of creating a supremely
convincing illusion of a functioning fictional community; and yet that an
examination of any of the novels will show how very significant a proportion of the book concerns the situation of a single character, alone, so that
such portions must either be irrelevant to the rest of the novel, or much of
the action must take place at the level of the individual and not society. A
second paradox emerges during an examination of the first, and that is
that the compelling illusion of reality is produced not by a specially intimate
connection with the world the reader inhabits, but by a technique of
including as many of the rules of operation of the fictional world as
possible in the novel itself, to obviate the necessity of constant and
disturbing reference to a world outside it. There is in fact less need for
reference from the world of a Trollope novel to the real world, than from
much other fiction.

One of the basic assumptions underlying Trollopian realism is that
for the sake of 'truth to life', fictional characters should be neither wholly
good nor wholly bad, but always 'mixed'. Trollope justified this type of
character on moral grounds, arguing that its didactic effect was greater.[1]
His interest in 'mixed' characters is not particularly original, nor does it
display in origin any specially profound psychological insight; but this
does not prevent it from forming the basis of an exceedingly interesting
fiction, of great social significance. The choice of imperfect heroes, sympathetic villains, and all manner of characters neither purely good nor bad
has been so extensively documented for over a century now, that there is

* From *Anthony Trollope and His Contemporaries* (London: Longman;
New York: St Martin's Press, 1972), abridged by the author from pp.
138–48. Reprinted by permission of the Longman Group Ltd and of the
author.

no need to demonstrate it again here. Certain of its implications, however, have been largely ignored.

The first of these implications is that 'natural justice' is now possible without theotechny, both on the social level, and within the individual character, who having (except in the cases of Mr Harding, Lizzie Eustace, and some of the characters in *The Way We Live Now*) conflicting impulses and standards, frequently judges himself, and condemns himself to mental torture, as Mark Robarts, Lady Mason, Julia Brabazon, Cousin Henry and John Caldigate do, to name but a few. Even Trollope's 'social justice' can operate better on mixed characters, who have something to lose, such as Julia Brabazon, again.[2]

The second and more important consequence of the mixed character is that much of the important action in a novel – which always in Trollope depends on moral decision and dilemma – is automatically played out at two levels, parallel to those on which 'natural justice' works – the social level of interaction between persons, and the private level of solitary debate with the self. The former has often been discussed, nowhere better than in R. H. Hutton's *Spectator* reviews such as that of *The Small House at Allington*,[3] while the private level has been curiously neglected, Hutton for instance complaining that Trollope did not take us 'into the world of solitary feeling at all'.[4] Most of this mental action takes place in internal monologues, consisting mainly of narrative report, which from time to time slips into direct speech, reported speech, or *erlebte Rede*. As these monologues always concern an individual's dilemma *vis-à-vis* a situation which has already been fully presented in narrative or summary, and as the individual's thoughts are therefore limited to these facts already known to the reader – usually events which have occurred within the action of the novel itself, and not even before the start of the first chapter – the reader can easily mistake the often long passages of internal debate for repetitive summary; although this is to mistake their function and structural importance. They can be long – several pages is not exceptional, or even half a chapter – and hence Trollope has been accused of tedious and unscrupulous padding. It is true that many of these passages are far less entertaining than his dialogue – there is less humour, for example, to enliven them – and if Trollope lacks any stylistic resource that his fiction seems to demand, it is a method of presenting these internal debates without slowness or repetition. He has a problem which the modern writer would probably solve by a 'stream of consciousness' technique.

There are various interesting narrative words used when a character is thinking in this way, to present his 'ideas, as expressed to himself in these long unspoken soliloquies' (*He Knew He Was Right*, Chap. lxxxiv). In her review of *Ayala's Angel* in the *Spectator*, Miss Dillwyn (herself a novelist) complains of 'Mr. Trollope's fondness for making people "tell", "teach", "encourage", or "bring" themselves to think this, that, or the other'; and she comments: 'It is a mode of expression which is excellent and effective in suitable places, but which loses its force, and becomes a mere mannerism, if constantly used where the various tenses of the verb "to think" would do equally well, without any "teaching", "telling", "educating", or "bringing".'[5] While accepting Miss Dillwyn's observation, I cannot agree with her adverse judgment, for in *Ayala's Angel* as elsewhere, these words are essential to Trollope's presentation of his characters' internal conflicts.

In the first half of *The Small House at Allington*, 'To teach oneself' occurs ten times, and 'to tell oneself' and its synonyms at least twenty, while such expressions as 'he argued the matter . . . within his own mind' (I, xii) are found some thirteen times in the same thirty chapters. There are in addition at least twenty-seven cases of characters deciding to control their own thoughts, and they or the narrator use intentional words to express this resolve. For example, after Crosbie has announced to Lily the need to delay their marriage for two years, she says to her sister, 'Don't talk to me, Bell . . . I'm trying to make myself quiet, and I half feel that I should get childish if I went on talking. I have almost more to think of than I know how to manage.' Then the narrator reports on her mental activity on going to bed:

And she had great matter for thinking; so great, that many hours sounded in her ears from the clock on the stairs before she brought her thoughts to a shape that satisfied herself. She did so bring them at last, and then she slept. She did so bring them, toiling over her work with tears that made her pillow wet, with heart-burning and almost with heart-breaking, with much doubting, and many anxious, eager inquiries within her own bosom as to that which she ought to do, and that which she could endure to do. But at last her resolve was taken, and then she slept. (I, xv).

This mental action is just as central to the whole action of the book as Lily's actual offer to set Crosbie free, later in the chapter, and is also essential to her characterization, since so much depends on her strong-minded resolves.

Again, a few chapters later, Crosbie has just completed a letter to Lily:

As he had waxed warm with his writing he had forced himself to be affectionate, and, as he flattered himself, frank and candid. Nevertheless, he was partly conscious that he was preparing for himself a mode of escape . . . I do not intend to say that he wrote with a premeditated intention of thus using his words [as an escape at some future time]; but as he wrote them he could not keep himself from reflecting that they might be used in that way. (I. xviii)

Here, in a passage of typically Trollopian insight, we find the language of self-persuasion ('forced himself', 'flattered himself', 'could not keep himself from reflecting') associated with semi-conscious motivation, which is described in almost Freudian terms. There are numerous cases of such unconscious or semi-conscious motivation in Trollope, frequently connected with the writing of letters, as though the act of letter-writing allowed the narrator more time to analyse such things than the fleeting act of speech did. The most striking example of all occurs in *Castle Richmond*, when Lady Desmond has written to her daughter, while subconsciously remembering how she had renounced all hope of Owen Fitzgerald's love so that her daughter might have him:

'My anxiety has been only for your welfare, [she writes] to further which I have been willing to make any possible sacrifice.' Clara when she read this did not know what sacrifice had been made, nor had the countess thought as she wrote the words what had been the sacrifice to which she had thus alluded, though her heart was ever conscious of it, unconsciously. (III, xiv)

But of all the novels, *The Small House* is one of those most occupied with mental struggles, and is thus most rich in striking examples of internal debates, mainly belonging to Lily, Johnny and Crosbie. Thus Trollope's concern with internal monologue not only has an important structural function, in providing a double plane of action, but has definite stylistic consequences as well, which deserve further investigation elsewhere.

A feature of Trollope's narrative which is almost necessarily connected with his use of internal monologue is the usually very simple chronology of the events recounted, by which nothing can feature in a character's thoughts which has not already been narrated before, so far is Trollope from using these monologues for narrative 'flashback'. Nearly everything a character thinks about is composed of events which have been part of the action of the novel, and everything else from an earlier past has been filled in as each character has been introduced, so that in this sense the novels are strictly unidirectional and self-enclosed. 'I would wish to have no guessing, and shall therefore proceed to tell all about it' (*The Bertrams*, opening to Chap. xiii) might be taken as Trollope's rule for more than just the avoidance of surprises, for it is his normal rule deliberately and openly to provide every particle of information that the reader needs in order to understand the events of the novel, and the interactions, conversations and thoughts of the characters, as they occur; and, in recounting things chronologically, he keeps the horse strictly before the cart, as he puts it in *The Duke's Children* (I, ix). As a result, to fulfil both these conditions, he must start off his novels with summary accounts of the past lives and so on of the chief characters, and every time he introduces a new person, he pauses to fill in the newcomer's background, sometimes, as with Mr Arabin in *Barchester Towers*, taking a full chapter to do so. These accounts partake very much of the nature of definitions, and very frequently end with a sentence like 'Such was Mr. Arabin, the new vicar of St. Ewald, who is going to stay with the Grantlys, at Plumstead Episcopi' (II, i). Similar sentences are found in most of the novels, right up to *The Landleaguers*, and signal the switch back from description to action again, once the process of making the character 'stand before the reader's eye' (*ibid.*) is complete. At this point the reader is in a position to understand all the future conduct, speech and thought of the character in question, so that a reading of the novel follows the same logical order as its composition, beginning with fully formed characters, which precede the action.

Writing from a vivid mental picture of a number of characters, whose personalities and interactions largely determine the course of the story, Trollope finally arrives at a working model of society; but it is not a total model. He prefers to describe the old vertical divisions of society into interest groups, rather than recognize the existence of classes in the modern sociological sense; and he is indeed staunch in his support of the interdependence of the gentry, their tenants and labourers, and the local tradespeople too, because this is the basis of the traditional rural society as he likes to see it. He omits industrial towns almost entirely from his model, and shows only a very small part of the life and work of the numerous class of servants who enable the lives of the gentry and aristocracy to be maintained. The tip of the iceberg that we can see consists of the interactions between master and servant, usually in matters outside daily routine, at times of crisis and so on, as well as the role of the servant class in conveying information, and retailing rumour: that is, servants as objects of the social perceptions of the higher classes, as the machinery whereby certain specific ends are achieved, and as an indication of the standing, prosperity and reputation of a family or individual. But in general they are seen very little in their own family lives.

It is not necessary, on the other hand, to prove at length the remarkable accuracy of the picture of upper- and middle-class society that Trollope conveys. This has been shown many times before, but it cannot be better demonstrated than with reference to F. M. L. Thompson's *English Landed Society in the Nineteenth Century*.[6] The reader of Trollope who opens this excellent study is struck by what Henry James called 'the surprise of recognition'. With everything that Thompson describes, the reader of Trollope is already familiar: the country estates, the location of the seats, the wealthy magnates, the less opulent squires, the parvenus of various ranks, the methods of estate management, the great aristocratic entertainments, the sale of land, the problems of entail and inheritance, and the striving for social status through land-ownership — all these things are in Trollope with an accuracy that is startling when one considers that he was an observer within the society, not a disinterested student of it from without. The fact that on reading Thompson one need not change the picture of nineteenth-century landed society that one has gathered from Trollope, or even very much alter the relative stress and emphasis given to each fact, is surely proof of the adequacy of Trollope's model of that social area.

The question that has interested Trollope's critics most, both in his own day and now, concerns how his novels work so well, and without any apparent fuss create such a perfect illusion of reality. Underlying this perplexity, I suspect, there is an important but unspoken assumption about the relationship of Trollope's novels — or, rather, the fictional worlds of Trollope's novels — to the real world. Because the illusion is so perfect, and — at the social level at least — the involvement of the reader so inexplicably complete, it has been assumed that therefore the world of a given novel is not only equivalent to reality in some way, but that it exists at a level particularly close to 'objective reality', or in a particularly close relationship to the real world. It is not sufficient to point out Trollope's factual accuracy on specific points. The phenomena of his fictional world are in one-one correspondence with those of the real world, and organized in much the same way as the phenomena of the real world can be .organized — indeed, rather in the way in which we normally do order the facts of our worlds (taught in this partly by our literature). But this correspondence does not imply that the fictional world is any the less an artistic construct, although the illusion of reality has usually directed attention away from one of the most important features of Trollopian realism — its independence, or autarky: in the sense that all the rules by which the fictional world runs, and the rules by which the reader can make moral and other judgments on the events of that world, are built into the book itself. Because these rules are in both cases generally valid in the readers' real worlds as well (or were, a hundred years ago) Trollope is a realist. We find his novels very substantial and comprehensible even in their presentation of, say, moral dilemmas we no longer share or fully understand, because we are taught by the narrator how to interpret what is happening.

The result is that the narrative presence of Trollope's persona in the novels is essential to their illusion, and not damaging to it. (It would in any case be absurd to discuss a Trollope novel without the narrator.) There is certainly one sort of authorial intrusion which does threaten the coherence of the work by admitting that it is fiction, but there are fewer of these harmful intrusions than is often supposed. They are different in kind from the narrative comments and that constant narrative presence which provide the stability and completeness of the fictional world, by stopping the reader going outside the book for his terms of reference. The narrative comments are often overtly didactic, but should not be seen as a moral additive, nor as the 'philosophic pill' which the fiction has to gild. They may sometimes be imperfectly fitted into the flow of the narrative, or even at times badly written, and can on occasion lead Trollope far away from his subject (as in the case of the essays on travelling in *The Bertrams*, which originally are relevant to the story, but expand eventually quite away from it). Yet they are not only an integral part of each novel, but are essential to its unity as well. And they mediate between the reader and the fiction, which they in fact establish as 'realistic'.

The essential thing about Trollopian autarky is that it gives a complete scheme of social and moral standards, by which to judge the characters and situations as each novel progresses. If the narrator gave us a judgment alone, we should be forced to go outside to whatever we knew of 'the Victorian way of thought' in order to understand its implications. As it is, the narrator usually does two things: he discusses the character or situation in concrete terms, using only that data which the reader already has at his disposal through the earlier part of the novel, and he writes short 'essays' (or makes even shorter passing comments) which put the problem in a wider perspective, and mediate between the fictional construct and the world of the reader.

Take questions of money, for example. In *Framley Parsonage* we know exactly the amount of Mark Robarts's income, and we know the precise amount he pays for his hunter, how much he signs a bill for, how much he eventually pays on it, and even how much his brother inherits from their father. Because we are given everybody's income and the prices of so many things, from houses to mutton, we have a good idea of what these sums mean. Moreover, the narrator often explains just what a character can and cannot expect to afford in terms of servants, carriages and horses of a given income, in the West End, St John's Wood, or the country. The account of Crosbie setting up house in *The Small House at Allington* is a wonderfully detailed and humorous example of this (II, x, 'Preparations for the Wedding'). In contrast, consider Thackeray's treatment of money in *Pendennis*. It is impossible to imagine Trollope leaving unknown the details of Pen's Oxbridge income, the amount of Major Pendennis's half-pay, and the size of the debt the Major settled for Captain Costigan, while the reader does not even know how much 'Arthur's Educational Fund' amounted to. Instead, Thackeray explains without giving precise figures, that Pen was living beyond his means, so that the reader must accept the narrator's judgment on trust – as is consonant with moral, satirical purpose. Trollope's narrator, on the other hand, includes all the necessary data for guiding the reader's judgment, in order to create his illusion. Trollopian realism does not work by referring outside itself to another world, but by absorbing the necessary facts and relationships of the world into the fiction itself.

Another example is embedded in the first paragraph of *The Claverings*:

> The gardens of Clavering Park were removed some three hundred yards from the large, square, sombre-looking stone mansion which was the country-house of Sir Hugh Clavering, the eleventh baronet of that name; and in these gardens, which had but little of beauty to recommend them, I will introduce my readers to two of the personages with whom I wish to make them acquainted in the following story. It was now the end of August, and the parterres, beds, and bits of lawn were dry, disfigured, and almost ugly, from the effects of a long drought. In gardens to which care and labour are given abundantly, flower-beds will be pretty, and grass will be green, let the weather be what it may; but care and labour were scantily bestowed on the Clavering Gardens, and everything was yellow, adust, harsh, and dry. Over the burnt turf, towards a gate that led to the house, a lady was walking, and by her side there walked a gentleman.

The narrator is explicitly addressing his reader, and introducing him to the persons and places – significantly, not them to him. First describing the unattractive state of the gardens, he proceeds to explain its significance in general terms, telling what abundant care and labour will effect; and then, pivoting his sentence expressively about a semicolon and a Trollopian 'but',[7] he particularizes on the Clavering Gardens, leaving the reader to draw his own conclusions – as he now must unambiguously – as to the quality of Sir Hugh's solicitude for his family seat, and hence as to his character. It is significant that this paragraph should be equally understandable by someone unacquainted with English gardens, or a dry English August. Next, the description concentrates on the burnt turf, and then the part of the turf near the gate on the house side, before finally focusing suddenly down on to the two walking figures to round off the paragraph. From the stylistic point of view it is worth noting the deceptively quiet precision of the last dozen words: 'a lady was walking, and by her side there walked a gentleman'. This is an exact statement of the situation where, it turns out, she is dismissing him, but he is succeeding in obtaining a final interview. It is also characteristic of Harry Clavering's life, for he is largely passive, and the decisions are all made by his womenfolk. Then the narrator disappears completely, and a long dramatic conversation takes over. This apparently simple paragraph, then, illustrates some of the fundamentals of Trollopian realism. So much meaning and development in a mere 170 words should help to banish the myth of Trollope's narrative dullness and inexpressiveness.

Having established the characteristics of Trollopian realism, and the twin levels of action — social interaction and internal monologue — it is now possible to see clearly what is the social significance of Trollope's vision of the world, by setting up a correspondence between his fiction and his society more satisfactory than the mere congruence of certain facts: that is, a correspondence between his views of society and his fictional method.

His vision of society shows human ties of love and respect in danger, and being replaced by money, ambition and power, while everybody is nonetheless tied together, willy-nilly, in a vast web of interdependence. Social pressures, even in the world of Barsetshire, deform individuals, as Hutton says, 'from their natural selves'.[8] The world of *The Way We Live Now*, with its all-involving title, is the ultimate fictional realization of this state. This novel is central to Trollope's whole corpus of work in that it is the purest embodiment of an idea which runs through all his fiction: a vision of modern life in which each man is an unwilling dependant on his fellows, and victim of all manner of social forces, inextricably part of society, yet increasingly cut off from his neighbours. So, in the midst of a crowded world, the individual is in the last analysis alone. In his novels, Anthony Trollope recognizes this as a central contradiction in modern existence, and his artistic methods correspond exactly to this important social observation.

NOTES

1. E.g. *Ralph the Heir*, III, xviii '. . . the faults of Ralph Newton, and
   not the vices of a Varney or a Barry Lyndon, are the evils against
   which men should in these days be taught to guard themselves; — which
   women also should be made to hate. Such is the writer's apology for
   his very indifferent hero, Ralph the Heir.'
2. See reviews of *The Claverings*, *Spectator*, xl, 4 May 1867, 498—9, and
   Saturday Review, xxiii, 18 May 1867, 638—9 (Julia Brabazon becomes
   Lady Ongar); see also Trollope's *An Autobiography*, ed. F. Page
   (Oxford University Press, 1950), pp. 197—8.
3. xxxvii, 9 Apr. 1864, 421—3; repr. *Critical Heritage*, pp. 197—201.
4. *Spectator* obituary, lv, 9 Dec. 1882, 1573—4.
5. Ibid., liv, 18 June 1881, 804—5.
6. Routledge & Kegan Paul, 1963. This work is chosen for comparison
   since it contains not a single reference to the novel for its evidence,
   but is drawn entirely from perfectly factual evidence such as estate
   records and account books.
7. See H. S. Davies, 'Trollope and his style', *Review of English Literature*,
   i, Oct. 1960, 73—85.
8. 'From Miss Austen to Mr. Trollope', *Spectator*, lv, 16 Dec. 1882,
   1609—11. See also G.-M. Tracy's comments on social 'cadres déformants',
   in his otherwise thin 'L'oeuvre de Trollope — ou le paradis perdu',
   Mercure de France, cccviii, Mar. 1950, 434—45.

C. P. SNOW
Trollope's Art*

. . . Critics, in his own time and since, have never been comfortable with Trollope, and have tended to take refuge in a kind of patronizing unease. During his career, nearly forty years, there was a good deal written about him. There couldn't help being. After all, he wrote forty-seven novels, and Victorian magazines and journals, the *Spectator*, the *Saturday Review, The Times*, many others, had plenty of space. The reviewers were usually sensible and literate men. But they were puzzled.

These novels were, most of them, clearly enjoyable and possibly admirable: but why? They lacked 'imagination' — a quality, it seems, which the non-creative are always seeking to discover in the creative. He didn't transfigure life, which even his supporters, such as R. H. Hutton in the *Spectator*, felt that he ought to. They had a remarkable gift for missing his own most remarkable gift. It was only distinguished fellow-writers, Henry James, above all Tolstoi (who, unknown to the public and to Trollope himself, was a great admirer), who could identify that.

It is wrong, however, to think that in his lifetime he had a bad press. It was rather uncomprehending, and it was sometimes delivered from a lofty height. Dickens's books were usually received with an approach to idolatry. (There is a legend that Dickens once had a bad review and never looked at another. Quite untrue. Dickens took considerable satisfaction in good reviews and went to some trouble to secure them.) Thackeray got an amount of unqualified adulation not granted to Trollope. So did George Eliot. Nevertheless, most of the time Trollope received serious and on the whole affectionate attention. At the age of about sixty, when his fortunes were on the decline . . . he began to have definitely hostile criticism, as for *The Way We Live Now* and *The Prime Minister*.[1]

* From *Trollope: His Life and Art* (London: Macmillan; New York: Scribner's, 1975), abridged from pp. 106–16. Reprinted by permission of the author.

It is a nice irony of literary history that when the English critics were being scornful about *The Prime Minister* (the entire press the worst he ever had for a serious novel, while modern opinion would rank it among his best) Tolstoi was overcome with enthusiasm for precisely the same book. 'Trollope kills me, kills me with his excellence.' Tolstoi was at that time writing *Anna Karenina*, and in the same correspondence there is a good deal of concern about 'the important thing'. That was the thing which will be mentioned soon. Tolstoi knew more about it than any writer.[2]

Even that period of disfavour for Trollope in England didn't last uninterrupted. There is a strong impression that his reputation was slipping precipitately years before his death. This was probably true in literary-intellectual circles, but it wasn't much reflected in the press. *The Duke's Children*, published at the age of sixty-five, attracted as much gratified praise (the note is always unmistakable, people can't disguise pleasure or the lack of it) as any of the books twenty years before. Which, incidentally, was entirely just.[3]

Throughout, the critics did their best, but they were puzzled as they had been in France about Balzac a generation before. As usual when puzzled, they produced a stereotype. Trollope was a photographer. It was a worthy thing to be, but not the highest. He could be respected for giving an exact replica of various sections of mid-century society, the clergy (that label clung to him right until death), the politicians, the aristocracy, the civil servants, the country gentry – a large slice, though not the whole, of the Victorian privileged world, roughly from the middle of the middle class up to the great landowners.

Well, that is true as far as it goes, or at least not demonstrably untrue. He was an unusually exact and pertinacious observer. He had seen a great deal of that part of England, and was good at making the most of what he had seen. He had the kind of detached uncensorious temperament which was more interested in what he saw than in his own views of what it ought to be. He had a real gusto for what was. He had, that is, a sense of fact, and took delight in it. To an extent, though a misleading extent, he, like Archdeacon Grantly, enjoyed the worldliness of the world.

He would have done that wherever and whenever he was put down. He would have relished the toings and froings of a Unitarian chapel just as much as Barchester Cathedral, if that had happened to come his way. To use a grandiloquent old phrase, he had a passion for the physiognomic charm of phenomena.

But he didn't need to observe like a private detective. There the critics mistook the nature of the imagination which they thought he lacked. The Civil Service he knew, of course, at first hand, and his accounts are the most accurate we have. His direct experience of politics, though he came to know secondary politicians like Sir Henry James (not to be confused with Trollope's most scrupulous nineteenth-century critic) pretty well, was limited to being an unsuccessful Liberal candidate for Beverley. That doesn't prevent his studies of the human political process − as opposed to his sketches of political ideas, in which he wasn't much interested − being, according to the shrewdest modern parliamentarians, right both in tone and detail.[4]

The same with the church, though . . . he made one or two administrative slips. And the same with the pattern of living in the great ducal houses, so we are told by those who grew up in them:[5] though Trollope himself can, at the very best, have had only an occasional visit there (there is little evidence even of that), and a visit, if it ever happened, when he was famous and had already written exactly how the Pallisers lived in such a house.

So we can take it that here are precise records of human beings moving about in many layers of society, *circa* 1850−80. They are the most precise records extant. But, if he was a photographer, he was a very odd one − because, as we have just seen, he often didn't have much acquaintance with the object photographed.

Still, he wouldn't have minded the description. He knew, better than anyone, that this social representation was a minor, though an essential part of what he was trying to do. But he was both a modest and a realistic man. 'To be known as somebody − to be Anthony Trollope if it be no more' − was the limit of his expectation. If people in his own time knew him as a social photographer, that was better than nothing. A writer like himself was lucky to be known for a tiny part of his intention. He would probably have been overjoyed and astonished if he could have known that a hundred years later he was still known as a social photographer. For that does remain − and may remain so, despite the efforts of brilliant young American critics, until readers acquire extra intuiton − a major part of his reputation.

In his modest fashion, he wouldn't have been surprised at that. He had been used to it in his own day. But he might have been surprised that this social photography, for which he is still being read and even cherished, is being surrounded by such an aura of nostalgia. Mid-Victorian England among Trollope's personages may seem desirable to us. It didn't seem specially so to them. Trollope was a much more acceptant man than Dickens, but he didn't like it overmuch, no more and no less than he would have liked any other period.

By and large, Victorians of his kind weren't overgiven to nostalgia, certainly not for recent historical periods. For instance, they didn't care for the eighteenth century in the sense we hanker after the nineteenth. They may have had more realistic historical memories or oral traditions. So far as they were nostalgic at all, it was for bogus Englands much further back. Trollope, for example, had a suppressed longing for the life of Saxon thanes surviving in their own land after the Conquest, living what he imagined to be an idyllic existence as medieval country gentlemen, their descendants represented lovingly in Trollope's novels by such families as the Thornes of Ullathorne. He wasn't for once inexact, he was just letting a romantic fancy run away with him.

Social representation, then, is the outer layer of Trollope's art. It is easy to recognize, and his readers did so from the beginning. They also felt a gratification at being let inside social groups, usually privileged and secretive social groups unknown to outsiders. Not many mid-Victorians had much idea of how people behaved inside a cathedral close, though the established church still had its hold on the country. They were quite ignorant about the Civil Service. They read the great speeches in parliament, but couldn't guess how those lofty figures talked to one another. So they took Trollope on trust – as it happened, rightly.

It was this aspect of Trollope that Nathaniel Hawthorne wrote about in a letter to James T. Fields, an American publisher. . . . The reference is well known, but it is worth noting, not only for what it says so generously, but also for what it leaves out.

It is odd enough that my own individual taste is for quite another class of works than those which I myself am able to write . . . Have you ever read the works of Anthony Trollope? They precisely suit my taste – solid and substantial, written on the strength of beef and through the inspiration of ale, and just as real as if some giant had hewn a great lump out of the earth, put it under a glass case, with all its inhabitants going about their daily business, and not suspecting that they were being made a show of.[6]

Of course, human beings live in society and are incomprehensible unless we understand it. But that is a platitude. We have to move another couple of layers inward before we come to what, as Trollope knew better than anyone, was his specific talent, his preoccupation and passion. Society, or a fraction of society, was useful to him on the way towards the central point, because human beings have to make choices and those choices are sometimes uniquely their own – in their freedom as the existentialists used to say – but more often conditioned by what society makes them do.

Trollope plays some marvellous moral and psychological conjuring tricks with these various kinds of choice — think of the old Warden, caught in an ingenious moral-social dilemma, or of Glencora, hesitating about running off with the man she loved, in essence though not appearance a purely human choice (where, despite Henry James, who wasn't rooted enough in sex to be infallible, she really could only choose one way), or Doctor Wortle, not certain how to treat justly a couple who by accident weren't married.

This layer of Trollope has recently become well recognized. . . . He had a delicate taste in the ethics of cases or, as one now says, situation ethics. It emerges in the autobiography as part of the process of building his own character: though sometimes his natural suspiciousness and scepticism make him doubt whether even honest men made their choices as they liked to think they did.

At last we come to what he set out to do and what he knew he did supremely well. For once, he half throws away his humility and tells us so. Before he speaks for himself, and before that is complemented by a statement from Henry James, who understood this depth of Trollope more profoundly than any English-speaking writer in the nineteenth century, the present writer wishes to make his own opinion clear. There is no simple term for Trollope's greatest gift — without which he would be an entertaining minor novelist.

When one says that no writer has been a better natural psychologist, that is saying something but not enough. He could see each human being he was attending to from the outside as well as the inside, which is an essential part of the total gift. That is, he could see a person as others saw him: he could also see him as he saw himself. He had both insight and empathy, working together in exceptional harmony. Further, and this may be even more uncommon, he could not only see a person in the here-and-now, with immediate impact, but also in the past and in the future. That diachronic vision is of course developed by experience and is impossible without it: but one can have all the experience in the world and still be completely lacking in it. In Trollope, the capacity must have been latent very early. It is already developed in his first book. Natural psychologists are fairly rare, but not too rare. Natural psychologists who have both insight and foresight combined are very rare indeed.

For want of a better shorthand expression, let us call this human equipment of Trollope's *percipience*. How many people possess it, even to a limited degree, we just don't know. He possessed it to an abnormal degree, perhaps as high as anyone on record. Those who don't possess a shred of it not unnaturally don't see anything in him. It is like people who can see only in black and white being asked to recognize the colour blue. On the other hand, people with more than the normal share of Trollopian percipience occur here and there in all kinds of places, often, and perhaps usually, right outside literary or aesthetic domains. Good priests, sometimes; doctors with an unusual diagnostic gift; some politicians who owe their survival to making the correct judgments of people round them; soldiers, ditto: sometimes people totally beaten by life, finding a fulfilment in being expert spectators. It may be more common in women than in men, and it may not be an accident that women often seem to understand Trollope's novels more naturally and deeply than men.

Trollope himself told us what he thought. The modesty drops away, as it should, when someone is certain, without assertion, that he knows exactly what he is talking about. He says:

He [Trollope is speaking of himself as novelist] desires to make his readers so intimately acquainted with his characters that the creatures of his brain should be to them speaking, moving, living, human creatures. This he can never do, unless he knows these fictitious personages himself, and he can never know them unless he can live with them in the full reality of established intimacy. They must be with him as he lies down to sleep and as he wakes from his dreams. He must learn to hate them and love them. He must argue with them, quarrel with them, forgive them, and even submit to them. He must know of them whether they be cold-blooded or passionate, whether true or false, and how far true and how far false. The depth and the breadth and the narrowness and shallowness of each should be clear to him. And, as here, in our outer world, we know that men and women change, – become worse or better as temptation or conscience may guide them, – so should these creations of his change, and every change should be noted by him. On the last day of each month recorded, every person in his novel should be a month older than on the first. If the would-be novelist have aptitudes that way, all this will come to him without much struggle: but, if it do not come, I think he can only make novels of wood.

It is so that I have lived with my characters, and thence has come whatever success I have obtained. There is a gallery of them, and of all in that gallery I may say that I know the tone of the voice, and the colour of the hair, every flame of the eye, the very clothes they wear. Of each man I could assert whether he would have said these or the other words: of every woman, whether she would then have smiled or so have frowned. When I shall feel that this intimacy ceases, then I shall know that the old horse should be turned out to grass. That I shall feel it when I ought to feel it, I will by no means say. I do not know that I am at all wiser than Gil Blas's canon: but I do know that the power indicated is one without which the teller of tales cannot tell them to any good effect.[7]

Trollope wasn't much given to rhetoric, but he is encouraged into rhetoric in that passage. He was even less given to boasting, but here he is boasting. On this subject few men have had more right to boast. Almost for the only time in his autobiography he is writing with unqualified confidence. In principle, perhaps not in detail (there are thousands of characters in the Trollope corpus, and he can't have known each one of them so perfectly), what he says is true. We can read the proof of it in the books. And the degree of obsessiveness is precisely what we should expect. It is perhaps essential, probably quite essential, to any kind of first-rate creative work. We have learned that from what so many of the greatest creative persons have told us, from Newton and Einstein downwards. The ability to keep the creative task obsessively in mind is one of the most cardinal of all abilities. Going to bed without being able to leave a fictional creation, nagging at how he could be made more truthful and living, isn't a rhetorical flourish. Trollope had done that.

It is necessary for anyone who is trying to reach a truth. In some of his characters, Trollope did reach a truth. That sounds a disparaging tribute. It isn't. There are very few novelists of whom it ought to be said. It was the reason why Tolstoi admired him so much. This was the important thing. Obviously Tolstoi would have been a great writer if, as part of his art, he hadn't had the identical purpose. Trollope would not have been a great writer without it. But it was enough.

There is an acute comment in Henry James' major essay on Trollope. This was written when James was forty,[8] confident of his own gift. He had always enjoyed Trollope, but as a young man had had all an aesthete's reservations. Anyway, Trollope is too difficult a writer for young men, even if they are as clever as Henry James.

In maturity James had developed some of his own percipience. He wrote, in the middle of a long essay, searching with Jamesian scrupulous anxiety to discover at last why Trollope actually was so good:

If he was in any degree a man of genius (and I hold that he was) it was in virtue of this happy, instinctive perception of human varieties. His knowledge of the stuff we are made of, his observation of the common behaviour of men and women, was not reasoned or acquired, not even particularly studied. All human beings deeply interested him, human life, to his mind, was a perpetual story; but he never attempted to take the so-called scientific view, the view which has lately found ingenious advocates among the countrymen and successors of Balzac.[9] He had no airs of being able to tell you *why* people in a given situation would conduct themselves in a particular way: it was enough for him that he felt their feelings and struck the right note, because he had, as it were, a good ear. If he was a knowing psychologist he was so by grace; he was just and true without apparatus and without effort . . . We care what happens to people only in proportion as we know what people are. Trollope's great apprehension of the real, which was what made him so interesting, came to him through his desire to satisfy us on this point – to tell us what certain people were and what they did in consequence of being so.

Right at the end of this examination – in which, as so often with James, conscience, taste and instinct aren't completely in unison – he finishes:

Trollope will remain one of the most trustworthy, though not one of the most eloquent, of the writers who have helped the heart of man to know itself.

There aren't many better statements about Trollope's percipience or the meaning of the realistic novel. Trollope never read that. It was written soon after his death, and published, in its final form, five years later. However, Trollope had written just one more boast, though a muted one, in the autobiography.

I do not think it probable that my name will remain among those who in the next century will be known as the writers of English prose fiction: but if it does, that permanence of success will probably rest on the characters of Plantagenet Palliser, Lady Glencora and the Reverend Mr Crawley.[10]

He wasn't at all a good judge of his novels as a whole, but on this he was on his home ground. Those three still seem, to readers in 1975, the height of his percipience. Others, such as Archdeacon Grantly, show at least as much projective power. Lucy Robarts is as good as Glencora, but without as much scope to display herself. For anyone who can take percipience at its least hopeful, Lady Mabel Grex is one of the best women in fiction.

It was his triumph to tell the truth about those characters and still leave them embossed in our experience. Both he and James would have agreed that some other characters in fiction, seen with visions not realistic, quite different from the Trollope percipient vision, have travelled further and will probably last longer − Don Quixote, Micawber, Sarah Gamp, Sherlock Holmes. But such figures depend on leaving things out − just as sentimentality does. The full truth about human beings depends on not leaving things out: and that is usually too difficult for our simple stereotype-attracted minds. It was Trollope's feat to tell so much of the truth about his great characters. There, not elsewhere, he achieved one of the peaks of realistic novel writing . . .

NOTES

1. *Trollope: The Critical Heritage*, ed. Donald Smalley (London, 1969), pp. 394−427. A number of complete reviews are quoted, nearly all of them dismissive.
2. N. N. Gusev, *Recollections*. Gusev was Tolstoi's secretary during the last years of his life. Gusev's memoirs, which are exceptionally informative though starry-eyed, are not available in English. They have not been used as a source by Troyat and other biographers of Tolstoi, which is a real omission. *Excellence*, in the sentence quoted, would be better translated as 'mastery'.
3. *Critical Heritage*, pp. 467−74.
4. Harold Macmillan, private communication.
5. Lady Dorothy Macmillan, in private conversation.
6. This gave Trollope a pleasure he wasn't used to. *An Autobiography*, ed. Bradford A. Booth (University of California Press, 1947), pp. 122−3.
7. *Autobiography*, pp. 194−5.
8. *North American Review*, 1883, revised and republished in *Partial Portraits*, 1888.
9. James was jeering at the bogus scientific determinism of Zola and others.
10. *Autobiography*, p. 300.

JOHN HALPERIN
Fiction that is True: Trollope and Politics*

Of all his literary creations, Trollope loved the Pallisers most. In his *Autobiography* he describes the string of characters who inhabit the Palliser novels as 'the best I ever made' and the novels in which they appear as 'the best work of my life'. He always had a special tenderness for these novels. And it is true that they represent the peak of his achievement — his widest canvas, his broadest range, his surest touch. The Barset novels, entertaining as they are, lean heavily upon caricature and farce. As tragedy is of higher seriousness than comedy, so the Palliser novels rather than the novels of Barchester represent Trollope's magnum opus.

No student of Trollope should be surprised by his interest in politics. Never satisfied to do just one thing at a time, he had a prodigious curiosity about people and places; this great vitality became channelled into many activities beyond the writing of fiction. Regularly he felt he must get out of his study and into the street — even into little-travelled corners of the world — to see life. Since he was always interested in the science of government, wherever he went on his travels — South Africa, Australia, New Zealand, the West Indies, North America, Italy, Iceland, the Sandwich Islands (Hawaii) — he observed carefully the political systems he saw, and wrote about them in his travel books. Indeed, the many tedious passages in these books recounting with unrelenting detail how various peoples govern themselves betray Trollope's failure to understand how uninteresting to others this subject might be. His *Life of Cicero* (1881) and his edition of Caesar's *Commentaries* (1870) touch more than lightly upon the problems of political principle and expediency; the bulk of his contributions to the *Pall Mall Gazette, Fortnightly Review,* and *St. Paul's Magazine* between

* From *Trollope and Politics: A Study of the Pallisers and Others* (London: Macmillan; New York: Barnes & Noble, 1977), abridged by the author from pp. 1–23. Reprinted by permission of Macmillan Press and the author.

1865 and 1869 are on political rather than literary matters. Always engaged by politics, Trollope was an informed political pundit and had opinions on a great many issues. From his earliest writings (articles on social and political conditions in Ireland; the *Dublin Review* asserted in 1869 that Trollope understood the Irish Tenant-Right question better than almost all Englishmen of his time) to his memoir of Lord Palmerston, almost the last thing he wrote, the novelist's fascination with politics is manifest. In the fifties he composed a series of essays on essentially political themes (written 1855–6; published for the first time in 1972 as *The New Zealander*); in the fifties and sixties he was a staunch defender of Palmerston and of Lord John Russell and his policies; also in the sixties he helped to found two politically progressive journals which characteristically supported the Liberal party (the *Fortnightly* and *St. Paul's* – he edited the latter); in the seventies he sided with Gladstone on the Eastern Question, speaking publicly on the issue and reading aloud to his family and some guests Gladstone's pamphlet on *The Bulgarian Horrors and the Question of the East* in 1876;[1] at the end of his life he broke explosively with Gladstone over matters essentially political. Trollope spoke no modern languages other than English, read little philosophy (nothing heavier than Bacon), knew no science; but on the subject of politics he was always well-informed.

Trollope says that 'in that work of choosing his ruler does it most behove [one] to use all the care and all the skill that he can compass'; and also that 'of all studies to which men and women can attach themselves, that of politics is the first and the finest.'[2] A well-known section of his *Autobiography* declares:

> to sit in the British Parliament should be the highest object of ambition to every educated Englishman ... The man in Parliament has reached a higher position than the man out ... To serve one's country without pay is the grandest work that a man can do ... Of all studies the study of politics is the one in which a man may make himself most useful to his fellow-creatures ... of all lives, public political life is capable of the greatest efforts.

This view – repeated again and again in various places, convinced as the novelist was that unpaid (as it was then) public service as a member of Parliament was the most disinterested and therefore the most patriotic activity for an educated man – led him to run for Parliament as a Liberal candidate in 1868. After 'wading through' a great deal of 'dirt and dishonour' in the borough of Beverley in Yorkshire – the voters of which were stunned by a bribeless campaign based on political principles clearly articulated – Trollope found his candidacy unequivocally rejected. He did not try again.

There can be no doubt that Trollope's frustrated political ambitions, both long before and long after Beverley, were sublimated in part into the writing of novels about politics. Having been 'debarred from expressing my opinions in the House of Commons, I took this method of declaring myself', the novelist says of his political novels in the *Autobiography*. Here the would-be politician spoke to the gallery of his readers; indeed, the Palliser novels, Trollope confesses, 'served me as safety-valves by which to deliver my soul.' These novels, which express so many of his political and social convictions, are in fact substitutes for political action; if Trollope could not air his political views in Parliament he could do so in his fiction.

In Trollope's day parliamentary White Papers were actually read by some laymen and portraits of leading politicians hung over the fireplaces of many homes. Like most of his contemporaries, Trollope believed instinctively in many of the institutions of his time (an attitude often satirized by Dickens; the two novelists have little in common). Unlike most of his fellow novelists, Trollope in his books expresses some of the normal qualities of these institutions and of those who believed in and peopled them (an employee of the Post Office for over thirty years, he was one of these people himself). It is unlikely that any other Victorian novelist could have put into the mouth of one of his heroes the following speech (from *The Claverings*): 'No man has a right to be peculiar. Every man is bound to accept such usage as is customary in the world.' Not surprisingly, then, Trollope's political novels introduce us to a great many ordinary politicians of middling stature whose convictions, abilities, and ambitions are equally ordinary. Bulging with detailed accounts of the everyday lives of such men and of the clubs and drawing-rooms they inhabit, these books have their settings in St Stephen's, Whitehall, Pall Mall, and the country houses where politicians and their hangers-on gather. As a sometime guest at political soirées and a constantly fascinated observer, Trollope knew how the powerful and great lived, and he is able to provide an account of them in these novels.

Even unfriendly critics have admitted that Trollope's political novels give more than a superficial picture of this segment of British life. In them we can learn a great deal about partisanship, coalitions, the maintenance of parliamentary majorities, the procedures of dissolution. And we can see how political ambitions work on the sensibilities of professional politicians – some of whom struggle to maintain exemplary ethical standards, some of whom have long since abandoned the struggle. Critics have often commented on Trollope's 'balance', his tendency to give both sides of a case, even to defend his own villains when no one else – not even his own characters – will do so. He typically saw politics as a continually shifting process of change and conciliation. And he typically saw personal life in political terms, unable as he was to imagine it as something separate from the life of the community. The theme of one of his last novels – *Dr. Wortle's School* – is that a bad life cannot be led in a good community without infecting that community, and he clearly believed the obverse of this too: a good life cannot be led in a bad community. In this novel Dr Wortle (often – but erroneously, despite the obvious sympathy with which he is drawn – assumed to be a self-portrait) tells Mr Peacocke that 'no man [has] a right to regard his own moral life as isolated from the lives of others around him . . . a man cannot isolate the morals, the manners, the ways of his life from the morals of others. Men, if they live together, must live together by certain laws.' Politics and social life – and thus the public and the private lives – are seen by Trollope as inextricably connected, interdependent. His politicians often seek political power primarily as a social tool – as a means of making peers, giving Garters, and so forth, and of depriving enemies of these good things – and it is in order to do this that the political parties chiefly compete in the Palliser novels. 'All political corruption resolves itself to this', Trollope says in *The New Zealander*. 'Men . . . desire the power of distributing [loaves] to others, and the distinction with which such power will invest themselves. To keep or achieve this politicians have . . . for many ages descended to falsehood, intrigue, and Machiavellian crookedness. Such is political corruption.'[3] Trollope understood that a politician must please both his own associates and the social Establishment if he is to succeed, and thus the political and social worlds are bound closely together in his novels. This has led some critics to think that Trollope's political novels, in the words of Bradford A. Booth, 'are not really "political" at all'. Politics is 'incidental' in these novels, Booth wrote; nor did he like them much as novels. His misleading and hostile account of them, coupled with the misreading of A. O. J. Cockshut and others, has helped to keep the Palliser novels in relative obscurity for years. Robert M. Polhemus, writing in 1968, was one of the first to point out that Trollope's political novels are concerned with such important questions as 'what politics should do and what motivates politicians . . . few other novelists give us such an acute sense of what it is like to live at the heart of a civilization's power elite'. Exactly; the novelists's awareness of the ways in which politics and society interact makes his political novels that much more politically sophisticated and knowledgeable. His recognition that politics is not always concerned with large issues and important ideas makes his account of it more, not less, authentic.[4] Unlike Disraeli, Trollope was a story-teller, not a pamphleteer.

Trollope's 'balance' — as well as a sort of creeping cynicism which increased as he grew older — also led the novelist to see the negative side of politics. If politics can be the grandest work that a man can put his hand to, it can also be the dirtiest. Trollope's judicious awareness of these contraries manifests itself in a curious sort of double vision which simultaneously admires and satirizes the profession of politics. So, despite his reverence, Trollope could also fill the Palliser novels with adventurers and opportunists who are never to be believed, men who regard politics as a huge game — 'an affair of expediency' from which sincerity, principle, and patriotism are always absent. This double vision runs through the Palliser novels and focuses on the abuses, tricks, and dishonesty of the average professional politician as well as on his rare virtues. Trollope saw politicians as buffoons as well as statesmen; indeed, no other English novelist — not even Disraeli — has left on record so many vivid and incisive portraits of political hacks or has written about them so mercilessly. Trollope saw that politics was often sham, mere theater, and settled nothing — that, in the words of *Phineas Finn*, 'The people can take care of themselves a great deal better than [politicians] can take care of them.' His politicians frequently speak glowingly of the practical advantages of doing nothing while seeming to do much. Thus a typical leitmotif of these novels is that of the *game* of politics — politics as a series of tricks conducted by ambitious and greedy men who seek to camouflage their real, selfish objects in dissembling. The image of the party 'game' recurs again and again throughout the political novels. For most of Trollope's politicians the game's the thing; party loyalty means choosing sides and sticking to one's friends.

In the *Autobiography* the novelist declares that 'A man who entertains in his mind any political doctrine, except as a means of improving the condition of his fellows, I regard as a political intriguer, a charlatan, and a conjurer.' The epithet 'conjurer' is applied throughout the Palliser novels to Trollope's most hated politicians, those who have taken the gamesmanship of politics beyond its usual bounds and turned it into a kind of sorcery whose selfish ends make it even more than ordinarily unwholesome and dangerous. It is only the exceptional individual in these novels who can remain aloof from the partisan contests over trivial issues which are seen to occupy so much time of political men. While Trollope reveres the occasional politician, his contempt for political *processes* and their paralyzing effects on individuals is manifest everywhere.

Politics breeds various kinds of dishonesty. Trollope hated most the ceremony of lying. He liked words to mean what they were supposed to mean, and he heard political rhetoric with contempt. His novels teem with instances of insulting partisan rhetoric spoken hotly in the House of Commons, followed immediately by normal and even friendly discourse among the combatants after adjournment out of the vision of the public eye – that organ for whose benefit parliamentary debates are largely staged. No man, he says, 'can hold a high position in the government who finds himself unable to defend honest intentions by false excuses, or to repel undeserved accusations by disingenuous sophistry'. Indeed, in the House of Commons 'the aggregate of untruth is very large . . . truth is not even expected'.[5] So Trollope thought that politics brings out the worst in most men – most men being ordinarily susceptible to its subtle corruptions. 'In the battle of politics,' says the *Autobiography*, 'men are led further and further away from first causes, till at last a measure is opposed by one simply because it is advocated by another.' The climactic political battles are fought over *who* is to do what is to be done – not *what* is to be done.

Most men, then, are not consciously dishonest from the first; through partisanship and contentiousness, they drift into insincerity. This is a lesson of *The Three Clerks*, in which many themes of the Palliser novels are given a dry run. Early on there is an interesting discussion between Harry Norman, the virtuous (but dull) hero, and Alaric Tudor, whose scruples succumb one after another to large ambitions. Justifying his scramble for place, Tudor remarks that 'when a man comes home from a successful chase, with his bag well stuffed with game, the women do not quarrel with him because there is mud on his gaiters . . . Men become mere vegetables by being too scrupulous.' A great man, he says, cannot afford to 'pick his steps' so carefully. Norman replies: 'Then I would not be great.'

> 'But surely God intends that there shall be great men on the earth?'
> 'He certainly wishes that there should be good men,' said Harry.
> 'And cannot a man be good and great?'
> 'That is the problem for man to solve.'
> . . . 'It is all a quibble about a word,' said Alaric.

But it is not just a quibble about a word. It is one of the questions to which the Palliser novels, one after another and in various ways, address themselves. Can a scrupulous man become a strong political leader? Is scrupulousness a weakness in politics? Can a great man also be a good man? Must a man become base in order to become 'great'? Tudor, who decides not 'to be impeded by small scruples', finds that as long as his villainy is both successful and undetected he can be lionized in society. Hostesses do not ask the man at the top how he got there; they are much more likely to ask him to dinner.

It may seem from all this that Trollope's 'balance' in politics is decidedly toward cynicism. This is true; but his idealism died hard. As late as the writing of the *Autobiography* he revered the profession of M.P., as we have seen. He also had great faith in the capacity of the unusual individual to withstand the immoralizing processes of the system and retain his integrity in the face of them all. Such a man may be forced out of the political Establishment; but the mere fact of his existence is cause for hope, even when things are at their worst.

As Trollope's reverence dimmed, so did his partisan loyalties. In his last novels real differences between the parties are few indeed. While they are finally seen to differ, as always, in terms of *personnel*, they are not seen to differ much in terms of *doctrine*. Yet throughout much of his writing life, Trollope's partisan stance was not balanced — despite his description of himself in the *Autobiography* as 'an advanced conservative liberal'. Until his last years he was an outspoken Liberal and an instinctive foe of the Conservative party and of what he conceived its few principles to be. This does not mean that Trollope, in today's terminology, could be described accurately as 'liberal'. On the contrary — though he was certainly 'advanced' on some issues, his was essentially a conservative temperament. The Liberal party of the time was no more 'liberal' than the Conservative party. Indeed, the oldest great landowning families in mid-Victorian England were Whigs; and many of the most radical measures of the nineteenth century were enacted by Tory ministries.

It is important to remember how little party labels meant, then as now. Victorian Liberalism included much that was conservative.

Trollope detested the Conservative party all of his life. Even when angry with the Liberals he refused to turn to their opponents. There is not much political theory in the Palliser novels, certainly, but there is a series of attacks on the Tories. One of the things Trollope disliked most about them was their tendency, as he saw it, to promote revolutionary measures for reasons of political expediency while in their hearts yearning for a return to past forms and values. Speaking in *The Bertrams* of the late forties and early fifties, Trollope comments bitterly:

> At that time men had not learnt by experience, as they now have, that no reform, no innovation, — experience almost justifies in saying, no revolution, strikes so foully in the nostrils of an English Tory as to be absolutely unreconcilable. When taken in the refreshing waters of office, any such pill can be swallowed. This is a fact now recognized in

politics; and it is a great point in favour of that party that their power of deglutition should be so recognized. Let the people want what they will, Jew senators, cheap corn, vote by ballot, no property qualifications, or anything else, the Tories will carry it for them if the Whigs cannot. A poor Whig premier has none but the Liberals to back him; but a reforming Tory will be backed by all the world – except those few whom his own dishonesty will personally have disgusted.

Unlike many of his literary contemporaries, Trollope had not been brought up in Liberal circles (Dickens and Thackeray, who had been, both ultimately attacked the Whig aristocracy – though Thackeray stood for Parliament as a Liberal). Trollope always revered the great Whig families and saw the Tory leaders as upstart con-men. He came especially to hate Disraeli. Indeed, the Conservative *volte-face* which helped to bring about the Second Reform Bill (1867; one of many instances in the Victorian period when Tories and Radicals worked together, a phenomenon alluded to in the passage quoted above) broadened his contempt for official Toryism and for Disraeli personally – and led him to make his Conservative Prime Minister in *Phineas Redux* bring in a bill for Disestablishment (Trollope at Beverley publicly accused Disraeli of being willing to disestablish anything for political ends).

In his official election address to the voters of Beverley, Trollope declared that 'Every Session during which a Conservative or Tory Government is in power, the political progress and improvement of the nation is impeded instead of furthered'; and he added that this feeling was 'a principal article of my political creed'. In a speech a few days later he said that 'to be Conservatives politically speaking seems to me to be unnatural'. Trollope had to take a partisan stand in the campaign, but he did not have to say these things. He believed that by definition 'A Conservative in Parliament is . . . obliged to promote a great many things of which he does not really approve . . . You can't have tests and qualifications, rotten boroughs and divine right of kings back again.'[6] The Conservative by his very nature is a sort of political dinosaur when he is not being a political chameleon, treacherous and dishonest. There is a long and whimsical aside in *The Eustace Diamonds* on the reactionary nature of Conservatives:

[Such men] feel among themselves that everything that is being done is bad, – even though that everything is done by their own party. It was bad to interfere with Charles, bad to endure Cromwell, bad to banish James, bad to put up with William. The House of Hanover was bad. All interference with prerogative was bad. The Reform Bill was very bad.

Encroachments on the estates of the bishops was bad. Emancipation of Roman Catholics was the worst of all. Abolition of corn-laws, church-rates, and oaths and tests were all bad. The meddling with the Universities has been grievous. The treatment of the Irish Church has been Satanic. The over-hauling of schools is most injurious to English education. Education bills and Irish land bills were all bad. Every step taken has been bad.

Thus Trollope on the Tory character.

None of this means that Trollope did not have genuinely progressive, even 'liberal', views on some issues. Again and again we encounter the novelist's feeling that while the stratification of society is inevitable, one should still do what one can to assist those at the bottom to help themselves upwards – and he saw the Conservatives as opposing such efforts, the Liberals as cooperating in them. He did not believe in 'equality', either absolute or otherwise; on the contrary, 'equality' is pronounced in several places to be a dream. But Trollope says that we must all believe in and help to defend 'liberty', especially the freedom of all people to create their own opportunities and to take advantage of those they find. While he accepted the existence of privileged classes, Trollope also felt that at least a theoretical entry into them by others should be possible. Thus he could believe simultaneously in aristocracy and 'Liberalism'. He favored universal free public education before the Forster Act of 1870 (W. E. Forster was a close friend) came along, as statements in *North America* in 1862 and on the hustings at Beverley in 1868 make clear. He attacked the Irish Church Establishment because, he said, it was anti-democratic, uncharitable, and unpopular. At Beverley he also declared his opposition to temperance legislation; and the position he took there on the ballot was actually a Radical one at the time (he opposed it because he wished workers to be able to vote for whom they liked *openly*, without fear of reprisals by employers). He criticized forced conscription. He sympathized with Garibaldi's cause in Italy against the attack by Napoleon III in 1867,[7] and with Turkey against the attack of Russia in 1877. He advocated the separation of 'power' and 'grandeur', approving of a constitutional monarch without real power and of a civil leadership which – like Palliser's in *The Prime Minister* – eschews personal grandeur in the exercise of real power. He generally supported moderately progressive politicians, and helped to found – and wrote for – several progressive journals, as we have seen. And he was one of the few prominent Englishmen of his time to support the North in the American Civil War. Indeed, he wrote *North America* in part to defend the North (at least its mission to preserve the Union, a cause he thought virtuous but lost) — and to mitigate the obvious Toryism of his mother's famous best-seller of 1832, *Domestic Manners of the Americans.* Frances Trollope's book had openly disparaged life in a democracy at a time when the Great Reform Bill was being hotly debated in England; of course the Tory press praised the book and the Whig press attacked it. Though in the preface to her *Belgium and Western Germany in 1833* Mrs Trollope denied having any 'strong party feeling' one way or the other, her satire of democratic life and American customs was carried on in *The Barnabys in America* and two later novels. In a sense Trollope was trying in *North America* to 'balance' the family's treatment of America — a fact which he readily admits in his preface to the book (though he too found much to dislike in America).[8]

It might be said that Trollope was a Liberal primarily because he was a conservative — the Conservatives seeming to him to be nothing at all. He became less optimistic as he got older, and certainly his preference for the Liberal party grew less energetic as the years went by. Finally, late in life, he broke explosively with Gladstone over Irish policy — in which, having lived in Ireland for so many years, he was greatly interested; and but for his friendship with Forster he might have publicly repudiated the Liberal party. He preferred it to the Conservative party, yes; but his attachment was less philosophical than social and temperamental. He knew many of the leading Liberal statesmen of the day and was invited to some of their homes. He disliked the unprincipled adventurers who seemed to have seized control of the Tory party. And he was a man who liked to belong to things in any case — the clubs, the Church, the hunts, the party — more for the sake of convenience than out of carefully developed conviction. He describes his own untheoretical nature in that of Sir Thomas Underwood in *Ralph the Heir.*

Trollope's essential conservatism is deep-rooted and consistent — much more consistent than his vague and spasmodic liberalism; indeed, it is the most consistent aspect of his thought from the beginning to the end of his life.

He always favored political rule by an oligarchy of aristocrats: 'all forms and manners of government . . . do and must . . . resolve themselves into oligarchies' of some sort, he says in *The New Zealander*; and 'The few best men of a people are always those who should rule.' Power is a 'privilege . . . of some few who are specially chosen' to govern; 'the best few' are always 'looked for, and in some sort found. And so the government goes on and is conducted in the one and only way in which the government of a great people can be managed.' Elsewhere in *The New Zealander* he says, simply: 'The aristocrat is . . . of all men the best able to rule.'[9]

This is certainly plain enough. It is an argument of each of the Palliser novels – in *Can You Forgive Her?*, for example, which asserts that a country is better off when its politicians have 'a personal stake' in it; in *Phineas Redux*, which declares that the rulers of England should be 'looked for among the sons of Earls and Dukes . . . as [they] . . . may be educated for such work almost from their infancy'; in the proclamation of the same novel that 'some men . . . seem to have been born to be Cabinet Ministers, – dukes mostly, or earls, or the younger sons of such, – who have been trained to it from their very cradles and of whom we may imagine that they are subject to no special awe when they first enter into that august assembly, and feel but little personal elevation'; in *The Duke's Children*, where Palliser argues eloquently that maintenance of the aristocracy is 'second only in importance to the maintenance of the Crown'. Put simply: 'the England which we know could not be the England that she is but for the maintenance of a high-minded, proud, and self-denying nobility' (this is *Phineas Redux*). In *The New Zealander* Trollope speaks to the 'danger' of aristocratic rule – so often a fact of nineteenth-century English life:

> We now hear much to the prejudice of the English aristocracy, and are told daily of our danger because the rule of the country is altogether in aristocratic hands. Would that it were! In what other hands can the rule of any country be safely placed? For what purpose have we an aristocracy here among us, if it be not that they may rule and guide us rightly? The main duty of all aristocrats, and we may say their only duty, is to govern; and the highest duty of any aristocrat is to govern the state.[10]

Critics have usually failed to comprehend this aspect of Trollope's thought – assuming, perhaps, that a man intelligent enough to write novels must also be a democrat.

Trollope's preference for aristocrats as political leaders has a partisan slant. The Pallisers have always been Whigs; and the great families which Trollope most admired were the old Whig familes, the conservative progenitors of Victorian Liberalism. His prejudices are discernible everywhere – even when, as in *Phineas Redux*, he is contemptuous of the political process; they testify to his belief that the two parties, in one respect at least, are not at all like one another.

> 'I do believe in the patriotism of certain families. I believe that the Mildmays, FitzHowards, and Pallisers have for some centuries brought up their children to regard the well-being of their country as their highest personal interest, and that such teaching has been generally

efficacious. Of course, there have been failures. Every child won't learn its lesson however well it may be taught. But the school in which good training is most practised will, as a rule, turn out the best scholars. In this way I believe in families.'

In this eloquent speech, Barrington Erle — though not always an admirable figure in these novels — articulates both a cardinal point of Trollope's political faith and the *donnée*, as it turns out, of one of his greatest novels: *The Duke's Children*.

The Mildmays, FitzHowards, and Pallisers — like Erle — are Liberals. While the days of the great Whig families are more or less over, Trollope acknowledges, some vestiges of their beneficent heritage yet remain.

> In former days, when there were Whigs instead of Liberals, it was almost a rule of political life that all leading Whigs should be uncles, brothers-in-law, or cousins to each other. This was pleasant and gave great consistency to the party; but the system has now gone out of vogue. There remains of it, however, some traces, so that among the nobler born Liberals of the day there is still a good deal of agreeable family connection. (*Phineas Redux*)

Trollope's complacent picture of government-by-family[11] expresses an obvious prejudice. Indeed, in a long passage later in *Phineas Redux* he pauses to discuss the superiority of Whig-Liberal governments to Tory governments specifically in terms of their usual aristocratic components:

> There is probably more of the flavour of political aristocracy to be found still remaining among our Liberal leading statesmen than among their opponents. A Conservative Cabinet is, doubtless, never deficient in dukes and lords, and the sons of such; but conservative dukes and lords are recruited here and there, and as recruits, are new to the business, whereas among the old Whigs a halo of statecraft has, for ages past, so strongly pervaded and enveloped certain great families, that the power in the world of politics thus produced still remains . . . . With them something of the feeling of high blood, of rank, of living in a park with deer about it, remains. They still entertain a pride in their Cabinets, and have, at any rate, not as yet submitted themselves to a conjuror. The Charles James Fox element of liberality still holds its own, and the fragrance of Cavendish is essential.

This is a crucial statement. Trollope at one stroke underscores his preference for the Liberals (in this respect not at all like the Conservatives, whose 'great' families are only the most recent *nouveaux riches* of the political arena), his admiration for the old families generally, and his approval of their exclusiveness. The passage demonstrates how Trollope's political Liberalism and temperamental conservatism are in perfect accord: he likes the Liberals better than the Tories because the aristocracy of the former is purer and older. The two admired Whigs evoked with such tenderness at the end of this passage are founding fathers of the Liberal party, not contemporary politicians. His preference for the Liberals has nothing to do with modern 'liberalism'. Indeed, as Donald Southgate has pointed out, mid-nineteenth-century Whiggery, being aristocratic in terms of 'personnel' and oligarchic in terms of 'influence', was 'the most ostentatious and self-conscious constituent of . . . "the Establishment" ' of the time.[12] And a most telling phrase is the one about the conjuror – a reference to Disraeli; the Liberals have never submitted themselves to such a leader, and Trollope hopes they never will. Certainly his hatred of Disraeli helped to color his view of the parties. Here the Conservatives and their leader are seen as upstart magicians and outsiders – while the Liberal leaders are portrayed as statesmen, products of an historical continuity which has eluded the Tories and which they can only ape.

In terms of what most Victorians thought, Trollope's own thinking was less reactionary than simply normal. As Lord Briggs has demonstrated[13] so well, Trollope believed heartily in Walter Bagehot's concepts of the 'old deference' and 'dignity' of the English constitution as safeguards against the barbarisms of rude democracy. 'Deference' meant habitual respect for social superiors and contempt for urban radicalism. Gladstone, no Radical, in the fifties was fond of referring to 'the strong prejudices in favour of the aristocracy which pervade all ranks and classes of the community'. The framers of the Second Reform Bill were no less aware in the sixties that the prestige of the aristocracy must not be tampered with. The best government – that most likely to bring social peace and political tranquility – was, in the opinion of Bagehot, Trollope, and many of their contemporaries, government by select few: upper-class members of Parliament who were alone sufficiently educated and experienced in life, as well as removed from the temptations of material greed, to undertake the work. Bagehot's *The English Constitution* appeared serially in 1867 in the *Fortnightly*, with which Trollope was closely connected; we may be sure that he read it. He accepted Bagehot's concept of the 'select few' and stressed the contrast between the elite classes and the demos. Like Bagehot, Trollope had little sympathy for the poor, cared little about them, and knew even less about the social problems caused by extreme poverty. Needless to say, he wished for no transfer of political power from rich to poor, no redistribution of wealth (there are no Marxist studies of Trollope). In his novels the working-class voter is portrayed as either greedy and unprincipled, or cretinous. Nor do the middle classes offer an alternative repository of faith. Indeed, they are seen by the novelist as especially unsuited to hold or exercise political power – being so vulnerable to the temptations of material speculation. Some of Trollope's harshest satire is directed against manipulative capitalists who are also would-be statesmen. Only a few members of the middle classes are able in these novels to resist temptation and work honestly for worthwhile political ends. A virtue of aristocratic rule in the eyes of Trollope and Bagehot was that it staved off the rule of mere wealth – 'the religion of gold', in Bagehot's phrase: both he and Trollope feared that the 'select few' might eventually be overwhelmed by the merely rich (a fear memorably articulated in *The Way We Live Now*).The upper middle classes were seen by Trollope as hopelessly enmeshed in speculation, stock-jobbing, and other commercial activities incompatible with honest political rule. He was afraid that the ruling classes might not escape such entanglements; the fact that the villains of his political novels are often middle-class businessmen with political aspirations expresses this fear.

The novelist accepted as a necessary fact of existence the stratification of society. 'I dislike universal suffrage; I dislike vote by ballot; I dislike above all things the tyranny of democracy', he proclaims in *North America*.[14] All his life Trollope hated the Radicals; those who appear in his novels are drawn unsympathetically. George Vavasor in *Can You Forgive Her?* is a criminal, Bott in the same novel is a toady, Turnbull in *Phineas Finn* is a demagogue, Moggs in *Ralph the Heir* is a fool, and Daniel Caldigate in *John Caldigate* is cold, humorless, and unappealing. Thomas Thwaite, the 'good' Radical tailor in *Lady Anna*, can be treated gently because 'no rational scheme of governance . . . had ever entered his mind, and of pure politics he knew [nothing]'. Rich, landed aristocrats are the proper rulers; they *must* serve or breach the trust between themselves and the country, out of which they have willingly been given so much. In order to perpetuate their ability to rule, they must also work to preserve their own order; Trollope's conscientious aristocrats do this. The few republicans who turn up in his novels – there is an odious collection of them in *Ralph the Heir*, and some plain silly ones in *He Knew He Was Right* – are treated with contempt, and often satirized.

On questions of the day such as the status of women and the rights of Jews, Trollope was unflinchingly reactionary: he hated the new feminism and shared many of the usual prejudices against Jews – attitudes clearly expressed in the Palliser novels. On the sticky question of Irish Tenant-

Right he is not altogether clear; but what he does say on the subject suggests that he disliked the system's injustices but not the system itself (he always opposed any attempt to tamper with free enterprise). Though he had little to say of them directly, throughout his life he detested the Evangelicals – favoring High Churchmen, as the Barset novels make clear (Disraeli, remember, was the great patron of the Low Church, while Gladstone appointed only High Churchmen – men like Archdeacon Grantly). In one of his election addresses at Beverley, Trollope declared that he 'would never be a member of any Church which is mixed up with and looks upon the state as its support'[15] – not so much advocacy of separation of church and state as an assertion that the church ought to seal itself off from the impurities of the civil power. He had said more or less the same thing in articles published in 1865 and 1866.

Trollope, then, was a political pundit all his life, though not always a political sage. Some of *The New Zealander* is simply silly; the political sections of the travel books are often incredibly tedious. And the novelist's prognostications in *North America* are, many of them, amusingly inept. He says here that the Gulf States of the South, even if subjugated, will never again be joined to the North; that in time 'the West' will also secede and form a third nation; that the Washington Monument will never be completed, and indeed that the city of Washington itself will never be rebuilt; that Lincoln, a mediocrity who should never have been elected, was wrong to relieve General McClellan, has conducted the war incompetently, and cannot possibly be re-nominated or re-elected: 'no man in the Union would be so improbable a candidate for the Presidency in 1864 as Lincoln'.[16] The leading politicians of Trollope's day did not seek him out for advice.

Trollope's interest in politics naturally spilled over into some of his novels. His critics have been fond of saying that his knowledge of the subject is so superficial that politics in these novels is really unimportant. How explain, then, the political issues they raise, the political characters who populate them, the extended commentaries in them on political questions? Trollope, remember, says in the *Autobiography* that in his political novels he expressed his political convictions, that in them he had been able to have a 'fling at the political doings of the day' – 'I took this method of declaring myself.' His two most purely political tales, *Phineas Finn* and *Phineas Redux*, treat issues actually being debated in the House of Commons as they appeared (e.g., parliamentary reform, the ballot, Irish land and church questions). And Trollope based some of his political characters on actual politicians of the day – though he says he did not do so. Trollope always denied specificity; regardless of his mendacity in this, it is true that the nature of the man himself, not his particular political philosophy, usually interests him most. His originality is in characterization rather than in ideas. So while there exist certain resemblances between Trollope's characters and real politicians of the day, it remains less important to make these identifications than to see these characters as illustrations of the interaction between certain types of men and certain social and political situations – a subject treated more than superficially in the political novels.

Trollope's habit of using real politicians as models for some of his fictional ones is yet another demonstration, should it be needed, of the closeness with which he followed politics. While his political novels stress and express a great many other themes – some of which, admittedly, have little to do with politics – it is hard to see how novels about Victorian politics and politicians could tell us much more about these subjects. Arthur Pollard has said that Trollope's political novels are 'historical as a faithful reflection of the life of their time'. If it is true, as Briggs has declared, that Trollope, more than any other Victorian writer, gives us a 'convincing impression' of what everyday life was like in England',[17] it is primarily the Palliser novels – focused as they so often are on real toads in real gardens – that make this so.

NOTES

1. See his notice of R. H. Hutton's *Studies in Parliament* in the *Fortnightly Review*, 4 (1 April 1886) and his letter to the *Examiner* (6 April 1850, written from Ireland) defending Russell's Irish policy. See also N. John Hall, 'Trollope Reading Aloud: An Unpublished Record', *Notes and Queries*, n.s. 22 (March 1975), 117–18. And – on the comment of the *Dublin Review* – see 'Trollope's Irish Novels', *Dublin Review*, 65 (October 1869).
2. 'The People and Their Rulers', in *The New Zealander*, ed. N. John Hall (Oxford, 1972), p. 13; and *St. Paul's Magazine*, 1 (October 1866), 4.
3. *The New Zealander*, p. 107.
4. See Bradford A. Booth, *Anthony Trollope: Aspects of His Life and Work* (Bloomington, Indiana, 1958), pp. 78 and 86–7, and Robert M. Polhemus, *The Changing World of Anthony Trollope* (Berkeley and Los Angeles, 1968), p. 150
5. *The New Zealander*, pp. 108 and 121.
6. Quoted by A. O. J. Cockshut in *Anthony Trollope: A Critical Study* (London, 1955), pp. 94–5. The two previous quotations are taken from the *Beverley Recorder*, 31 October 1868, and the *Hull & Eastern Counties Herald*, 3 November 1868.
7. See *The Letters of Anthony Trollope*, ed. Bradford A. Booth (London, 1951), p. 206.

8. The discussion of Mrs Trollope's books is indebted in part to Donald Smalley's informative Introduction to his paperback edition of *Domestic Manners of the Americans* (New York, 1949; repr. 1960).

9. *The New Zealander*, pp. 135, 144—5, and 13.

10. *The New Zealander*, p. 18.

11. Undoubtedly some of his pleasant associations with the great Whig-Liberal families came from his going so frequently to Lady Stanley of Alderley's political salon. The Stanleys — like the fictional Standishes, FitzHowards, Mildmays, etc. — were related to all the great Liberal families of the day, and Trollope surely met there many of the family members (including the Russells).

12. Donald Southgate, *The Passing of the Whigs, 1832—1886* (London, 1962), p. 77. On Trollope's reference in the passage from *Phineas Redux* quoted above in the text: Fox and Sheridan led the formation in 1794 — after George III's break-up of the supremacy of the old Whig party — of what was called the New Whig party, which after 1820 developed into the Liberal party.

13. See Asa Briggs, 'Trollope, Bagehot, and the English Constitution', in *Victorian People* (Chicago, 1955), pp. 87—115.

14. *North America*, ed. Robert Mason (Harmondsworth, England, 1968; abridged), p. 188.

15. *Beverley Recorder*, 7 November 1868.

16. *North America*, p. 211 *passim*.

17. Arthur Pollard, 'Trollope's Political Novels', Inaugural Lecture, University of Hull (April 1968), p. 25; and Briggs, pp. 93—4.

JAMES R. KINCAID
Trollope's Narrator*

The Trollope problem has always been defined most forcefully by passages like this one:

> But let the gentle-hearted reader be under no apprehension whatsoever. It is not destined that Eleanor shall marry Mr. Slope or Bertie Stanhope. And here perhaps it may be allowed to the novelist to explain his views on a very important point in the art of telling tales. (*Barchester Towers*, I, xv).

This narrative voice, interrupting, defining, applying, complicating, anticipating, parodying the action, playing with the conventions the novel is at the same time exploiting ruthlessly, has been to readers and critics both a joy and an embarrassment. Why does that voice so continually disrupt the illusion, reminding us that the novel is not history at all, but just art, mere make-believe? Why does it so deliberately attack not only the plot of that particular novel but all plots, as if Trollope were conducting a running battle with Aristotle?

The narrator is not, of course, the only source of worry in Trollope. There is the nondescript style, the absence of symbolism, the refusal to abandon certain low-mimetic and ironic views, and the consequent failure to reach the sublimity of tragedy, and, perhaps worst of all, the attachment to romantic comedy formulas, an attachment apparently so fixed that those formulas are shamelessly duplicated in novel after novel. 'The heroine', says the narrator of *Orley Farm*, 'must by a certain fixed law be young and marriageable' (I, ii). But who so set the law? And if indeed one determines to obey this law, why call our attention to it and thus increase its unnaturalness and diminish its force? Why, finally, all this artificiality

* From *The Novels of Anthony Trollope* (Oxford: Clarendon Press, 1977), pp. 3–5, 32–44. Reprinted by permission of Oxford University Press and of the author.

coupled with such apparently lifelike realism? If one accepts as accurate
Hawthorne's famous argument that Trollope's art was 'just as real as if
some giant had hewn a great lump out of the earth, and put it under a
glass case, with all its inhabitants going about their daily business, and not
suspecting that they were made a show of',[1] why is it we are so very much
aware of the giant, the difficulties he has with the hewing, and the shape
and form of the glass case?

Is Trollope the last of the old-fashioned novelists, working snugly within
safe conventions and allowing to his readers a full indulgence in the
nostalgic pleasure of recognition, or is he the first of the practitioners of
'open form', anticipating the freest experiments in fiction and holding a
moral outlook so advanced it is best understood as 'situation ethics'? The
first conclusion is the one given most commonly in Trollope's own century
and ours — until the last decade, when the second suspicion has grown
upon us. My own sense is that both answers are, in their way, correct.
Trollope clearly does not abandon the assumptions of the comedy of
manners tradition nor the aesthetics of closed form, but neither does he
fully accept them. The result is an exposition of the traditional values of,
say, Jane Austen, with a running counter-exposition which casts doubt on
the validity or existence of these values; the secure formal pattern, correspondingly, is made fluid, pried open in various places and with various
tools. Values are countered but not subverted; the shape of the whole is
made elastic, but it is not destroyed. Though this mixed form is, in fact,
characteristic of the Victorian novel in general, Trollope's use of it is
perhaps both the subtlest and the most radical.

Also, one should add, the most slippery. Though the final effect is
generally harmonious, the means to this complex harmony are often found
through disruption. The rhetoric, like the apparent pattern, shifts direction
quietly but with startling effects, and we come to recognize as typical
passages like the following, where comfort is being given to travellers
ashamed of their ignorance and provinciality: 'Why be discomforted
because you cannot learn the mysteries of Italian life, seeing that in all
probability you know nothing of the inner life of the man who lives next
door to you at home? There is a whole world close to you which you have
not inspected. What do you know of the thoughts and feelings of those
who inhabit your own kitchen?' (*Travelling Sketches*, p. 108). Is this
passage satiric, a disguised call to action, introspection, and increased
sympathy? Is it cynical, a rhetorical attack on the reader? Or is it genuinely
chummy and sophisticated, taking the edge off the point by repeating it
several times and thus really meaning to tell us, 'Be happy in your prejudice'?
Or is it neutral, moving us away from the promised comfort ('Why be

discomforted . . .') to a desolate reminder of our aloneness, and then
removing the emotional force, asking simply that we recognize that though
we do not now and never will join with other human life, we should not be
too disappointed in this condition? While on the whole I prefer the last
alternative, it is clearly neither fine nor comprehensive enough to catch
the actual effect of the passage. And such a passage represents the difficulty
and challenge of Trollope. His obvious modernity is combined with a
resolute and equally obvious old-fashionedness, and we are as unlikely now
to find secure and simple 'comfort' in the total effect of a Trollope novel
as we are in the passage of presumed consolation just quoted.

At one point in Trollope's last, unfinished novel, *The Landleaguers*, the
narrator breaks into the action to give his views on a political policy,
'cordially' agreeing here and violently disagreeing there. 'Of my disagreement', he says, 'no one will take notice; — but my story cannot be written
without expressing it' (Chap. xxxix). Why not? The story itself does not
in any sense depend on his expression of disagreement, and it appears that
he means to tell us only that he cannot go on with the story until he gets
this argument out of his system. The point of view becomes dislocated and
the use of the narrator self-indulgent, out of control, illegitimate. The
instance seems to deserve all the witty attacks ever made on Trollope's
intrusive narrators, but, by itself, it hardly seems to justify them fully. In
fact, such passages are almost as rare as examples of blasphemy or indec-
ency. Trollope's most serious and pressing claim to be recognized as a
major artist rests principally with his subtle and organic use of the dramatized narrator. Still, the attacks have been so effective that early admirers
of Trollope were sometimes forced to defend him, somewhat comically it
now appears, by hailing him as the first of the disappearing authors.[2]
    Even though it is no longer so necessary to mount a general defence of
Trollope's practice, there is still little agreement as to the actual effect of
these narrators. The four most important modern Trollope critics line up
two against two on the question of whether the narrator is used to achieve
'aesthetic distancing' or to pull us directly into the work. Cadbury and
apRoberts are on the distancing side; Hillis Miller and Polhemus argue for
immersion.[3] The suggestion that they both are right, depending on which
passage one examines, and that Trollope's narrator in fact draws us into
the fiction or distances us from it according to the demands of the moment
is embarrassingly obvious, but, I think, accurate. It should be noted,
however, that the argument for distancing is especially valuable, since
Trollope's deceptively gregarious narrator has so often deluded commentators.

Many critics who disliked Trollope's narrator intruding at all disliked even more his intruding in such a vulgar way and assuming such an unwarranted chumminess. The assumption made most often is that the narrator is there to make things easy, to give assurances, to comfort, even to flatter.[4] James, naturally, capitalized on this misreading of Trollope's effects, claiming with his characteristic waspish sarcasm that Trollope's realism allowed him to catch an 'exact and on the whole becoming image'.[5] James's remarks on the flattering narrator seem to me less clever, however, than the narrator's own: the typical novel reader, he says, desires amusement, disdains education, and wants a story in which 'elevated sentiment prevails'; he must be made to feel, of course, 'that the elevated sentiments described are exactly his own' (*Ralph the Heir*, III, xviii). The chummy narrator, it appears, can be deceptively nasty. The 'good-humoured geniality' of Thackeray seemed to Trollope to be a defect, causing 'the reader to be almost too much at home with his author' (*Thackeray*, Chap. ix). Trollope's own narrators are neither so matey nor so consistent.

It is true that the narrator is often charged with the responsibility of making whatever connections there are. Characters tend to wheel about in space, each imagining that he is the isolated centre of some tragedy or wild romance. The narrator characteristically corrects that tendency and provides some sense of community. But it is often an ironic community of the exact sort being resisted by the main plot, which is most often comic. Neither formally nor thematically nor rhetorically do the narrator and the major action co-ordinate. The chief function of the narrator, on all levels, is to disrupt. The easy geniality, the flattering warmth is largely of the surface. Frank O'Connor brilliantly points out that Trollope's narrator's 'favorite device is to lead his reader very gently up the garden path of his own conventions and prejudices and then to point out that the reader is wrong'.[6] Though this is naturally not the single narrative strategy, one observes how very often Trollope's objective descriptions, particularly of bizarre persons or unsavoury motives, imperceptibly alter, drop the objectivity gradually, and move us inward. We suddenly realize that it is not 'it' being discussed but 'we'. Trollope does literally shift the pronouns, adopting a technique of the sermon, a standard device of application. He so disguises the technique, however, that we are led not to contemplation, the end desired by the sermon, but to radical identification — with Ferdinand Lopez, for instance, one of the most repellent of his characters: 'And so he taught himself to regard the old man as a robber and himself as a victim. Who among us is there that does not teach himself the same lesson?' (*The Prime Minister*, III, v). We come to recognize as symptomatic Trollope's repeated use of 'And so he taught himself', suggestive as it is of the irrational way people form their beliefs and the foundations for their behaviour. It is suggestive as well of the quiet and artful way in which the narrator is seeking to educate the reader by establishing control over his imagination. Controlling the imagination, he can thus educate it, make it grow. The strategy is typically Romantic, as are the pedagogical principles: educate the imagination by stretching it, pushing it away from customary positions and values, and making it live with wild old mariners, idiot boys, and mad mothers, 'rendering it the receptacle of a thousand unapprehended combinations of thoughts'. On the face of it, Trollope's novels and works like 'Alastor' or 'Christabel' are poles apart. But the serenity and ordinariness of Trollope's world often cover perverse identifications he expects us to make or highly unusual values we are forced to accept. One important use of the narrator is to nudge us, against our conscious knowledge and probably against our will, into accepting a most extraordinary value system. Perhaps the clearest example is found in *Barchester Towers*, where the exceptionally friendly and chatty narrator is used with great subtlety, and we are forced to relax into heightened insight. The narrator works from the beginning to establish a surface rhetoric of intimacy and relaxation. 'Our doctrine', he says, 'is, that the author and the reader should move along together in full confidence with each other' (I, xv). The point of this comment and, to a large extent, of the novel itself is that we are all of us men, whether bishops, archdeacons, authors, or readers. He denies explicitly the author's special claim to knowledge and authority, and also appears to deny his fiction the prerogative to surprise, lecture, and edify. On the first level, the rhetoric works by direct flattery, giving the sense that we – the author and the reader – are undeluded, tolerant, realistic, and not bamboozled, as are the characters, by power or position. Since this comfortable rhetorical assumption appears to demand so little, the reader can easily enough accept it. The point of view thus establishes not only a sense of clear and typical realism but a relaxation of the reader's cautions and an easy identification with the novel's most important point: that the joy of life comes in renouncing power and its corollary notions of progress and in accepting the common, the kindly, and the established. Unlike most moral comedies, where the dominant rhetorical mode is attack and where the reader is asked to sharpen his critical faculties, here we are especially asked not to be so eager to judge. The tactful comedy involving Mr. Quiverful and the wardenship, for instance, makes just this point. Trollope brilliantly establishes the entirely understandable impatience of Mrs. Quiverful with her husband's apparent 'sentimental pride' and over-scrupulousness. At the same time, he shows the equally understandable judgement of 'the outer world' that Mr. Quiverful was rapacious and dishonourable. The narrator concludes, 'It is astonishing how much difference the point of view makes in the aspect of all that we look at!' (II, v). The rhetorical insistence is on moderation and acceptance.

At the same time, however, this basic relaxation is used to promote a clear and startling set of values. For example, the narrator early injects some facetious and good-natured complaints about sermons: 'There is, perhaps, no greater hardship at present inflicted on mankind in civilised and free countries, than the necessity of listening to sermons. No one but a preaching clergyman has, in these realms, the power of compelling an audience to sit silent, and be tormented' (I, vi). He goes on through a rather long paragraph on this 'bore of the age', working exactly for the expansive, unbuttoned attitude in the reader that can recognize the experience as a common one and respond to that recognition with laughter. The next paragraph begins clearly in the same vein, and the reader is encouraged to lean back and companionably agree some more. But the tone and direction are quietly changed. The 'preaching clergyman' becomes the 'young parson', 'my too self-confident juvenile friend', 'my insufficient young lecturer', and the attack is shifted from the general target of boring preachers to the quite specific one of ignorant youth presuming to lecture age. Young clergymen are advised to 'read to me some portion of those time-honoured discourses which our great divines have elaborated in the full maturity of their powers'. Otherwise, 'it all means nothing'. The true harshness and severity of the last comment and of the pervasive assault on youth are masked not only by the light tone but by the introductory rhetoric, which leads us so very gently into the subject. The initial chummy platitudes do disappear, but the tone remains the same and the reader is encouraged to slide into the narrator's position and recognize a 'secret' set of values altogether different from those in the romantic comedy being carried out in the plot. Later in the novel, then, the issue can be brought up without the elaborate introduction. When Mr. Arabin is preparing to read himself in at St. Ewold's, the narrator reflects with deceptively genial irony on the fact that 'it often surprises us that very young men can muster courage to preach for the first time to a strange congregation' (II, iv). He again goes on and on in mock wonder at how those 'who have never yet passed ten thoughtful days' 'are not stricken dumb by the new and awful solemnity of their position'. After a few paragraphs the irony becomes much sharper, though, as the reader is led to the very ungenial reflection that perhaps the process of ordination 'banishes the natural modesty of youth'. We are thus urged to relax into positions which are finally very aggressive and specialized.

As the major action of the novel becomes more idealized, the tone of the narrator becomes sharper and more cynical, so as to insist on his opposition. *The Small House at Allington*, for instance, locates the major action in the highly principled loyalty and constancy of Lily Dale, a romantic image so exalted that it might be incredible, were it not for the very crusty narrator: 'But men are cowards before women until they become tyrants; and are easy dupes, till of a sudden they recognise the fact that it is pleasanter to be the victimiser than the victim – and as easy' (I, xiv). It is this narrator who allows us to see the major action of the novel as a record both of romantic loyalty and of neurotic perversity.

The values are not always this aggressive, of course; particularly in the very late, 'dark' novels the narrator sometimes adopts a distinct mildness. His apologies to the reader no longer carry the mock humility of *Barchester Towers*, but a genuine courtesy, as if seeking to re-establish through the reader a league of gentlemen in order to confront a novelistic world where gentlemen no longer exist. Such a narrative tone is especially apparent in *Mr. Scarborough's Family* and *The Landleaguers*. Instead of forcing the reader to act with Mr. Harding, in other words, the narrator seeks to create Mr. Harding in his narrator and in his reader.

But many narrative comments have no apparent relation to values. They seem to have no thematic function at all and act only to remind us that we are reading a novel. Passages of this sort are very common: 'As the personages of a chronicle such as this should all be made to operate backwards and forwards on each other from the beginning to the end, it would have been desirable that the chronicler should have been able to report that the ceremony was celebrated by Mr. Emilius. But as the wedding did not take place till the end of the summer, and as Mr. Emilius at that time never remained in town, after the season was over, this was impossible' (*The Eustace Diamonds*, Chap. 1 xxvii). Mr. Emilius is clearly an excuse for a joke on the structure of the novel itself, a joke that is used deliberately to make us think of fabricated plots, crude artistic manipulations. Sometimes the narrator will offer some burlesque critical commentary, as in *The Three Clerks*, where he compares at some length his 'devil', Undy Scott, to Varney and Bill Sykes [*sic*], suggesting that he would have hanged the villain, 'had I drunk deeper from that Castalian rill whose dark waters are tinged with the gall of poetic indignation' (III, xv). Just as James said, Trollope took delight 'in reminding the reader that the story he was telling was only, after all, a make-believe'. Those 'suicidal' 'little slaps at credulity'[7] are basic to Trollope's art and to the aesthetic assumptions we must grant if we are to appreciate that art.

'It is impossible to imagine what a novelist takes himself to be unless he regard himself as an historian and his narrative as a history.'[8] The venerable analogy that James here ignores and tries to dismiss to the realm of impossibility is provided by the image of the artist as maker.[9] The shoemaker gave Trollope his favourite sarcastic reference, but the assumption that art is not something observed but something made is a serious one. Such art is what Albert Cook calls 'reflexive'; 'it *considers itself*'.[10] Many characters think of themselves as actors in stories, and at one remarkable point in *Lady Anna* a group of lawyers are urged to remember that they are characters in a comedy and that 'generosity and valour always prevailed over wealth and rank with ladies in story' (Chap. xxx). All this has the slightly dizzying effect of holding one mirror up not to life but to another mirror. Art reflects art. The major role in constructing this reflexive mirror is borne not by the characters, however, but by the narrator. He reminds us over and over that what we are engaged with in reading this novel is art, not life, and that art, unlike life, is an affair of convention, tradition, pure artifice.[11]

In *Doctor Thorne*, for example, we are promised right off that the 'hero' (lots of discussion given on that point, of course) will avoid an unhappy end, since the narrator is 'too old now to be a hard-hearted author' (I, i). Similarly, he says of Mary, 'she is my heroine, and, as such, must necessarily be very beautiful' (I, iii). The artifice is deliberate and dramatic; there is no possibility *at these moments* of imagining that the action has an autonomous life, of confusing art and life. Again and again, the reader is reminded of the very large gap separating the two. In *Doctor Thorne* the narrator interrupts a vital courtship scene to remind us of the difference between narrative and real time. It takes him a long time to tell about some hand-squeezing, he says, but in life it would take only a moment. Failing 'a quick spasmodic style' where 'five words and half-a-dozen dashes and inverted commas' (I, viii) could simulate a correspondence, his art must, sadly, differ greatly from life. Not only is no attempt made to simulate action, but he very pointedly wants us to recognize the divorce here of art and life, as he does also in a famous passage in *Phineas Finn*, where he admits that his recounting of a cabinet assembly probably does not bear much relation to actuality. 'But then, again,' he adds, 'there is this safety': no one in the general public will ever know whether he was accurate or not (Chap. xxix).

Lest we become too involved in the action, the narrator is always round the corner with the signs reminding us that such a response would be far too simple. At moments of most intense emotion, when the action threatens to become what we might call 'tough' or 'honest', that is, when we forget most completely that this is art, the narrator finds some way to slide between us and our absorption. In the very touching scene where the pathetic and courageous Marie Melmotte is beaten by her father, for instance, the narrator offers us a discussion of the propriety of depending on 'spectacle', a quotation from Horace to support his argument, then a translation of it – 'Let not Medea with unnatural rage/Slaughter her mangled infants on the stage' – and finally an assurance that he will not 'harrow' us with such details. The playful language and the grotesque inappropriateness of Medea's tragic exaltation to Marie's pointless struggle for tiny, grubby rewards make it appear almost as if the narrator were making fun of the action. Well, he almost is. As the action pulls us in more strongly, the narrator pushes back on us all the harder.

The effect of this technique is to create a balance in our response, complicating greatly our participation in the action without simply overturning and thus inverting our position. The narrator never gives a sense that he can quite manipulate at will; it is always clear that, even if he is subject to no laws, he will good-naturedly agree to abide by certain conventions. Why? Because we, as readers, are more comfortable that way. 'Since you demand it, I'll provide it', he says. But he says it, in effect, openly, thus calling our attention to the artificiality not only of the convention but of our demands as well. He will give us happy endings, plenty of marriages, punishments for villains, and the like, but not without letting us see that one source of these patterns is the simple egoism inside ourselves. The effect is the exact opposite of reassurance. We are urged, on one hand, to find full meaning in pattern suggested by the action, but there is a concurrent sense of the artificiality, even falseness of that pattern, a sense that genuine life is to be found only outside all pattern. The narrator counters the notion that life or its true reflection in fiction can be explained by easily perceived form: 'The editor specially insists on a Nemesis' (II, iii), according to the literary parody in *The Three Clerks*. At the same time, life is not certainly altogether without form either. The attack really is upon simple and regular patterns, upon certainty itself, either of a controlled or uncontrolled life. The hypnotic plain narrative, the beautifully transparent style, and all the power of the traditional narrative myths are balanced against this playful narrator and his cunning reminders of the irrational and the unformed. He not only reminds us of these frightening qualities but locates them within ourselves. There is, thus, on the most general level, a formal opposition between the demands and promises of the action and the corrosive remarks of the narrator. The battle is never won, and the disruption is never conclusive. We are engaged in reading a Trollope novel not in the simple and final subversion of the main action but in the richer and more demanding *process* whereby the conflict between art and life is carried out.

The process is made most evident to us as the plot is worked out alongside a running commentary on the mere artificiality of that plot. For instance, the narrator reminds us in novel after novel that he despises all secrets and that he will therefore, 'for the comfort of my readers', tell us all right away (*Miss Mackenzie*, II, ii). Those who like plots should close the book; those more adventurous should 'look for your interest' elsewhere in the story (*Dr. Wortle's School*, I, iii). The reason for all this, presumably, is the author's disdain for artificiality: 'I abhor a mystery. I would fain, were it possible, have my tale run through, from its little prologue to the customary marriage in its last chapter, with all the smoothness incidental to ordinary life' (*The Bertrams*, I, xiii). He deliberately refuses to withhold information, he says, because such selection and ordering is unnatural. But of course by calling our attention to that presumed naturalness and congratulating himself on it, he is exposing the fact that even apparent naturalness is the artificial semblance of nature. Thus he is merely emphasizing a different sort of control, a different artifice.

For it is the total form of the novel that the narrator is finally interested in disrupting. In order to open the closed form, its symmetry must be attacked, and we therefore expect and indeed find the narrator going to work vigorously on all the essential parts of the form, particularly those places where we are, in any case, most conscious of form: the beginning and the end. Trollope's novels customarily begin with a beginning that includes some discussion of the nature of beginnings. Though often moderate in comparison with the attacks on endings, opening commentary always at least notes that the beginnings *are* beginnings, and more elaborate essays are sometimes included, as in *Doctor Thorne, The Eustace Diamonds*, and *Mr. Scarborough's Family*, three novels which, because they are unusual in being highly 'plotted', therefore require special attention from the artificer. The opening of *Is He Popenjoy?* contains an amusing passage discussing the relative advantages of various opening strategies, an idea expanded to considerable length in *The Duke's Children*, where an entire chapter, entitled 'In Medias Res', is devoted to a discussion of the problem and a jocular demonstration of its difficulties. It even contains a sample opening for analysis: 'Certainly, when I threw her from the garret window to the stony pavement below, I did not anticipate that she would fall so far without injury to life or limb' (I, ix).

But the endings draw much more attention, suggesting as they do the notion of completion, the confirmation of pattern. Here Trollope's narrator brings forth the critical machinery with great display in almost every novel. 'The last details' of romance, he says in *The Last Chronicle of Barset*, 'if drawn out to their natural conclusions, are apt to be uncomfortable, if not dull' (Chap. 1i), and he good-naturedly protects us from the discomfort and the dullness. By doing so, of course, even greater discomfort is added — but never dullness. In many endings the narrator calls attention to artificiality by suggesting that such conclusions are simply unnecessary (*The Bertrams*, for instance); in *John Caldigate* he says he will add the ending just so readers will not think him indolent or cold-hearted. More pointed is the ending of *The Three Clerks*: 'It need hardly be told in so many words to an habitual novel-reader that Charley did get his bride at last.' The narrator in *The Warden* plainly says that he would leave out the ending altogether 'were it not for the custom of the thing'. Occasionally he suggests that he allows things to happen simply because of the artificial convention: 'And of whom else must we say a word? Patience, also, of course, got a husband — or will do so' (*Doctor Thorne*). *Barchester Towers* similarly ends with some facetious remarks on giving rose-coloured endings, false as they are, because that colour is in fashion. The light jokes on marriage that obtrude at the end of *Ayala's Angel* subtly disrupt the integrity of the comic solution; the dark jokes on the same subject at the end of *Framley Parsonage* have the same effect but are far less subtle: 'when the husband walks back from the altar, he has already swallowed the choicest dainties of his banquet. The beef and pudding of married life are then in store for him; — or perhaps only the bread and cheese. Let him take care lest hardly a crust remain — or perhaps not a crust.' The disruption is, however, just that; it is never destruction. The form is opened, but not parodied, At the conclusion of *Dr. Wortle's School*, for instance, the narrator says, 'I cannot pretend that the reader shall know, as he ought to be made to know, the future fate and fortunes of our personages. They must be left still struggling.' He goes on refusing to tell the future of this person, guessing at what might happen to another. In one sense this is rather a fake openness, since we have a very good idea what will happen, and all the commentary about the continued 'struggling' of these people is not totally discordant with the dynamic quality usually striven for in a comic ending. If struggling, they are still living, even if not quite happily ever after. Even this most extreme form of the narrator's call to artificiality, therefore, functions to provide a balance; full parody is never allowed.

   This formal result is supported by a very strong and very unusual rhetoric. Trollope almost surely found this mixed form, in fact, not through thinking about form at all but through a concentration on the effect of his work on the reader. His comments on form are occasional and perfunctory, but he was most interested in rhetoric and spoke on it often and with intensity. He emphasized over and over that the reader's sympathy is the crucial matter, without which 'no novel is anything'.[12] For Trollope as for many other Victorians, art now had to shoulder responsibilities once taken by religion; novels, Trollope said, 'have in great measure taken the place of sermons'.[13] He exposes his own religious method most openly in *The Eustace Diamonds*, where he addresses 'my reader, whose sympathies are in truth the great and only aim of my work' (Chap. xxxv), explaining that by identifying with the very imperfect (very imperfect indeed in *The Eustace Diamonds*) characters in these novels we learn instinctively and gradually a greater tolerance and charity for the very imperfect people around us and for our very imperfect selves. Even when our imaginations are quite weak we benefit, very much as does Mrs. Wortle who, bewildered by her husband's charity towards the erring Mrs. Peacocke, tries to put herself in that poor woman's place: she finds it 'extremely difficult to imagine herself to be in such a position'. But she does as well as she can: 'It was terrible to think of, – so terrible that she could not quite think of it; but in struggling to think of it her heart was softened towards this other woman' (*Dr. Wortle's School*, II, vii). This is the paradigm for Trollope's rhetorical strategy: just as James said, an artist creates his readers just as he creates his characters.

The moral heart-softening is a task undertaken jointly by the narrative itself and the commenting narrator. The end in view is to make us active, not contemplative, and it is principally up to the narrator to get us in motion, to force us into final collaboration[14] with the artist. He must make us willing to undergo the terrible difficulty of imagining and forging the work. To force us into this most taxing and dangerous endeavour, the narrator must be as sly and as devious as possible. James's notion that Trollope 'never played with a subject, never juggled with the sympathies or the credulity of his reader'[15] could not be more wrong; in fact many of the early objections to Trollope's use of point of view seem to stem from some vague sense that the narrator is far too devious, asking the reader for far too much. Such deviousness is 'extra-professional'; it violates 'the contract of the writer with the reader'.[16] It does indeed, and we are often so battered by this rhetoric and its great demands that we might feel like joining in the protest. Sometimes a single passage is so vigorously sentimentalized and then so joltingly desentimentalized, it all seems unfair. The lonely and supersensitive Duke of Omnium, for instance, forms a warm friendship with the impoverished Lady Rosina De Courcy, even though she has nothing at all to give: 'But nevertheless he liked Lady Rosina, and was never bored by her. She was natural, and she wanted nothing from him.

When she talked about cork soles she meant cork soles. And then she did
not tread on any of his numerous corns' (*The Prime Minister*, II, vii). A
cartoon caption that could measure a reader's response might read, 'Sigh –
Ahh – Biff – Oof – Grunt'. The attack on convention is made in order
finally to support it in a renewed, revitalized form; and the attack on the
reader is conducted in order to make him finally into the artist. So it is all
worth it.

NOTES

1. Trollope was so fond of this quotation that he used it twice with
   obvious approval, in 'The Genius of Nathaniel Hawthorne', *North
   American Review*, 129 (1879), 205, and, with minor variations, in
   An Autobiography, ed. Frederick Page and Michael Sadleir (London:
   Oxford University Press, 1950), p. 145.
2. Wilbur L. Cross, *The Development of the English Novel* (New York:
   Macmillan, 1924), praises Trollope's 'withdrawal, so to speak, behind
   the scenes' (p. 216); Richard Burton, *Masters of the English Novel: A
   Study of Principles and Personalities* (New York: Holt, 1909) goes
   further: 'First among modern novelists, Trollope stands invisible
   behind his characters' (p. 253).
3. William Cadbury, 'Character and the Mock Heroic in *Barchester
   Towers*', *TSLL*, 5 (1963–4), 509–19; Ruth apRoberts, *The Moral
   Trollope* (Athens, Ohio: Ohio University Press, 1971), p. 55; J. Hillis
   Miller, *The Form of Victorian Fiction* (Notre Dame, Ind.; University
   of Notre Dame Press, 1968), p. 85; Robert M. Polhemus, *The Changing
   World of Anthony Trollope* (Berkeley: University of California Press,
   1968), p. 5. The best and most flexible practical criticism on this
   point is in Arthur Mizener's 'Anthony Trollope: The Palliser Novels',
   From Jane Austen to Joseph Conrad, ed. Robert C. Rathburn and
   Martin Steinmann, Jr. (Minneapolis: University of Minnesota Press,
   1958), pp. 160–76.
4. See, for example, Geoffrey Tillotson, 'Trollope's Style', *Mid-Victorian
   Studies*, by Geoffrey and Kathleen Tillotson (London: Athlone Press,
   1965), pp. 56–61.
5. Henry James, 'Anthony Trollope', *Partial Portraits* (London: Macmillan,
   1888), p. 101.
6. Frank O'Connor, *The Mirror in the Roadway: A Study of the Modern
   Novel* (New York: Knopf, 1956), pp. 167–8.
7. *Partial Portraits*, p. 116.
8. *Partial Portraits*, p. 116.
9. Robert Scholes and Robert Kellogg, *The Nature of Narrative* (New
   York: Oxford University Press, 1966), examine the tradition of the
   novelist as maker as an alternative to the bard and *histor*. They also

give a tightly reasoned attack on the narrow dogmatism of 'disappear-
ance-of-the-author' aesthetics (pp. 265–79).

10. *The Meaning of Fiction* (Detroit: Wayne State University Press, 1960),
    p. 25; see pp. 24–37.

11. It has been argued by an early reviewer (rev. of *The Small House at
    Allington, Saturday Review*, 17, 14 May 1864, 595–6) and more
    recently by both Robert Polhemus (*The Changing World*, p. 6) and
    Wayne C. Booth (*The Rhetoric of Fiction* [Chicago: University of
    Chicago Press, 1961], p. 206), that such commentary has the opposite
    effect, demonstrating that the characters and action are so real that
    the narrator cannot manipulate them if he would. Obviously as long as
    the argument is carried on at this level of generality, the coin can be
    turned over and over. Conviction in this case must depend on concrete
    demonstration.

12. 'On English Prose Fiction as a Rational Amusement', *Anthony Trol-
    lope: Four Lectures*, ed. Morris L. Parrish (London: Constable, 1938),
    p. 124.

13. 'Novel-Reading', *The Nineteenth Century*, 5 (Jan. 1879), 27.

14. R. G. Collingwood has a famous discussion of this strategy in art
    generally: *Principles of Art* (Oxford: Clarendon Press, 1938),
    pp. 311–15.

15. *Partial Portraits*, p. 103.

16. The first complaint was in 'Mr Trollope's Novels', *The National Review*
    (Oct. 1858), reprinted in *Trollope: The Critical Heritage*, ed. Donald
    Smalley (London: Routledge & Kegan Paul, 1969), p. 83; the second
    in the *Saturday Review*'s notice of *Doctor Thorne*, 5 (12 June 1858),
    618.

JULIET McMASTER
The Author in his Novel*

Notwithstanding the critical orthodoxy of the first half of this century, which has advocated the total withdrawal of the artist from his work, I find that our sense of an authorial presence has a great deal to do with Trollope's artistic success, and with his achievement in being, as C. P. Snow calls him, obsessively readable.[1] Trollope, like most Victorian novelists, would have reacted strongly against the Joycean image for the artist as a being remote and, to all outward appearances, detached from his own work, 'invisible, refined out of existence, indifferent, paring his fingernails'.[2] He, like his model Thackeray, valued a close relation with his readers, and took pains to create it and maintain it. David Aitken has pointed out. 'Trollope's writing has a marked personal quality, which is difficult to describe in general terms – and difficult, indeed, quite to put one's finger on at the outset – and yet is unmistakably there and unmistakably appealing'.[3] I will make my own attempt at trying to characterize that personal quality in the novels.

Occasionally, as a slightly embarrassed and self-effacing figure thrust in from the wings onto his own stage, he introduces himself among his own characters, as to a cry for 'Author!' from the audience. Remember Mr. Pollock, the hunting novelist in *Can You Forgive Her?*. The Pollock/ Trollope name juggle is not unlike the Popplecourt/Palliser one in *The Duke's Children*. We hear of one insignificant Mr. Grindley that he is inferior to a banker and to two brewers and 'even to Mr. Pollock the heavy-weight literary gentleman' (I, xvi). That 'even' is Trollope's little joke, like Johnson's definition of a lexicographer as 'a harmless drudge'. The hunting episode at Edgehill is delightful for the Trollopian, as there Trollope puts into the mouth of his characters all the mockery that he knew his club acquaintances aimed at him. 'By George, there's Pollock!' says Maxwell.

* From *Trollope's Palliser Novels: Theme and Pattern* (London: Macmillan; New York: Oxford University Press, 1978), abridged by the author from pp. 202–18. Reprinted by permission of the author.

'I'll bet half a crown that he's come down from London this morning, that he was up all night last night, and that he tells us so three times before the hounds go out of the paddock' (I, xvi). True to form, Pollock burbles, 'By George, . . . just down from London by the 8.30 from Euston Square, and got over here from Windsor in a trap. . . . I had to leave Onslow Crescent at a quarter before eight, and I did three hours' work before I started' (I, xvii).[4] On this occasion Pollock takes a bet that he will see more of the hunt than Maxwell, and loses it. His fifteen stone prove too much for his horse, which at last 'refused a little hedge, and there was not another trot to be got out of him' (*Ibid.*). Trollope allows himself a little lyric outburst about his on-stage self: 'few knew the sad misfortunes which poor Pollock sometimes encountered; – the muddy ditches in which he was left; the despair with which he would stand by his unfortunate horse when the poor brute could no longer move across some deep-ploughed field . . .' (*Ibid.*). There is the writer of the *Autobiography* plainly enough: the brash and extrovert exterior, the boasting about early morning labours, the apparent cheerful indifference to the opinion of others; and behind that, the hint of the weary effort by which it must all be maintained, and the acute sensitivity to judgment that is testified by this very image of himself as he supposes others see him.

Another novelist who appears briefly as a harmless drudge, convenient to be made into mincement under Chaffanbrass's examination, is Mr. Bouncer in *Phineas Redux*. Mr. Bouncer, who also has some Trollopian attributes, attempts to stand on his dignity, a posture which Chaffanbrass will by no means allow. This 'unfortunate author' makes no very brilliant showing, and is dismissed with insulting patronage.

'The poor fictionist' alike calls for our tolerant sympathy when he talks explicitly and as the present author about the pitfalls of the novelist's career. As James Kincaid has forcefully demonstrated, Trollope is very much a self-conscious author, and is not shy of talking about the process of writing while he is in the midst of it.[5] But here too his characteristic tone is self-deprecatory and apologetic:

> The poor fictionist very frequently finds himself to have been wrong in his description of things in general, and is told so roughly by the critics, and tenderly by the friends of his bosom. . . . He catches salmon in October; or shoots his partridges in March. . . . He opens the opera-houses before Easter, and makes Parliament sit on a Wednesday evening. And then those terrible meshes of the Law! How is a fictionist, in these excited days, to create the needed biting interest without legal diffi-culties; and how again is he to steer his little bark clear of so many rocks . . . ? (*Phineas Finn*, Chap. xxix).

Of course this is to a large extent a front. Trollope, as he knows in his heart of hearts, is better able than most poor fictionists to steer his little bark through the terrible meshes of the law, as through the hunting field, the partridge-shooting, and the Cabinet meetings. In the same novel, *à propos* of Phineas's improvement in parliamentary speaking, he tosses off the comparison, 'He knew that words would come readily enough to him, and that he had learned the task of turning his thoughts quickly into language while standing with a crowd of listeners around him, — as a practised writer does when seated in his chair' (Chap. lxxv). The analogy comes readily to hand, because there he is, the practised writer, turning out the right rhythms at that moment. We are reminded of the passage in the *Autobiography* on the uses of familiarity, which are so to train the writer's ear 'that he shall be able to weigh the rhythm of every word as it falls from his pen' (Chap. xii). But the self-deprecatory pose suits Trollope, and he adopts it often. It is an appeal for sympathy.

Trollope's authorial tone is not chatty and colloquial like Thackeray's; on the contrary, his diction in the narration (dialogue is another matter) is rather formal than otherwise, and abounds in decorative inversions and slightly archaic usage. Still less is he outrageously erratic, like Sterne. And yet a close relation with his reader is as much part of his strategy as theirs. 'Oh, thou, my reader, whose sympathies are in truth the great and only aim of my work', he apostrophises us, at one point (*The Eustace Diamonds*, Chap. xxxv). In spite of the deliberate inflation of style, I am inclined to believe that, 'in truth', he meant what he said, — as much as he could mean any such large generalization. The sympathies of his reader were immensely important to him, even if they were not quite the only aim of his work. George Bartley's letter, which condemned *The Noble Jilt* on the grounds that there was no character with whom the audience could sympathize, had early been declared 'gospel' in Trollope's critical creed (*Autobiography*, Chap. v).

Can You Forgive Her?, with its personal appeal directed at the reader in the second person, is one of the few novels extant that gets the reader right into the title. That appeal is followed up in the novel itself in the discussion of Alice's misdemeanours:

> But can you forgive her, delicate reader? Or am I asking the question too early in my story? For myself, I have forgiven her. The story of her struggle has been present to my mind for many years. . . . And you also must forgive her before we close the book, or else my story will have been told amiss. (I, xxxvii).

The young James's irritable reaction to this kind of appeal — 'The question is, Can we forgive Miss Vavasor?' Of course we can, and forget her, too, for that matter' — is quite in character with his later strictures against Trollope for his 'terrible crime' in admitting his novels are fictions.[6] Both the question and the admission are authorial intrusions of the kind that Jamesian critics deplore. But by such 'intrusions' Trollope maintained his necessary contact with his reader. In his apostrophe to the reader he has included other figures of his own particular rhetoric. 'Am I asking the question too early?' — he wonders, pausing, as in a lecture, for the slower students to catch up and for the faster ones to respond. 'For myself, I have forgiven her' — he confesses: not that I would want to bully you into my position — I realize you have your own opinions. For himself, he is also ready to add the personal touch about the many years that Alice's struggle has occupied his mind. (He does not at this point include the painful story of the rejection of *The Noble Jilt* a dozen years before — but the acquaintance has so far advanced that the reader feels such intimate revelations are only just round the corner.) 'My story will have been told amiss' — he admits humbly, envisaging the possibility of failure, in order to capture his audience's compassion. And throughout such a passage runs the earnest and almost spoken plea that we shall allow our author to convince us: that we should listen to him, hear his case, understand his point of view. That is often Trollope's tone; and not just in visible and explicit appeals like this, but invisibly, in the choice of words, the time he takes to explain, the filling in on background information, the painstaking attention he pays to the business of keeping his reader with him, even if it means repeating information. For instance, late in the same novel, and on our second meeting with a very minor character, he is cheerfully ready to furnish this timely reminder: 'Then he . . . walked up the street till he reached the house of Mr. Jones, the pugilistic tailor. The reader, no doubt, has forgotten all he ever knew of Mr. Jones, the pugilistic tailor. It can soon be told again. . . . ' (II, xxxii). And he proceeds to tell it.

His use of the summing-up final sentence of a paragraph, so that his prose moves in long rhythms like Spenserian stanzas, is another sign of the same solicitude. His paragraphs are generally models of lucidity, beginning with a sentence that introduces a proposition or a problem, proceeding with an elaboration of its intricacies, ending with a summary or at least an overview of ground covered. Here is an opening sentence from near the beginning of *The Eustace Diamonds*, on Lizzie's covert use of jewels to trap Sir Florian when she is supposed to be in mourning: 'Lady Linlithgow saw the jewels come back, one by one, ring added to ring on the little taper fingers, the rubies for the neck, and the pendant yellow earings.' Now the complications are unfolded: as a conscientious woman Lady Linlithgow disapproves of Lizzie's use of lures, but she also partly enters into Lizzie's campaign to catch a rich husband. The conflict of the guardian's worldliness with her conscience is then elaborated, and in the process we come to know a good deal of her character, and Trollope has some fun in the crackling enumeration of her vices and virtues:

> Lady Linlithgow was worldly, stingy, ill-tempered, selfish, and mean. Lady Linlithgow would cheat a butcher out of a mutton-chop, or a cook out of a month's wages, if she could do so with some slant of legal wind in her favour. . . . But nevertheless she recognized certain duties, – and performed them, though she hated them. She went to church, not merely that people might see her there, – as to which in truth she cared nothing – but because she thought it was right. (Chap. i)

Understand this exactly, insists the narrator: it may seem like a contradiction, and certainly it is surprising that she should be both so bad and yet by her own lights a dutiful woman; but people are not simple organisms, and you must understand the balance of contrary motives in this one. From your own knowledge of human nature you may conclude that so mean and wordly an old harridan, if she goes to church, must go there only for another wordly motive. But no, in this case that's not how it was; strange as it may seem, in fact – 'in truth' – she went there because she thought it was right. (I exaggerate the explaining tone for emphasis, but that tone is there, running beneath the vision and its expression.) The final sentence neatly rounds off the paragraph, bringing Lizzie's jewels and Lady Linlithgow's character together: 'Now a marriage with Sir Florian Eustace would be very splendid, and therefore [Lady Linlithgow] was unable to go into the matter of the jewels with that rigour which in other circumstances she would certainly have displayed.' But it is more than a summary – its force and irony can be grasped only if one has carefully followed the preceding matter. The opening 'now' is characteristic too: it asserts again the stance of explainer to eager audience. The word has virtually lost its use as an adverb of time, to become a comfortable conjunction with no more force than as a mild appeal that we should pay special attention to what follows. ('Now you must know and understand, O Best Beloved . . . ' – as Kipling addresses his child reader in the *Just So Stories*.)[7]

Trollope reminds one often of an accommodating lecturer, a personal presence responding to the needs of a present audience, humorous often, and patient and engagingly concerned with his students' full understanding of the subject in hand. Are you with me? Am I going too fast? Shall I explain that again? Don't hesitate to ask a question. Such is the tone behind the narration. And such solicitude and accommodation cannot but win the attention and loyalty of his hearers. You have to keep listening, keep reading — the fellow obviously cares so much about you.

His tone of careful explanation is often perceptible when he is accounting to the reader for his characters' behaviour by drawing attention to their limited points of view. The reader has been given such complete information about surrounding characters and events that he has to be reminded how small a proportion of knowledge falls to the share of the participating characters. Why is Frank Greystock fool enough to be attracted by so manifest a little liar as Lizzie, the reader may wonder. The narrator explains: 'It can hardly be too strongly asserted that Lizzie Greystock did not appear to Frank as she has been made to appear to the reader. In all this affair of the necklace he was beginning to believe that she was really an ill-used woman; and as to other traits in Lizzie's character . . . it must be remembered that beauty reclining in a man's arms does go far towards washing white the lovely blackamoor' (Chap. xxxv). Even so disgusting a character as Quintus Slide of the People's Banner, when he is gnashing his teeth at being prevented from publishing his ugly gossip, gains this con-scientious concession from his creator: 'It must be acknowledged on behalf of this editor that he did in truth believe that he had been hindered from doing good' (*Phineas Redux*, I, xxvii). There follows a fine ironic passage, written from Slide's point of view, on the irreproachable moral standing of the editor of the People's Banner. 'It must be remembered . . .', 'It must be acknowledged . . . ' — those are the characteristic little phrases by which Trollope keeps his reader's attention, alerts him to conflicting views and extenuating circumstances. He really is a very good lecturer.

Trollope's characteristic phrase 'in truth' is one more of his little holds on our attention, his signals that our author is to be trusted. A much larger proportion of the narrative commentary than one at first realizes is dramatic, in the sense that it proceeds not direct from an omniscient author but as sifted through the consciousness of the characters. Such is Slide's self-righteous reflection that I have just referred to. But Trollope is careful to flag his internal monologues as not carrying the full authority of the author. The 'in truth' phrase generally marks the insight that we can rely on. So in an interview between Phineas and Lady Laura when she begins by rebuking him for the duel, and then trails off: 'Neither of them knew what was taking place between them; but she was, in truth, gradually submitting herself again to this man's influence' (*Phineas Finn*, Chap. xxxix).

It is not surprising that Trollope should have irritated some readers by defeating their expectation for the long-term suspense created by the whodunnit. Don't worry, he tells us; 'let the gentle-hearted reader be under no apprehension whatsoever. It is not destined that Eleanor shall marry Mr. Slope or Bertie Stanhope' (*Barchester Towers*, I, xv). That passage, it is traditionally supposed, is the one James had in mind when he spoke of the terrible crime of the author in conceding to the reader 'that he and this trusting friend are only "making believe".'[8] Similarly, 'The reader need hardly be told that, as regards this great offence [the murder of Bonteen], Phineas Finn was as white as snow' (*Phineas Redux*, II, ix). That one irritated Hugh Walpole.[9] And, in case we are fretting about the whereabouts of Lizzie's necklace, our author sets our minds at ease: 'The Eustace diamonds were locked up in a small safe . . . beneath the establishment of Messrs. Harter and Benjamin. . . . The chronicler states this at once, as he scorns to keep from his reader any secret that is known to himself' (*The Eustace Diamonds*, Chap. lii). This stated policy of openness has its uses; our author reminds us again that *he* is no remote and godlike artist paring his fingernails, but a very human presence, concerned for the trust and loyalty of his audience. Of course he manages to have it both ways: he enters into a compact of frankness with his readers, *and* he maintains his own kind of suspense. He tells us whom Eleanor Bold won't marry, but he keeps us interested on the question of whom she will; he tells us Phineas didn't do the murder, but not how the trial will come out; he tells us where the diamonds are, but not how they got there. He knows to a nicety just which beans he can afford to spill — just enough of them to serve his purpose.

One of his strengths is the running commentary, a kind of practical criticism on the course of an argument, the turns of thought in a passage of reflection, the composition or reception of a letter. The reader is not allowed to skim; he is made to sit down with the author and characters to respond in detail to this or that appeal or turn of phrase. The letter with commentary, for instance, is a minor genre of which Trollope must be the master. Spooner's letter of proposal for Adelaide Palliser is directly followed by a record of the argument between Spooner and his cousin on its composition. The letter ends with a postscript:

'As I believe that Miss Palliser is fond of books, it may be well to tell her that there is an uncommon good library at Spoon Hall. I shall have no objection to go abroad for the honeymoon for three or four months in the summer.'

The postscript was the Squire's own, and was inserted in opposition to the cousin's judgment. 'She won't come for the sake of the books,' said the cousin. But the Squire thought that the attractions should be piled up. 'I wouldn't talk of the honeymoon till I'd got her to come round a little,' said the cousin. The Squire thought that the cousin was falsely delicate, and pleaded that all girls like to be taken abroad when they're married. (*Phineas Redux*, I, xxix)

The whole Spooner-Adelaide subplot is not one of Trollope's most successful pieces of comic writing, but it has its moments, like this debate on the art of letters of proposal. Behind such a scene is Trollope's implied faith that if you only look at something closely enough it will become interesting: something like Constable's belief that there is nothing ugly — no object or scene that the effects of light and perspective will not make beautiful and significant. It is that quality of Trollope's that James called 'his great, his inestimable merit . . . a complete appreciation of the usual'[10] — (a tribute which I find more appreciative and less patronizing than some of Trollope's apologists). The commentaries on letters are often included in parenthesis in the letter itself, and again we are made aware of Trollope's painstaking concern to keep the reader with him: Lady Midlothian writes to Alice on her engagement to Grey, ' "I was heartily glad to find that your choice had done you so much credit." (If the reader has read Alice's character as I have meant it should be read, it will thoroughly be understood that this was wormwood to her)' (*Can You Forgive Her?* I, xviii). In this case the commentary is explicitly directed to the reader, but often it proceeds as a running record of the correspondent's reaction, so that we have something like dialogue, but with one of the participants limited for the moment to mental notes. I allow myself one more example, from Silverbridge's letter to his father on the election campaign at Polpenno:

'It was beastly work!' The Duke made another memorandum to instruct his son that no gentleman above the age of a schoolboy should allow himself to use such a word in such a sense. 'We had to go about in the rain up to our knees in mud for eight or nine days, always saying the same thing. And of course all that we said was bosh.' Another memorandum — or rather two, one as to the slang, and another as to the expediency of teaching something to the poor voters on such occasions. 'Our only comfort was that the Carbottle people were quite as badly off as us.' Another memorandum as to the grammar. The

absence of Christian charity did not at the moment affect the Duke.
'I made ever so many speeches, till at last it seemed to be quite easy.'
Here there was a very grave memorandum. Speeches easy to young
speakers are generally very difficult to old listeners. 'But of course it
was all bosh.' This required no separate memorandum. (*The Duke's
Children*, III, iii)

There is the author as critic of his own text, though managing the proceeding through another character, and supplying his readers with full and
explicit notes on the minutiae of this communication and its reception. I
have used the letter with commentary as an example, because it is convenient in being especially characteristic of Trollope; but the same close
attention to phrasing and timbre may be found in the recording of dialogue
or passages of reflection. Listen; read carefully; respond — he keeps asking
us, tacitly.

Trollope manages to maintain close contact with the reader on the one
hand, and with the content of his story on the other. He often writes, both
sympathetically and satirically, of people who buttonhole one another:
lovers do it — 'she twisted one of her little fingers into one of his button-
holes' (*Orley Farm*, II, xl) — and bores do it, like Sir Timothy Beeswax
(*The Duke's Children*, III, xvii) and the American minister in *He Knew He
Was Right*. But he is himself one of the most practised buttonholers in the
history of English fiction. It is his ability to stay *in touch* that partially
accounts for his obsessive readability.

The sense of touch is always important in the content of Trollope's
novels. He has a sensitivity almost like Sterne's to the human skin and the
human fingers as mediums of communication: he probably borrowed the
Warden's gesture of playing on an imaginary violoncello when at a loss for
words from Uncle Toby's whistling of Lillabullero. There are memorable
touches in the novels, both tender, like the intertwinings of lovers' fingers,
and aggressive, like Johnny Eames' fist planted in Crosbie's eye, or Eleanor
Bold's slap in the face to Mr. Slope — the only language he could understand at that moment. When Madame Max lays a finger on the Duke of
Omnium's sleeve, he becomes putty in her hands.

But I am concerned with Trollope's particular sensitivity to contact in a
figurative as well as a literal sense. My comments here are bound to be
impressionistic, but it is an impression I am talking about, an impression
that Trollope keeps his own tenacious hand on your sleeve, a touch as
irresistible as Madame Max's to the Duke, and makes you want to keep
listening, keep hearing. He is like the Ancient Mariner. First he holds you
with his skinny hand: then he fixes you with his glittering eye.[11]

How does he do it? The answer must be enormous and multiform, but I think that one decisive constituent is his choice of proximity, both to his readers and to the action he describes. A writer like Fielding chooses characteristically to stand rather far from the events he describes (though close to his reader), and gives one a sense of nations and classes marshalling for and against the Jacobite cause as a continuing context for the less distanced depiction of the loves and adventures of Tom Jones. Others — say like Sterne in the eighteenth century or Virginia Woolf in our own — specialize in the close-up vision of men and women in the intimacies of their conduct, in the minute fluctuations of warmth and withdrawal that are the moment to moment history of human consciousness. Thackeray is one who, as it were, uses the zoom lens, so that he can display before us the whole panoply of the armies clashing on the field of Waterloo ('the columns of the Imperial Guard marched up the hill of St. Jean, at length and at once to sweep the English from the height . . . '), and then focus minutely on the significant detail of George Osborne, 'lying on his face, dead, with a bullet through his heart' (*Vanity Fair*, Chap. xxxii). Proust is I suppose the closest observer of the detail of human sensibility, and he includes the reflective and analytic faculty, so that the instantaneous perception of finger, tongue or nostril can become the impulse of pages of introspective analysis.

Trollope has made up his mind how closely he wants to watch, how much of the life of a given character he has room to show us. He has not opted for the microscopic examination of subject matter, or the most intimate proximity to his reader. But what he has achieved, I think, is a choice of proximity, not quite intimate, not too distant, that will have the maximum appeal for most people. We all know how we are apt to be more engaged in the workings and personal conflicts of a department or college than of an institute or a whole university, more absorbed in the life of a village or a local chapter than of a city or a national organization. Trollope certainly ranged well beyond the 'two or three families in a country village' that Jane Austen said were the very thing for a novelist; but like her he had the instinct to place himself close to his subject. Though he may range over continents and aspire to describe alike low life and the conduct of cabinet meetings, whatever he observes he observes as though he were there at the same time, in the same room or the same lane, within earshot. He puts us close, close to his people and their lives. He explains, not from second to second but from movement to movement, just what motives move them, just what stimuli make them wince with embarrassment or throb with delight. He does not make them our brothers and sisters, fathers and uncles, as Sterne seems to do; nor does he try, like Charlotte

Brontë, to make us identify ourselves with the characters. But he does keep us close enough to them to make us feel *in touch* – to maintain the connection we feel with friends and acquaintances who keep us regularly informed of their movements with just enough detail to keep awake our absorbed interest.

Look at Sexty Parker signing a bill, for instance. Sexty Parker is only a minor character in a vast novel, and one who in aggregate, and in looking back on the novel, is perhaps not very vivid or memorable. But for the moment in which he is observed, the observation is total and engrossing.

> 'Oh, I ain't afraid,' said Sexty, taking his pen and writing his name across the bill. But even before the signature was finished, when his eye was taken away from the face of his companion and fixed on the disagreeable piece of paper beneath his hand, he repented of what he was doing. He almost arrested his signature half-way. He did hesitate, but had not pluck enough to stop his hand. (*The Prime Minister*, I, i)

Perhaps the reader does not care one way or the other about the ultimate fate of Sexty; but for these moments – watch him! will he stop in mid-signature? – we are spellbound. Just look at something closely enough, and it is bound to be interesting.

Trollope can retain our fascinated attention in passages of reflection too, like the long one in *The Prime Minister* in which Glencora ponders the Duke's charge of 'vulgarity', rejects it, accepts it, justifies herself in the face of it. The mental journey is anchored at key points by reference to the physical occupation of letter-writing: 'She escaped, to the writing of her letters she said, almost before the meal was done. "Vulgarity!" she uttered the word aloud to herself, as she sat herself down in the little room upstairs.' As her mind explores the charge and its implications, we keep hearing of that unfinished correspondence: 'The letters remained long unwritten, and then there came a moment in which she resolved that they should not be written. The work was very hard, and what good would come from it? . . . But at last, before she had abandoned her desk and paper, there had come to her another thought. . . . Having in this way thought it all out, she took up her pen and completed the batch of letters before she allowed herself to go to bed' (I, xix). The chronicle of the writing of the letters, which accompanies the more subtle but less concrete chronicle of Glencora's inward debate, is Trollope's way of fixing the attention of the novel-reader, who craves events as well as ideas. But the reflection also is dramatic and minutely fascinating, for we follow it through the fluctuations of Glencora's resolution: 'Was her courage already gone from her? Was she so weak that a single word should knock her over, – and a word evidently repented of as soon as uttered? Vulgar! Well, let her be vulgar as long as she gained her object.' Such a passage bears out Trollope's claim to have *lived* with his characters, 'in the full reality of established intimacy'.

It is so that I have lived with my characters, and thence has come whatever success I have attained. There is a gallery of them, and of all in that gallery I may say that I know the tone of the voice, and the colour of the hair, every flame of the eye, and the very clothes they wear. Of each man I could assert whether he would have said these or the other words; of every woman, whether she would then have smiled or so have frowned. When I shall feel that this intimacy ceases, then I shall know that the old horse should be turned out to grass. (*Autobiography*, Chap. xii)

His novels tell us enough of the tones of the voice, the tilt of the eyebrows, the tricks of phrasing and passing effects of gesture and expression, to bear out his claim. As sober critics we know that there is no Glencora, no Plantagenet Palliser, or the rest, only beguiling arrangements of words that create an illusion of men and women. But as Trollope's readers, the sympathetic readers that his own solicitous and disarming tone persuades us to be, we can hardly resist being convinced that they live and breathe, that we could be close to them as their author is close to them, listening in on their thoughts and entering into their motives. By creating and maintaining our sympathy, as well as by surrounding himself with his own illusion, he has endowed us with his own sense of his characters' life. That we can so respond to his characters, and become so minutely interested in their concerns, is a result both of his proximity to them, and of his proximity, created and maintained so quietly but so continuously, to us.

NOTES

1. *Trollope: His Life and Art*, p. 166.
2. *A Portrait of the Artist as a Young Man*, ch. 5.
3. ' "A Kind of Felicity": Some Notes About Trollope's Style', *Nineteenth-Century Fiction*, 20 (1966), p. 345.
4. Trollope at this time was actually living in the country at Waltham Cross; but Onslow Crescent may be a reminiscence of another large literary man (though no hunter), Thackeray, who lived at 36 Onslow Square from 1854 to 1862.

5. James R. Kincaid, 'Bring Back *The Trollopian*', *Nineteenth-Century Fiction*, 31 (1976), 12ff. 'He reminds us always that art is art' (p. 12).
6. *Nation*, September 28, 1865, or *Critical Heritage*, p. 249; 'The Art of Fiction', *Longman's Magazine*, 4 (September, 1884), p. 504.
7. David Aitken perceptively notes that in his frequent use of repetition Trollope is 'inviting us to regard his characters with affectionate sympathy. The trick induces a kind of warmth of feeling which is like the irrational, sentimental warmth that nursery talk can sometimes inspire even in adults.' ' " A Kind of Felicity": Some Notes About Trollope's Style', p. 348.
8. 'The Art of Fiction', op. cit., p. 504.
9. *Anthony Trollope* (London, 1928), p. 109.
10. 'Anthony Trollope', *Partial Portraits* (1888); *Critical Heritage*, p. 527.
11. It is a byword that Trollope was read avidly and compulsively in the underground shelters in London during the Second World War. Those who have fallen under his spell, in those or other circumstances, will sympathize with General Liddament, the Trollopian in Anthony Powell's novel, *The Soldier's Art* (London, 1966), who 'read from a small blue book that had the air of being a pocket edition of some classic' (familiar prop!):

> 'What do you think of Trollope?'
> 'Never found him easy to read, sir.' . . .
> *'You've never found Trollope easy to read?'*
> 'No, sir.'

He was clearly unable to credit my words. (pp. 45–6)

Notes on the Authors

Henry James (1843–1916), novelist and critic. His criticism is collected in *Partial Portraits* (1888), *Notes on Novelists* (1914) and *The Art of the Novel* (edited by R. P. Blackmur, 1934).

Frederic Harrison (1831–1923), writer and positivist. His books include *Cromwell* (1888), *Studies in Early Victorian Literature* (1895), *Ruskin* (1902) and *Theophano: The Crusade of the Tenth Century* (1904).

W. P. Ker (1855–1923), late Quain Professor of Language and Literature, University College, London. His books include *Epic and Romance* (1897), *The Dark Ages* (1904), *English Literature: Medieval* (1912) and *On Modern Literature: Lectures and Addresses by W. P. Ker* (edited by T. Spencer and J. Sutherland, 1955).

Michael Sadleir (1888–1957), writer and publisher. His books include *Excursions in Victorian Bibliography* (1922), *Trollope: a Commentary* (1927), *Trollope: a Bibliography* (1928) and *XIX Century Fiction: a Bibliographical Record* (1951).

Paul Elmer More (1864–1937), literary critic and philosopher. His books include *Shelburne Essays* (8 vols, 1904–21) and *New Shelburne Essays* (3 vols, 1928–36).

Lord David Cecil (*b.* 1902), Goldsmiths' Professor of English Literature, Oxford, 1948–69, now Honorary Fellow, New College, Oxford. His books include *Early Victorian Novelists* (1934), *The Young Melbourne* (1939), *Max: a Biography* (1964) and *A Portrait of Jane Austen* (1979).

Chauncey Brewster Tinker (1876–1963), late Professor of English and Keeper of Rare Books, Yale University. His books include *Young Boswell* (1922), *A New Portrait of James Boswell* (co-author, 1927) and *The Good Estate of Poetry* (1929).

A. O. J. Cockshut (*b.* 1927), Lecturer in nineteenth-century literature, Oxford, and Fellow of Hertford College, Oxford. His books include *Anthony Trollope: a Critical Study* (1955), *The Imagination of Charles Dickens* (1961) and *Truth to Life: the Art of Biography in the Nineteenth Century* (1974).

Frank O'Connor, pseudonym of Michael O'Donovan (1903–66), Irish short story writer and critic. His books include *Guests of the Nation* (1931), *Bones of Contention* (1936), *The Mirror in the Roadway: a Study of the Modern Novel* (1956) and *The Lonely Voice* (1963).

Bradford Allen Booth (1909–67), late Professor of English, University of California, Los Angeles, and founder and editor of *The Trollopian* (later renamed *Nineteenth-Century Fiction*). His books include *The Letters of Anthony Trollope* (1951) and *Anthony Trollope: Aspects of His Life and Art* (1958).

Gerald Warner Brace (1901–78), novelist and late Professor of English, Boston University. His books include *The Garretson Chronicle* (1947), *Bell's Landing* (1955), *The Age of the Novel* (1955) and *Winter Solstice* (1960).

Gordon N. Ray (*b.* 1915), President, the John Simon Guggenheim Memorial Foundation, Professor of English, New York University. His books include *The Letters and Private Papers of William Makepeace Thackeray* (4 vols, 1945–6), *Thackeray: The Uses of Adversity* (1955), *Thackeray: The Age of Wisdom* (1958) and *The Illustrator and the Book in England, 1790–1914* (1976).

J. Hillis Miller (*b.* 1928), Frederick W. Hilles Professor of English and Professor of Comparative Literature, Yale University. His books include *Charles Dickens: the World of His Novels* (1958), *The Disappearance of God: Five Nineteenth-Century Writers* (1963), *The Form of Victorian Fiction* (1968) and *Thomas Hardy: Distance and Desire* (1970).

Ruth apRoberts (*b.* 1919), Professor of English, University of California, Riverside. Her publications include *Trollope: Artist and Moralist* (1971).

James Gindin (*b.* 1926), Professor of English, University of Michigan, Ann Arbor. His publications include *Postwar British Fiction: New Accents and Attitudes* (1962), *Harvest of a Quiet Eye: The Novel of Compassion* (1971) and *The English Climate: an Excursion into a Biography of John Galsworthy* (1979).

David Skilton (*b.* 1942), Professor and Head of the Department of English, St. David's University College, Lampeter, in the University of Wales. His publications include *Anthony Trollope and His Contemporaries* (1972) and *The English Novel: Defoe to the Victorians* (1977).

C. P. Snow, Baron Snow (1905–80), the writer. His books include the eleven-volume sequence of novels *Strangers and Brothers* (1940–70), *The Two Cultures and the Scientific Revolution* (1959), *Public Affairs* (1971) and *Trollope: his Life and Art* (1975).

John Halperin (*b.* 1941), Professor of English, University of Southern California. His publications include *The Language of Meditation: Four*

Studies in Nineteenth-Century Fiction (1973), *Egoism and Self-Discovery in the Victorian Novel* (1974) and *Trollope and Politics* (1977).

James R. Kincaid (*b.* 1937), Professor and Chairman of the Department of English, University of Colorado, Boulder. His publications include *Dickens and the Rhetoric of Laughter* (1971), *Tennyson's Major Poems* (1975) and *The Novels of Anthony Trollope* (1977).

Juliet McMaster (*b.* 1937), Professor of English, University of Alberta. Her publications include *Thackeray: The Major Novels* (1971) and *Trollope's Palliser Novels* (1978).

Selected Bibliography

This bibliography lists chiefly twentieth-century material on Trollope. Although substantial, it is by no means all-inclusive. The following bibliographical studies have been helpful: James Kincaid, appendix to *The Novels of Anthony Trollope* (1977); J. C. Olmsted and J. E. Welch, *The Reputation of Trollope: An Annotated Bibliography, 1925–1975* (1978), Ruth apRoberts, Trollope chapter in *Victorian Fiction: A Second Guide to Research* (1978); Donald Smalley, Trollope chapter in *Victorian Fiction: A Guide to Research* (1964).

For a bibliography of nineteenth-century criticism of Trollope, see David Skilton, *Anthony Trollope and His Contemporaries* (1972), and Donald Smalley (ed.), *Trollope: The Critical Heritage* (1969); the latter reprints many contemporary reviews.

For a detailed bibliography of Trollope's own works, see Michael Sadleir, *Trollope: A Bibliography* (1928).

Books and Monographs

Biography, Bibliography and Letters

Escott, T. H. S., *Anthony Trollope: His Work, Associates and Literary Originals* (London: John Lane, 1913).
Pope Hennessy, James, *Anthony Trollope* (Boston, Mass.: Little, Brown, 1971).
Sadleir, Michael, *Trollope: A Bibliography* (London: Constable, 1928; rpt. London: Dawsons, 1964).
———, *Trollope: A Commentary* (London: Constable, 1927; 3rd edn, rpt., London: Oxford University Press, 1961).
Snow, C. P., *Trollope: His Life and Art* (London: Macmillan, 1975).
Stebbins, Lucy and Stebbins, Richard Poate, *The Trollopes: The Chronicle of a Writing Family* (New York: Columbia University Press, 1945).

Trollope, Anthony, *The Letters of Anthony Trollope*, ed. Bradford Allen Booth (London: Oxford University Press, 1951). A new edition of Trollope's letters is in preparation, edited by N. John Hall.

Criticism

apRoberts, Ruth, *Trollope: Artist and Moralist* (London: Chatto & Windus, 1971); published in America as *The Moral Trollope* (Athens, Ohio: Ohio University Press, 1971).

Booth, Bradford A., *Anthony Trollope: Aspects of His Life and Art* (Bloomington, Ind.: Indiana University Press, 1958).

Bowen, Elizabeth, *Anthony Trollope: A New Judgement* (New York and London: Oxford University Press, 1946).

Brown, Beatrice Curtis, *Anthony Trollope* (London: Arthur Barker, 1950).

Clark, John W., *The Language and Style of Anthony Trollope* (London: André Deutsch, 1975).

Cockshut, A. O. J., *Anthony Trollope: A Critical Study* (London: Collins, 1955; rpt. New York: New York University Press, 1968).

Cohen, Joan M., *Form and Realism in Six Novels of Anthony Trollope* (The Hague: Mouton, 1976).

Davies, Hugh Sykes, *Trollope*, Writers and their Work, No. 118 (London: Longmans Green, 1960).

Edwards, P. D., *Anthony Trollope*, Profiles in Literature Series (London: Routledge & Kegan Paul, 1969).

——, *Anthony Trollope: His Art and Scope* (St. Lucia: University of Queensland Press, 1977).

Fredman, Alice Green, *Anthony Trollope*, Columbia Essays on Modern Writers, No. 56 (New York: Columbia University Press, 1971).

Gerould, Winifred Gregory and Gerould, James Thayer, *A Guide to Trollope* (Princeton, N. J.: Princeton University Press, 1948).

Hall, N. John, *Trollope and his Illustrators* (London: Macmillan, 1980).

Halperin, John, *Trollope and Politics: A Study of the Pallisers and Others* (London: Macmillan, 1977).

Helling, Rafael, *A Century of Trollope Criticism*, Commentationes Humanarum Litterarum, 22, No. 2 (1957), 1–203.

Hennedy, Hugh L., *Unity in Barsetshire* (The Hague: Mouton, 1971).

Irwin, Mary Leslie, *Anthony Trollope: A Bibliography* (New York: H. W. Wilson, 1926).

Kincaid, James R., *The Novels of Anthony Trollope* (Oxford: Clarendon Press, 1977).

McMaster, Juliet, *Trollope's Palliser Novels: Theme and Pattern* (London: Macmillan, 1978).

Nichols, Spencer Van Bokkelen, *The Significance of Anthony Trollope* (New York: D. C. McMurtrie, 1925).

Olmsted, John Charles and Welch, Jeffrey Egan, *The Reputation of Trollope: An Annotated Bibliography 1925–1975* (New York and London: Garland, 1978).

Polhemus, Robert M., *The Changing World of Anthony Trollope* (Berkeley and Los Angeles: University of California Press, 1968).

Pollard, Arthur, *Anthony Trollope* (London: Routledge & Kegan Paul, 1978).

Skilton, David, *Anthony Trollope and His Contemporaries: A Study in the Theory and Conventions of Mid-Victorian Fiction* (London: Longman, 1972).

Smalley, Donald (ed.), *Trollope: The Critical Heritage* (London: Routledge & Kegan Paul; New York: Barnes & Noble, 1969).

Terry, R. C., *Anthony Trollope: The Artist in Hiding* (London: Macmillan, 1977).

Tracy, Robert *Trollope's Later Novels* (Berkeley, Los Angeles, and London: University of California Press, 1978).

Walpole, Hugh, *Anthony Trollope* (New York: Macmillan, 1928).

Wildman, John H., *Anthony Trollope's England*, Brown University Studies, vol. v (Providence, R. I.: Brown University Press, 1940).

Articles, Chapters of Books, and Works Containing Important References to Trollope

Critical and Biographical Studies

Aitkin, David, 'Anthony Trollope on "the Genus Girl" ', *Nineteenth-Century Fiction*, 28 (1974), 417–34.

Allen, Walter, *The English Novel: A Short Critical History* (London: Phoenix House, 1954), pp. 190–8.

apRoberts, Ruth, 'Anthony Trollope', *Victorian Fiction: A Second Guide to Research*, ed. George H. Ford (New York: Modern Language Association of America, 1978), pp. 143–71.

——, 'Carlyle and Trollope', *Carlyle and His Contemporaries*, ed. John Clubbe (Durham, N.C.: Duke University Press, 1976), pp. 204–26.

——, 'Trollope Empiricus' *Victorian Newsletter*, 34 (1968), 1–7.

——, 'Trollope's Casuisitry', *Novel*, 3 (1969), 17–27.

Atlee, Clement R., 'The Pleasure of Books', *National and English Review*, 142 (1954), 17–21.

Auchincloss, Louis, 'Americans in Trollope', *Reflections of a Jacobite* (Boston: Houghton Mifflin, 1961), pp. 113–25.

Baker, Ernest A., 'Trollope', *From the Brontës to Meredith: Romanticism in the English Novel. The History of the English Novel* (London: H. F. and G. Witherby, 1937), viii, 112–60.

Baker, Joseph Ellis, *The Novel and the Oxford Movement*, Princeton Studies in English, No. 8 (Princeton, N.J.: Princeton University Press, 1932), pp. 136–44.

——, 'Trollope's Third Dimension', *College English*, 16 (1955), 222–5, 232.

Banks, J. A., 'The Way They Lived Then: Anthony Trollope and the 1870s', *Victorian Studies*, 12 (1968), 177–200.

Belloc, H., 'Anthony Trollope', *London Mercury*, 27 (1932), 150–7.

Betsky, Seymours, 'Society in Thackeray and Trollope', *From Dickens to Hardy: A Guide to English Literature*, ed. Boris Ford (London: Cassell, 1963), vi, 144–68.

Blair, Frederick G., 'Trollope on Education: An Unpublished Address', *Trollopian*, 1 (1947), 1–9.

Boll, Ernest, 'The Infusions of Dickens in Trollope', *Trollopian*, 1 (1946), 11–24.

Booth, Bradford A., 'Anthony Trollope', *Victorian Newsletter*, 13 (1958), 24–5.

——, 'The Parrish Trollope Collection', *Trollopian*, 1 (1945), 11–19.

——, 'Trollope', *The English Novel: Select Bibliographical Guides*, ed. A. E. Dyson (London: Oxford University Press, 1974), pp. 200–17.

——, 'Trollope and "Little Dorritt" ', *Trollopian*, 2 (1948), 237–40.

——, 'Trollope and the "Pall Mall Gazette" ', *Nineteenth-Century Fiction*, 4 (1949), 51–69, 137–58.

——, 'Trollope and the Royal Literary Fund', *Nineteenth-Century Fiction*, 7 (1952), 208–16.

——, 'Trollope in California', *Huntington Library Quarterly*, 3 (1939), 117–24.

——, 'Trollope on "Emma"': An Unpublished Note', *Nineteenth-Century Fiction*, 4 (1949), 245–7.

——, 'Trollope on Froude's "Caesar" ', *Trollopian*, 1 (1946), 33–47.

——, 'Trollope on the Novel', *Essays Critical and Historical Dedicated to Lily B. Campbell*, University of California Publications: English Studies, No. 1 (Berkeley and Los Angeles: University of California Press, 1950), pp. 219–31.

——, 'Trollope on Scott: Some Unpublished Notes', *Nineteenth-Century Fiction*, 5 (1950), 223–30.

——(ed.), 'Author to Publisher: Anthony Trollope and William Isbister', *Princeton University Library Chronicle*, 24 (1962), 51–67.

Brace, Gerald Warner, 'The World of Anthony Trollope', *Texas Quarterly*, 4 (1961), 180–9.

Briggs, Asa, 'Trollope, Bagehot and the English Constitution', *Cambridge Journal*, 5 (1952), 327–38; rpt. *Victorian People: A Reassessment of Persons and Themes, 1851–67* (Chicago: University of Chicago Press, 1955), pp. 87–115.

Burn, W. L., 'Anthony Trollope's Politics', *Nineteenth Century and After*, 143 (1948), 161–71.

Burton, Richard, *Masters of the English Novel: A Study of Principles and Personalities* (New York: Holt, 1909), pp. 252–8.

Cadbury, William, 'Shape and Theme: Determinants of Trollope's Forms', *PMLA*, 78 (1963), 326–32.

Cecil, David, 'Anthony Trollope', *Early Victorian Novelists: Essays in Revaluation* (London: Constable, 1934); rpt. *Victorian Novelists: Essays in Revaluation* (Chicago: University of Chicago Press, 1958), pp. 245–79.

Chapman, Raymond, 'Trollope', *The Victorian Debate: English Literature and Society 1832–1901* (London: Weidenfeld & Nicolson, 1968), pp. 181–93.

Church, Richard, *The Growth of the English Novel* (London: Methuen, 1951), pp. 168–74.

Cooper, Harold, 'Trollope and Henry James in 1868', *Modern Language Notes*, 58 (1943), 558.

Coyle, William, 'Trollope and the Bi-columned Shakespeare', *Nineteenth-Century Fiction*, 6 (1951), 33–46.

——, 'Trollope as Social Anthropologist', *College English*, 17 (1956), 392–7.

Cross, Wilbur L., 'Anthony Trollope', *The Development of the English Novel* (New York: Macmillan, 1924), pp. 215–24.

Darbishire, Helen, 'Anthony Trollope', *Somerville College Chapel Addresses and Other Papers* [1925] (London, 1962), pp. 105–10.

Davidson, J. H., 'Anthony Trollope and the Colonies', *Victorian Studies*, 12 (1969), 305–30.

Dustin, John E., 'Thematic Alternation in Trollope', *PMLA*, 77 (1962), 280–8.

Edwards, P. D., 'Trollope and "All the Year Round" ', *Notes & Queries*, 221 (1976), 403–5.

——, 'Trollope and the Reviewers: Three Notes', *Notes & Queries*, 213 (1968), 418–20.

Fraser, Russell A., 'Anthony Trollope's Younger Characters', *Nineteenth-Century Fiction*, 6 (1951), 96–106.

——, 'Shooting Niagara in the Novels of Thackeray and Trollope', *Modern Language Quarterly*, 19 (1958), 141–6.

Gindin, James, 'Trollope', *Harvest of a Quiet Eye: The Novel of Compassion* (Bloomington, Ind.: Indiana University Press, 1971), pp. 28–56.

Gragg, Wilson B., 'Trollope and Carlyle', *Nineteenth-Century Fiction*, 13 (1958), 266–70.

Green, Gladys, 'Trollope on Sidney's "Arcadia" and Lytton's "The Wanderer" ', *Trollopian*, 1 (1946), 45–54.

Gordon, Albert H., 'Anthony Trollope: The Fall and Rise of His Popularity', *The Gazette of the Grolier Club*, 24–25 (1976), pp. 60–73.

Grossman, Richard H. and Wright, Andrew, 'Anthony Trollope's Libraries', *Nineteenth-Century Fiction*, 31 (1976), 48–64.

Hagan, John, 'The Divided Mind of Anthony Trollope', *Nineteenth-Century Fiction*, 14 (1959), 1–26.

Hall, N. John, 'Millais' Illustrations for Trollope', University of Pennsylvania *Library Chronicle*, 42 (1977), 23–46.

——, *Salmagundi: Byron, Allegra, and the Trollope Family* (Pittsburgh: Beta Phi Mu, 1975).

——, 'Trollope and Carlyle', *Nineteenth-Century Fiction*, 27 (1972), 197–205.

——, 'Trollope as Critic of the Novel', *Revue Belge de Philologie et d'Histoire*, 53 (1975), 776–90.

——, 'Trollope Reading Aloud: An Unpublished Record', *Notes & Queries*, 220 (1975), 117–18.

——, 'Trollope's Commonplace Book, 1835–1840', *Nineteenth-Century Fiction*, 31 (1976), 15–25.

——, 'An Unpublished Trollope Manuscript on a Proposed History of World Literature', *Nineteenth-Century Fiction*, 29 (1974), 206–10.

Halperin, John, 'Trollope and Feminism', *South Atlantic Quarterly*, 77 (1978), 179–88.

——, 'Politics, Palmerston, and Trollope's Prime Minister', *Clio*, 3 (1974), 187–218.

——, 'Trollope, James, and the International Theme', *Yearbook of English Studies*, 7 (1977), 141–7.

Hamer, Mary, 'Forty Letters of Anthony Trollope', *Yearbook of English Studies*, 3 (1973), 206–15.

——, 'Number-Length and Its Significance in the Novels of Anthony Trollope', *Yearbook of English Studies*, 5 (1976), 178–89.

Harrison, Frederic, 'Anthony Trollope's Place in Literature', *Forum*, 19 (1895), 324–37; rpt. *Studies in Early Victorian Literature* (London and New York: Edward Arnold, 1895), pp. 183–204.

Harvey, G. M., 'Scene and Form: Trollope as Dramatic Novelist', *Studies in English Literature, 1500–1900*, 16 (1976), 631–44.

Hawthorne, Julian, 'The Maker of Many Books', *Confessions and Criticisms* (Boston: Ticknor, 1887), pp. 140–62.

Hennedy, Hugh L., 'Trollope Studies, 1963–73', *British Studies Monitor*, 6 (1975), 3–27.

Herbert, Christopher, 'Trollope and the Fixity of the Self', *PMLA*, 93 (1978), 228–39.

Howells, William Dean, 'Effectism', *Harper's Monthly*, November 1889; rpt. *W. D. Howells as Critic*, ed. Edwin H. Cady (London: Routledge & Kegan Paul, 1973), pp. 169–71.

——, *Heroines of Fiction* (New York and London: Harper, 1901), II, 94–137.

——, *My Literary Passions* (New York: Harper, 1895) p. 247.

——, 'Novel-Writing and Novel-Reading: An Impersonal Explanation', ed. William M. Gibson, *Bulletin of the New York Public Library*, 62 (1958), 15–34.

Humphreys, Susan L., 'Trollope on the Sublime and Beautiful', *Nineteenth-Century Fiction*, 33 (1978), 194–214.

James, Henry, 'Anthony Trollope', *Century Magazine*, 4 (1883), 385–95; rpt. slightly different form in *Partial Portraits* (London: Macmillan, 1888), pp. 97–133.

Jillson, Frederick F., 'The "Professional" Clergyman in Some Novels by Anthony Trollope', *Hartford Studies in Literature*, 1 (1969), 185–97.

Johnson, Pamela Hansford, 'Anthony Trollope, an Odd Fish', *New York Times Book Review*, 25 Apr. 1965, p. 2.

——, 'Trollope's Young Women', *On the Novel: A Present for Walter Allen on his 60th Birthday from his Friends and Colleagues*, ed. B. S. Benedikz (London: J. M. Dent, 1971), pp. 17–33.

Jones, Frank Pierce, 'Anthony Trollope and the Classics', *Classical Weekly*, 37 (1944), 227–31.

Jones, Iva G., 'Trollope, Carlyle, and Mill on the Negro: An Episode in the History of Ideas', *Journal of Negro History*, 52 (1967), 185–99.

Kenney, Mrs. David J. 'Anthony Trollope's Theology', *American Notes & Queries*, 9 (1970), 51–4.

Kincaid, James R., 'Bring Back *The Trollopian*', *Nineteenth-Century Fiction*, 31 (1976), 1–14.

King, Helen Garlinghouse (ed.), 'Trollope's Letters to the *Examiner*', *Princeton University Library Chronicle*, 26 (1965), 71–101.

Koskimies, Rafael, 'Novelists' Thoughts about Their Art', *Neuphilologische Mitteilungen*, 57 (1956), 148–59.

Lee, James W., 'Trollope's Clerical Concerns: The Low Church Clergymen', *Hartford Studies in Literature*, 1 (1969), 198–208.

Letwin, Shirley Robin, 'Trollope on Generations Without Gaps', *Daedalus*, 107 (1978), 53–70.

Mason, Michael, 'The Way We Look Now: Millais' Illustrations to Trollope', *Art History*, 1 (1978), 309–40.

More, Paul Elmer, 'My Debt to Trollope', *Demon of the Absolute*, New Shelburne Essays, vol. 1 (Princeton, N.J.: Princeton University Press, 1928), pp. 89–125.

Newbolt, Sir Franics, *Out of Court* (London: Philip Allan, 1925), pp. 1–82.

O'Connor, Frank, 'Trollope the Realist', *The Mirror in the Roadway: A Study of the Modern Novel* (New York: Knopf, 1956), pp. 165–83.

Park, Clara Claiborne, 'Trollope and the Modern Reader', *Massachusetts Review*, 3 (1962), 577–91.

Parks, Edd Winfield, 'Trollope and the Defense of Exegesis', *Nineteenth-Century Fiction*, 7 (1953), 265–71.

Pollard, Arthur, 'Thackeray and Trollope', *The Victorians*, ed. Arthur Pollard, *History of Literature in the English Language* (London: Barrie and Jenkins, 1970), vi, 107–39.

Praz, Mario, 'Anthony Trollope', *The Hero in Eclipse in Victorian Fiction*, trans. Angus Davidson (London: Oxford University Press, 1956), pp. 261–318.

Pritchett, V. S., 'Trollope was Right', *The Working Novelist* (London: Chatto & Windus, 1965), pp. 109–20.

Ray, Gordon N., 'Trollope at Full Length', *Huntington Library Quarterly*, 31 (1968), 313–40.

Robinson, Clement Franklin, 'Trollope's Jury Trials', *Nineteenth-Century Fiction*, 6 (1952), 247–68.

Sadleir, Michael, 'Anthony Trollope', *Things Past* (London: Constable, 1944), pp. 16–53.

——, 'Trollope and Bacon's Essays', *Trollopian*, 1 (1945), 21–34.

Saintsbury, George, *Corrected Impressions: Essays on Victorian Writers* (London: Heineman, 1895; New York: Dodd, Mead, 1895), pp. 172–7.

——, 'Trollope Revisited', *Essays and Studies By Members of the English Association* (Oxford: Clarendon Press, 1920), vi, 41–66.

Shumaker, Wayne, *English Autobiography: Its Emergence, Materials and Form*. University of California Publications: English Studies, No. 8 (Berkeley and Los Angeles: University of California Press, 1954), pp. 158–84.

Slakey, Roger L., 'Trollope's Case for Moral Imperative', *Nineteenth-Century Fiction*, 28 (1973), 305–20.

Smalley, Donald, 'Anthony Trollope', *Victorian Fiction: A Guide to Research*, ed. Lionel Stevenson (Cambridge, Mass.: Harvard University Press, 1964), pp. 188–213.

Smith, Sheila M., 'Anthony Trollope: The Novelist as Moralist', *Renaissance and Modern Essays Presented to Vivian de Sola Pinto in Celebration of His Seventieth Birthday*, ed. G. R. Hibbard (New York: Barnes & Noble, 1966), pp. 129–36.

Snow, C. P., 'Trollope: The Psychological Stream', *On the Novel: A Present for Walter Allen on His 60th Birthday from His Friends and Colleagues*, ed. B. S. Benedikz (London: J. M. Dent, 1971), pp. 3–16.

Stebbins, Richard Poate, 'Trollope at Harrow School', *Trollopian*, 1 (1945), 35–44.

Stephen, Leslie, 'Anthony Trollope', *National Review*, 38 (1901), 68–84.

Stevenson, Lionel, *The English Novel: A Panorama* (London: Constable, 1960), pp. 318–24.

——, 'Trollope as a Recorder of Verbal Usage', *Trollopian*, 3 (1948), 119–25.

Stone, Donald D., 'Trollope as a Short Story Writer', *Nineteenth-Century Fiction*, 31 (1976), 26–47.

——, 'Trollope, Byron, and the Conventionalities', *The Worlds of Victorian Fiction*, Harvard English Studies 6, ed. Jerome H. Buckley (Cambridge: Harvard University Press, 1975), pp. 179–203.

Sutherland, J. A., *Victorian Novelists and Publishers* (London: University of London, Athlone Press, 1976).

Taylor, Robert H., 'Letters to Trollope', *Trollopian*, 1 (1946), 5–9.

——, 'The Trollopes Write to Bentley', *Trollopian*, 3 (1948), 83–98, 201–14.

Thale, Jerome, 'The Problem of Structure in Trollope', *Nineteenth-Century Fiction*, 15 (1960), 147–57.

Thorp, Willard and Drinker, Henry S., *Two Addresses Delivered to Members of the Grolier Club: I. Trollope's America by Willard Thorp; II, The Lawyers of Anthony Trollope by Henry S. Drinker* (New York: The Grolier Club, 1950).

Tillotson, Geoffrey, 'Trollope', *A View of Victorian Literature* (Oxford: Clarendon Press, 1978), pp. 255–85.

Tingay, Lance O., 'Trollope and the Beverley Election', *Nineteenth-Century Fiction*, 5 (1950), 23–37.

——, 'Trollope's Popularity: A Statistical Approach', *Nineteenth-Century Fiction*, 11 (1956), 223–9.

Tinker, Chauncey Brewster, 'Trollope', *Yale Review*, 36 n.s. (1947), 424–34.

Trollope, Muriel R., 'What I Was Told', *Trollopian*, 2 (1948), 223–35.

Trollope, Thomas Adolphus, *What I Remember*, 3 vols (London: Richard Bentley, 1887–9).

Vincent, C. J. 'Trollope: A Victorian Augustan', *Queen's Quarterly*, 52 (1945), 415–28.

Wall, Stephen, 'Trollope, Balzac, and the Reappearing Character', *Essays in Criticism*, 25 (1975), 123–44.

Welsby, Paul A., 'Anthony Trollope and the Church of England', *Church Quarterly Review*, 163 (1962), 210–20.

West, Rebecca, 'A Nineteenth-Century Bureaucrat', *The Court and the Castle: Some Treatments of a Recurrent Theme* (New Haven: Yale University Press, 1957), pp. 133–64.

Wildman, John H., 'Anthony Trollope Today', *College English*, 7 (1946), 397–9.

Wittig, Ellen W., 'Trollope's Irish Fiction', *Erie*, 9 (1974), 97–118.

Woolf, Virginia, 'The Novels of George Meredith', *Collected Essays* (London: Chatto & Windus, 1966; New York: Harcourt, Brace and World, 1967), 1, 224–32.

——, 'Phases of Fiction', *Collected Essays*. II, 56–102.

Wright, Andrew, 'Anthony Trollope as a Reader', *Two English Novelists* (Los Angeles: William Andrews Clark Memorial Library, 1974), pp. 45–68.

Studies of Trollope's Style

Aitken, David, ' "A Kind of Felicity": Some Notes About Trollope's Style', *Nineteenth-Century Fiction*, 20 (1966), 337–53.

apRoberts, Ruth, 'Anthony Trollope, or the Man with No Style at All', *Victorian Newsletter*, No. 35 (1969), pp. 10–13.

Davies, Hugh Sykes, 'Trollope and His Style', *Review of English Literature*, 1 (1960), 73–85.

Klinger, Helmut, 'Die Umschreibung als Stilmittel in den Romanen

Anthony Trollopes', *Weiner Beitrage zur englischen Philologie*, 75 (1973), 124–35.

Tillotson, Geoffrey, 'Trollope's Style', *Ball State Teachers College Forum*, 2, No. 2 (Winter 1961–2), 3–6; rpt. *Mid-Victorian Studies*, Geoffrey and Kathleen Tillotson (London: Athlone Press, 1965), pp. 56–61.

See also John W. Clark, *The Language and Style of Anthony Trollope* (London: André Deutsch, 1975).

Studies of Individual Novels

The American Senator

    apRoberts, Ruth, 'Trollope's One World', *South Atlantic Quarterly*, 68 (1969), 463–77.

    Greenberg, Clement, 'A Victorian Novel', *Partisan Review*, 11 (1944), 234–8.

    Harden, Edgar F., 'The Alien Voice: Trollope's Western Senator', *Texas Studies in Literature and Language*, 8 (1966), 219–34.

    Stryker, David, 'The Significance of Trollope's "American Senator" ', *Nineteenth-Century Fiction*, 5 (1950), 141–9.

    Taylor, Robert H., 'The Manuscript of Trollope's *The American Senator*. Collated with the First Edition', *Papers of the Bibliographical Society of America*, 41 (1947), 123–39.

    Wildman, John H., 'Trollope Illustrates the Distinction', *Nineteenth-Century Fiction*, 4 (1949), 101–10.

Ayala's Angel

    Miller, J. Hillis, *The Form of Victorian Fiction: Thackeray, Dickens, Trollope, George Eliot, Meredith, and Hardy* (Notre Dame, Ind.: University of Notre Dame Press, 1968), pp. 124–39.

Barchester Towers

    Bankert, M. S., 'Newman in the Shadow of *Barchester Towers*', *Renascence*, 20 (1968), 153–61.

    Cadbury, William, 'Character and the Mock Heroic in *Barchester Towers*', *Texas Studies in Literature and Language*, 5 (1964), 509–19.

    Kincaid, James R., '*Barchester Towers* and the Nature of Conservative Comedy', *Journal of English Literary History*, 37 (1970), 595–612.

    Knoepflmacher, U. C., 'Introduction: Entering a Victorian Novel – *Barchester Towers*'; '*Barchester Towers*: The Comedy of Change', *Laughter and Despair: Readings in Ten Novels of the Victorian Era* (Berkeley and Los Angeles: University of California Press, 1971), pp. 3–49.

Kronenberger, Louis, 'Barchester Towers', *The Polished Surface: Essays in the Literature of Worldliness* (New York: Knopf, 1969), pp. 217–32.

Shaw, W. David, 'Moral Drama in *Barchester Towers*', *Nineteenth-Century Fiction*, 19 (1964), 45–54.

Taylor, Robert H., 'On Rereading *Barchester Towers*', *Princeton University Library Chronicle*, 15 (1953), 10–15.

The Barsetshire Chronicle

Borinski, Ludwig, 'Trollope's Barsetshire Novels', *Die Neueren Sprachen*, n.s.II (1962), pp. 533–53.

Knox, Ronald A., 'The Barsetshire Novels', *Literary Distractions* (London: Sheed & Ward, 1958), pp. 134–44.

Quiller-Couch, Sir Arthur, 'Anthony Trollope: The Barsetshire Novels', *Charles Dickens and Other Victorians* (Cambridge: Cambridge University Press, 1925), pp. 219–34.

Sherman, Theodore A., 'The Financial Motif in the Barchester Novels', *College English*, 9 (1948), 413–19.

See also Hugh L. Hennedy, *Unity in Barsetshire* (The Hague: Mouton, 1971).

Can You Forgive Her?

Chamberlain, David S., 'Unity and Irony in Trollope's *Can You Forgive Her?*', *Studies in English Literature, 1500–1900*, 8 (1968), 669–80.

Hoyt, Norris D., ' "Can You Forgive Her?": A Commentary', *Trollopian*, 2 (1947), 57–70.

Levine, George, 'Can You Forgive Him? Trollope's "Can You Forgive Her?" and the Myth of Realism', *Victorian Studies*, 18 (1974), 5–30.

McMaster, Juliet, ' "The Meaning of Words and the Nature of Things": Trollope's *Can You Forgive Her?*', *Studies in English Literature, 1500–1900*, 14 (1974), 603–18.

Castle Richmond

Hennedy, Hugh L., 'Love and Famine, Family and Country in Trollope's *Castle Richmond*', *Erie* 7 (1972), 48–66.

Cousin Henry

apRoberts, Ruth, '*Cousin Henry*: Trollope's Note from Antiquity', *Nineteenth-Century Fiction*, 24 (1969), 93–8.

Polhemus, Robert M., '*Cousin Henry*: Trollope's Note from Underground', *Nineteenth-Century Fiction*, 20 (1966), 385–9.

Doctor Thorne

   Dixon, Sir Owen, 'Sir Roger Scatcherd's Will, in Anthony Trollope's
      Doctor Thorne', *Jesting Pilate, and Other Papers and Addresses*
      (Sydney: Law Book Co., 1965), pp. 71–81.
   Melada, Ivan, '*Dr. Thorne*', *The Captains of Industry in English Fiction,
      1821–1871* (Albuquerque: University of New Mexico Press, 1970),
      pp. 166–71.

Dr. Wortle's School

   Maxwell, J. C., 'Cockshut on "Dr. Wortle's School" ', *Nineteenth-
      Century Fiction*, 13 (1958), 153–9.

The Duke's Children

   Hagan, John H., '*The Duke's Children*: Trollope's Psychological Master-
      piece', *Nineteenth-Century Fiction*, 13 (1958), 1–21.
   Kenney, Blair Gates, 'The Two Isabels: A Study in Distortion', *Victorian
      Newsletter*, No. 25 (1964), pp. 15–17.

The Eustace Diamonds

   Milley, Henry J. W., '*The Eustace Diamonds* and *The Moonstone*',
      Studies in Philology, 36 (1939), 651–63.

The Fixed Period

   Skilton, David, '*The Fixed Period*: Anthony Trollope's Novel of 1980',
      Studies in the Literary Imagination, 6 (1973), 39–50.

Framley Parsonage

   Bićanić, Sonia, 'Some New Facts about the Beginning of Trollope's
      Framley Parsonage', *Studia Romanica Et Anglica Zagrabiensia*, 9–10
      (1960), pp. 171–6.
   Glavin, John J., 'Trollope's "Most Natural English Girl" ', *Nineteenth-
      Century Fiction*, 28 (1974), 477–85.
   Hamer, Mary, '*Framley Parsonage*: Trollope's First Serial', *Review of
      English Studies*, 26 (1975), 154–70.

He Knew He Was Right

   apRoberts, Ruth, 'Emily and Nora and Dorothy and Priscilla and
      Jemima and Carry', *The Victorian Experience: The Novelists*, ed.
      Richard A. Levine (Athens: Ohio University Press, 1976),
      pp. 87–120.

Is He Popenjoy?
D., T. C., 'Victorian Editions and Victorian Delicacy', *Notes & Queries*, 187 (1944), 251–3.

The Last Chronicle of Barset
Corsa, Helen S., ' "The Cross-Grainedness of Men": The Rev. Josiah Crawley – Trollope's Study of a Paranoid Personality', *Metapsychological Literary Criticism – Theory and Practice: Essays in Honor of Leonard Falk Manheim*, ed. Melvin Goldstein (Hartford, Conn.: University of Hartford, 1973), pp. 160–72.
Hamer, Mary, 'Working Diary for *The Last Chronicle of Barset*', *Times Literary Supplement*, 24 Dec. 1971, p. 1606.
Harvey, G. M., 'The Form of the Story: Trollope's *The Last Chronicle of Barset*', *Texas Studies in Literature and Language*, 18 (1976), 82–97.
West William A., '*The Last Chronicle of Barset*: Trollope's Comic Techniques', *The Classic British Novel*, ed. Howard M. Harper, Jr and Charles Edge (Athens: University of Georgia Press, 1971), pp. 121–42.

The Macdermots of Ballycloran
Donovan, Robert A., 'Trollope's Prentice Work', *Modern Philology*, 53 (1956), 179–86.
Terry, R. C., 'Three Lost Chapters of Trollope's First Novel', *Nineteenth-Century Fiction*, 27 (1972), 71–80.
Tingay, Lance O., 'The Publication of Trollope's First Novel', *Times Literary Supplement*, 30 Mar. 1956, p. 200.
——, 'The Reception of Trollope's First Novel', *Nineteenth-Century Fiction*, 6 (1951), 195–200.
——, 'Trollope's First Novel', *Notes & Queries*, 195 (1950), 563–4.

Orley Farm
Adams, Robert M., ' "Orley Farm" and Real Fiction', *Nineteenth-Century Fiction*, 8 (1953), 27–41.
Booth, Bradford A., 'Trollope's *Orley Farm*: Artistry *Manqué*', *From Jane Austen to Joseph Conrad: Essays Collected in Memory of James T. Hillhouse*, ed. Robert C. Rathburn and Martin Steinmann, Jr (Minneapolis: University of Minnesota Press, 1958), pp. 146–59.

The Palliser Chronicle

Borinski, Ludwig, 'Trollope's Palliser Novels', *Die Neueren Sprachen*, n.s.12 (1963), pp. 389–407.

Chapman, R. W., 'Personal Names in Trollope's Political Novels', *Essays Mainly on the Nineteenth Century: Presented to Sir Humphry Milford* (London: Oxford University Press, 1948), pp. 72–81.

Dinwiddy, J. R., 'Who's Who in Trollope's Political Novels', *Nineteenth-Century Fiction*, 22 (1967), 31–46.

Kenney, Blair G., 'Trollope's Ideal Statesmen: Plantagenet Palliser and Lord John Russell', *Nineteenth-Century Fiction*, 20 (1965), 281–5.

Kleis, John Christopher, 'Passion vs. Prudence: Theme and Technique in Trollope's Palliser Novels', *Texas Studies in Literature and Language*, 11 (1970), 1405–14.

Laski, Audrey L., 'Myths of Character: An Aspect of the Novel', *Nineteenth-Century Fiction*, 14 (1960), 333–43.

Mizener, Arthur, 'Anthony Trollope: The Palliser Novels', *From Jane Austen to Joseph Conrad: Essays Collected in Memory of James T. Hillhouse*, ed. Robert C. Rathburn and Martin Steinmann, Jr (Minneapolis: University of Minnesota Press, 1958), pp. 160–76.

Mohan, Ramesh, 'Trollope's Political Novels (Chronicles of Parliamentary Life)', *Indian Journal of English Studies*, 1 (1960), 57–69.

Pollard, Arthur, 'Trollope's Political Novels', Inaugural Lecture, University of Hull, April 1968, pp. 3–25.

See also John Halperin, *Trollope and Politics: A Study of the Pallisers and Others* (London: Macmillan, 1977) and Juliet McMaster, *Trollope's Palliser Novels: Theme and Form* (London: Macmillan, 1978).

Phineas Finn

Bloomfield, Morton W., 'Trollope's Use of Canadian History in "Phineas Finn" (1867–1869)', *Nineteenth-Century Fiction*, 5 (1950), 67–74.

Borinski, Ludwig, 'Anthony Trollope: *Phineas Finn: The Irish Member*', *Der englische Roman im 19. Jahrhundert: Interpretationen*, ed. Paul Goetsh *et al.* (Berlin: E. Schmidt, 1973), pp. 199–213.

Halperin, John, 'Trollope's *Phineas Finn* and History', *English Studies*, 59 (1978), 121–37.

The Prime Minister

Klinger, Helmut, 'Varieties of Failure: The Significance of Trollope's *The Prime Minister*', *English Miscellany*, 23 (1972), 167–83.

Ralph the Heir
  Booth, Bradford A., 'Trollope, Reade, and "Shilly-Shally" ', *Trollopian*,
    1 (1947), 45–54; 2 (1947), 43–51

The Small House at Allington
  McMaster, Juliet, ' "The Unfortunate Moth": Unifying Theme in *The
    Small House at Allington*', *Nineteenth-Century Fiction*, 26 (1971),
    127–44.

The Vicar of Bullhampton
  Cadbury, William, 'The Uses of the Village: Form and Theme in Trol-
    lope's *The Vicar of Bullhampton*', *Nineteenth-Century Fiction*, 18
    (1963), 151–63.

The Warden
  Best, G. F. A., 'The Road to Hiram's Hospital: A Byway of Early
    Victorian History', *Victorian Studies*, 5 (1961), 135–50.
  Ganzel, Carol H., '*The Times* Correspondent and *The Warden*', *Nine-
    teenth-Century Fiction*, 21 (1967), 325–36.
  Goldberg, M. A., 'Trollope's *The Warden*: A Commentary on the "Age
    of Equipoise" ', *Nineteenth-Century Fiction*, 17 (1963), 381–90.
  Hawkins, Sherman, 'Mr. Harding's Church Music', *Journal of English
    Literary History*, 29 (1962), 202–23.
  Heilman, Robert B., 'Trollope's *The Warden*: Structure, Tone, Genre',
    Essays in Honor of Esmond Linworth Marilla, ed. Thomas Austin
    Kirby and William John Olive (Baton Rouge: Louisiana State Univer-
    sity Press, 1970), pp. 210–29.
  Houston, Maude, 'Structure and Plot in *The Warden*', *University of
    Texas Studies in English*, 34 (1955), 107–13.
  Marshall, William H., *The World of the Victorian Novel* (South Bruns-
    wick, N.J. and New York: A. S. Barnes, 1967), pp. 322–36.
  Pickering, Samuel F., Jr, 'Trollope's Poetics and Authorial Intrusion in
    The Warden and *Barchester Towers*', *Journal of Narrative Technique*,
    3 (1973), 131–40.
  Sharp, R. L., 'Trollope's Mathematics in *The Warden*', *Nineteenth-
    Century Fiction*, 17 (1962), 288–9.
  Stevenson, Lionel, 'Dickens and the Origin of "The Warden" ', *Trollopian*,
    2 (1947), 83–9.

The Way We Live Now

Edwards, P. D., 'The Chronology of "The Way We Live Now" ', *Notes & Queries*, 214 (1969), 214–16.

——, 'Trollope Changes His Mind: The Death of Melmotte in *The Way We Live Now*', *Nineteenth-Century Fiction*, 18 (1963), 89–91.

Hornback, Bert G., 'Anthony Trollope and the Calendar of 1872: The Chronology of "The Way We Live Now" ', *Notes & Queries*, 208 (1963), 454–7.

Nathan, Sabine, 'Anthony Trollope's Perception of *The Way We Live Now*', *Zeitschrift fur Anglistik und Amerikanistik* (East Berlin), 10 (1962), 259–78.

Slakey, Roger, L., 'Melmotte's Death: A Prism of Meaning in *The Way We Live Now*', *Journal of English Literary History*, 34 (1967), 248–59.

Tanner, Tony, 'Trollope's *The Way We Live Now*: Its Modern Significance', *Critical Quarterly*, 9 (1967), 256–71.

Wolff, Robert Lee, 'The Way Things Were: The Hundredth Anniversary of a Classic: Anthony Trollope's *The Way We Live Now*', *Harvard Magazine*, 77 (1975), 44–50.

Index